BASIC
Pastrywork
TECHNIQUES

BASIC
Pastrywork
TECHNIQUES

Second Edition

L G NICOLELLO F.H.I.M.A., L.C.G., C.G.L.I. 152
J DINSDALE F.H.I.M.A., Cert. Ed.

Hodder & Stoughton
LONDON SYDNEY AUCKLAND TORONTO

Preparation of food is an art.
The art of preparing food is knowledge.

British Library Cataloguing in Publication Data

Nicolello, L. G.
  Basic pastrywork techniques. –2nd. ed.
  1.   Pastries
  I.   Title   II. Dinsdale, J.
  641.865

  ISBN 0–340–53741–8

First published 1984
This edition 1991

Typeset by Taurus Graphics, Abingdon, Oxon.
Printed for the educational publishing division of Hodder and
Stoughton Ltd, Mill Road, Dunton Green, Sevenoaks, Kent by
St Edmundsbury Press.

CONTENTS

To my wife Olwen and sons Stephen and Clive

ACKNOWLEDGMENTS

I wish to thank all the colleagues with whom I have worked over the years, for my knowledge has been gained by working with, and learning the craft from, some of the best pastry chefs in the catering industry.

My thanks also to colleagues with whom I have worked in departments of catering studies at Ealing College of Higher Education, London and at South Fields College of Further Education, Leicester. I acknowledge also the students I have taught for their desire for knowledge has stimulated this work.

I would like to record my gratitude to Julia Dinsdale, my former colleague at South Fields, for collaborating with me in this project and who, with unfailing support and able assistance, has played a large part in the compilation of the contents. She has reviewed scripts and prompted me to provide additional information and specific details which I might otherwise have overlooked.

I am also grateful to George Ingham, former Deputy Head of Department of Catering Studies, South Fields College of Further Education, for his expert guidance and valued help.

Thanks also to Paul Farrell the Principal of South Fields College, Leicester for encouragement given.

I thank D R Gregory of the Environment Health Department, Leicester City, for literature with information regarding safe food, hygiene and safety at work.

I am most grateful to A Barker, Environmental Health Department, Delyn Borough Council, for his expertise and invaluable help in reading the script on safe food, hygiene and safety at work and amending any errors and omissions.

Finally I thank my wife and sons for their patience and understanding, which undoubtedly has kept me going.

L G Nicolello

The Publishers would like to thank the Hotel Catering and Institutional Management Association for permission to reproduce copyright material on pages 38–41 and Paul Wilson, Head of Crawley Hotel School, for permission to use the kitchen facilities.

INTRODUCTION

This book aims to provide thorough but basic information on the techniques of pastry work.

It is intended as an instruction manual which will complement recipe books. It covers the principles of practice and the techniques of production, while giving information on the finer points of work required to achieve a high standard of professionalism.

Its aim is to give an understanding, by use of cross reference of ingredients, techniques and methods used by the pastry cook. It also sets out to develop an awareness in the student of the reasons for any fault which may occur.

The book gives information on the selection and use of tools and on careful upkeep and maintenance of equipment.

No book can cover every aspect of pastrywork but an attempt has been made here to include most of the information required by novice pastry cooks who are ambitious and aspire to improve and develop their skills in pastry work.

The book may also be useful to bridge the gap of knowledge between the basic cookery book and the more expensive pastry recipe book. It could be of value to the lecturer or cook in an establishment which has no pastry specialist. It is not intended to cover in depth the theory relating to nutritional value of foods, applied science, structure or composition of the commodities, or to give lists of recipes and methods.

I THE PASTRY SECTION

The pastry section in a catering establishment, although part of the kitchen and under the supervision of the head chef or catering manager, is considered to be a separate unit. The main reasons for this are because of the specialist staff and equipment required for it to work efficiently and to avoid contamination of sweet goods by the savoury smells and flavours of the foods being prepared in the kitchen and larder areas.

The purpose of the pastry section is to prepare and serve all hot and cold sweet dishes, pastries, cakes, gâteaux, petits fours, ice-cream dishes, confectionery and yeast goods. Often this includes breads and special customer requirements such as celebration cakes.

The section has specialist facilities, equipment and staff, and will therefore liaise with the kitchen and larder sections on the production of savoury items; for example, pie coverings, vol-au-vents, sausage rolls, choux paste, cheese straws, fleurons, savoury flans and tartlets, pizzas and pastas. Pastes and other items will be supplied by the pastry section. In some cases they will be prepared and baked by them for completion and service in the main kitchen.

Depending on the type of establishment, the section would provide food for lunch, dinner and supper menus, afternoon teas, buffets, banquets and possibly outdoor catering functions.

If stewed fruits, croissants and brioche rolls are served at breakfast, these would also be prepared by the pastry section.

■ THE PASTRY BRIGADE

The number of staff working in the pastry kitchen will vary depending on the type and size of the establishment, the number and expectations of its customers, the variety and size of menu and the type of service given. Often the quality of products rather than the quantity will determine the number of persons required to staff the section.

The usual brigade in a busy first class hotel or restaurant pastry kitchen will consist of staff who tend to specialise in this field of work. It will consist of a chef de partie, a first commis, who should have sufficient experience to take control when the chef pâtissier is away, several second commis and apprentices. In smaller pastry kitchens there may only be one or two persons employed. In some cases the preparation and service of sweets is taken over by one of the kitchen cooks.

This breakdown of a full brigade gives their French titles and describes the areas of work for which they are responsible.

Chef pâtissier (chief pastry cook)

This person is responsible to the head chef for the efficient running of the section; controlling and co-ordinating staff, ordering commodities, and liasing with other departments. The chef pâtissier plans menus, controls expenditure and waste to meet the profit percentage required. The chef pâtissier must be a specialist in pastrywork, should possess initiative and imagination, be creative and artistic. A good knowledge of commodities and equipment is very important, but above all he or she should be conscientious, loyal and self reliant.

Pâtissier (pastry cook)

This area is usually covered by the first commis who would generally assist the chef pâtissier in running the section. He or she would prepare hot and cold sweets, sweet sauces, pastries for afternoon teas, gâteaux and cakes. He or she would also supervise the preparation of the sweet trolley or buffet table and control the service of food.

Confiseur (confectioner)

This area of work needs great skill, experience and artistry. The chef pâtissier normally undertakes this in addition to organizational duties. The work involves the preparation of sugar, marzipan, chocolate, pastillage, decorative and display items, petits fours, wedding, birthday and celebration cakes.

Tourier (paste handler)

This person is responsible for the preparation and manipulation of all pastes required for the making of flans, tartlets, pies and puff pastry items. If no baker is employed he or she would also prepare fermented goods.

Boulangère (baker)

Only very large establishments employ a person for this area. The duties would be to tend to the ovens, make breads, make speciality and breakfast rolls and all yeast goods.

Glacier

This person is involved in the preparation and service of dishes which include ice-cream in its composition. He or she would have to be knowledgeable and skilled in the making of various ice-creams, sorbets, bombes, biscuits glacé and other moulded ice-creams. A good glacier will have artistic ability for ice carving. Because of hygiene laws and production costs, it is generally accepted these days that manufactured ice-cream is bought in. The pastry cook and glacier must, however, know the care and conditions required for storing and service of ice-creams.

2 HYGIENE AND SAFETY

■ HYGIENE

Staff must know that germs, given the correct conditions, multiply rapidly and this could result in widespread food contamination. It is important to remember that germs are everywhere, and harmful bacteria are transferred easily to foods, possibly causing serious illnesses. To safeguard the consumer, a food handler is therefore responsible for taking precautions against the risks of food contamination and must pay special attention to the commodities used, food preparation, working areas and personal health and hygiene. All food handlers have a responsibility to maintain good hygiene. Food hygiene legislation, lays down legal standards, which have to be met.

It is most advisable to purchase foods from reputable firms that have efficient and qualified staff, maintain a high standard of hygiene and follow strict quality control in their transactions between their suppliers and their consumers.

Foods should be checked on arrival, to ensure they are wholesome, of good quality and applicable within the 'use by' date codes.

Fresh food supplies are best delievered in the amounts for immediate use and close to the day required for preparation. They should be checked on arrival for any sign of deterioration before they are accepted. Once on the premises, correct storage procedures should be adopted.

■ PERSONAL HYGIENE

Good hygiene practices are vital in all catering establishments to prevent food from becoming contaminated. Therefore, a high standard of personal health and hygiene must be maintained.

Staff should be educated in basic health and hygiene procedures and are advised to take formal training — to study for the Institution of Environmental Health Officers Certificate for Food Handlers, for example.

Professional craftspersons will take a personal pride in being clean and neat in appearance, will make sure that they pay special attention to personal health and hygiene and will try to promote the same approach and habit in others. Caterers have a great responsibility towards customers and consumers, and to prevent the spread of infection, a high standard of hygiene must be maintained at all times.

The following points should be observed and should form the basis of good practice:

1 Always maintain a high standard of personal cleanliness. Shower or bath frequently, keep your hair clean and wear clean clothes.

2 Keep your nails cut short and always ensure that they are clean and free from nail varnish.

3 Hair must be kept clean, neat and contained totally within a head covering, if necessary secured by a hairnet, clip or bands. This prevents the hair from contaminating food and protects it from grease and steam.

4 Always wash hands on entering a food room, before commencing work and regularly throughout the working day. Most importantly, they should be washed after using the toilet, after using a handkerchief, after coughing and sneezing, after smoking and after handling rubbish.

5 It is most essential to wash hands and utensils between handling raw and cooked foods.

6 To clean hands effectively, wash thoroughly with hot water and soap and scrub with a nail brush, then dry them on a clean hand towel, or use a disposable towel or hot air blower.

7 Hand washing facilities must be made available in and out of the kitchens and should be easily accessible to all food handlers.

8 Always start work wearing clean, protective clothing either washable or disposable.

9 Outdoor clothes should never be brought into a food preparation area, and working clothes must not be worn outside the working environment.

10 It is most important that a carrier of an infectious disease does not handle food. If suffering from an illness, diarrhoea, vomiting, sores, boils, rashes, septic cuts, colds, sore throats or other infections, DO NOT WORK. Inform the supervisor and seek medical advice. It is most advisable to seek advice if any close family contacts are suffering from a possible infectious illness.

11 Cover cuts, burns and abrasions with an approved waterproof dressing whenever handling foods.

12 Do not sneeze, cough or spit over or near foods.

13 Never touch the mouth, nose, ears, or hair during food preparation, these contacts could contaminate foods.

14 Keep fingers out of food as much as possible; use clean utensils to handle and to taste foods.

15 Never smoke in food areas or while handling food. It is illegal to do so and is one method of transferring germs from mouth to food.

16 Jewellery should never be worn while preparing foods. Food can easily collect in the crevices, and the jewellery might fall into a mixture without being noticed.

■ KITCHEN HYGIENE

To facilitate effective cleaning and safe food working procedures, it is essential that all equipment, walls, floors, windows and ceilings, and general production, service and storage areas are constructed of suitable materials, maintained to a high standard of cleanliness and kept in good repair.

Items that are not movable, such as shelves of cupboards, should be filled so that they are flush to the floor or wall. The entry of moisture and materials into any gaps, makes an ideal breeding ground for germs and insect pests, which could cause contamination and, possibly, contribute to food poisoning. Alternatively, sufficient space should be allowed between the items and the surfaces, to allow thorough cleaning with ease.

It is essential that in any part of the kitchen or stores, food residues and dirt are not allowed to accumulate to levels which expose the foods being prepared to the risks of contamination. Cleaning processes must therefore be thorough. They must include not only places that are easy to reach, but also places such as under equipment, between shelves, in and around cupboards, behind and under refrigerators and freezers, sinks and equipment, and all areas where access is difficult.

All corners, crevices and joints are danger areas and must be checked and cleaned thoroughly.

Fans, canopies and ventilator shafts should be kept free of dust and grime.

When cleaning refrigerators and freezers, door seals must be cleaned and checked for efficiency.

For safety's sake, when cleaning electrically powered equipment, always disconnect the power supply before dismantling. When reassembling, make sure that the parts are put together correctly and that any safety devices are locked correctly and securely in position.

Take care not to turn on electrical switches or gas taps during cleaning.

A good routine should be planned to clean all surfaces and equipment that come close to or in contact with food at least once a day. Constantly used surfaces must be cleaned more frequently, especially when handling different types of foods.

Floors should be cleaned daily with a thorough cleansing every week. In all cases, clean hot water must be used, together with the correct amount of a suitable detergent and disinfectant if appropriate. Renew the water frequently, as washing the floor or any item with cold or dirty water is ineffective.

Refuse and swill bins, or disposable plastic refuse bags, should be sited well away from food areas, preferably outside the kitchen. They should be make of a suitable material and have a close-fitting cover. Bins and bags must be kept covered at all times to avoid attracting rodents, insects and other pests. A smaller type of receptacle fitted with a foot-operated lid opener is advised for immediate use in the kitchen. This eliminates using the hands and soiling them on the lid. The bins should be emptied frequently.

Emptied bins should be cleaned, washed and sterilized inside and out. Bags should be closed and tied when full, ready for collection.

Neither pets nor other live animals should be allowed on premises where food is prepared or stored.

Rats, mice, ants, flies, cockroaches and other pests are possible carriers of disease, and will enter a building to find food and warmth. Dirt and scraps of food left around, or uncleaned equipment or premises, will encourage them into the buildings.

When infestation is apparent, the Environmental Health Officer should be contacted immediately, who will then advise on the action to adopt. It is most advisable to leave the treatment to the experts and only use chemical bait poisons or pesticide sprays in food rooms on advice from a qualified person and under strict supervision and control.

Brushes, brooms, mops, cloths and all cleaning items should be stored in an appropriate cleaning cupboard, preferably outside the kitchen. Cloths and mops must be washed after use, sterilized frequently and allowed to dry before storing away. Dish cloths should be changed and sterilized regularly.

■ CLEANING PROCEDURES

Equipment and tools should be prepared for washing by pre-cleaning and/or soaking. To wash:

Prepare two sinks, one for washing and one for rinsing. Change the water in the sinks frequently to keep them clean and hot, — 60° C (140° F) for washing and 82° C (180° F) for rinsing. Use the correct quantity of an appropriate detergent.

Before washing, always remove any foodstuffs left in or on the equipment, paying special attention to particles that have become lodged in crevices or in the mesh of sieves and strainers. If foods have stuck, burnt or dried on the equipment, or when utensils have been used for cake mixes, eggs or milk, they must be pre-soaked in cold or lukewarm water immediately after use. Do not use very hot water as this will harden the foods and make the equipment more difficult to clean.

Greasy pots, pans, trays, etc should always be soaked in very hot detergent water to loosen and disperse the grease. Knives and other metal utensils that have been used for acidic fruits such as lemons, pineapples, apples, will stain if left unwashed. To avoid this wash or rinse immediately after use.

Metal trays and pans, china, glass or earthen ware that are very hot should never be placed in cold water. The sudden change of temperature may cause the metals to distort out of shape or cause the china, glass or earthen ware to crack.

Small metal tools such as piping tubes, cutters, fragile items or knives and other sharp tools, should never be left in the sink to soak. If a heavy item were placed on top, the piping tube, cutters or fragile items could easily be squashed, broken or distorted, and therefore become useless. Knives or sharp tools may not be noticed in the sink and cut hands could be the result.

Utensils made of wood or part wood, such as rolling pins, spatulas, knives, sieves, etc should never be allowed to soak for too long in water. This causes the wood to swell and on drying out, the wood may split or warp, and in the case of knives, the handle may come apart.

After washing, rinse thoroughly with clean, hot water and ensure that the equipment is wiped dry before storing. In the case of metals which could go rusty, it is advisable to heat dry them by standing the items in front of an open oven or by other means of dry gentle heat. Items made from wood should always be dried naturally before being stored.

Always keep equipment in a dust free cupboard or keep it covered. Store tidily and whenever possible stack the items so that space is not wasted. There is a saying 'everthing has a place and there is a place for everything'. This is a good rule to follow so that items may be quickly found.

Special care of different materials

Some of the materials used in the manufacture of equipment, and the way that certain utensils are made, necessitates special care and treatment to maintain them and to prevent their premature deterioration.

ALUMINIUM

Soda must never be used as this causes the aluminium to corrode, become pitted and develop holes. Aluminium equipment should be washed in hot detergent water, rinsed well and immediately dried. It is a soft metal so avoid using wire wool and coarse abrasive cleaning materials.

TINNED WARE

Some items such as moulds, whisks, strainers, sieves and certain copper pans are coated with a layer of tin. Wash these in mild detergent or soda solution, taking care that excessive abrasion is not used on the tin coating. Damage to the tin coating is also caused if the items are empty and exposed to high temperatures (tin will melt if the temperature is above 230° C (446° F)).

It is important that utensils are re-tinned when the coating wears off as the bare metal exposed would contaminate, discolour and spoil any contents. With copperware this process is worthwhile; with other metals it may be more economical to purchase replacements.

COPPER AND TINNED COPPER

This equipment should be soaked in very hot water to which a little soda has been added, brushed clean, rinsed in very hot water and dried.

Copper is a good conductor of heat but has the disadvantage that it tarnishes easily. To brighten copper, rub with a mixture of salt and lemon juice or vinegar, rinse in clean water then dry.

STAINLESS STEEL

Clean in hot water and detergent, rinse with very hot water and dry. Steel wool and harsh abrasive agents are best avoided.

PLASTICS

Wash in a weak solution of detergent or warm soapy water immediately after use. Rinse in clean warm water and dry. Some plastic utensils are not affected by temperatures a little above the boiling point of water, but they should never be subjected to any form of dry heat. Other plastics cannot withstand heat of any kind.

ENAMEL

Very little use is made of utensils made from enamel in a production kitchen. It is used mainly for cabinets, ovens and boiling grid tops. Providing it is washed regularly, all that is required is washing with hot detergent water and wiping dry. Care should be taken as enamel chips easily if knocked and may drop or fly into foods.

IRON

This is one of the most favoured metals for omelette and pancake pans and for baking trays, but it is prone to rust. After washing the equipment should be rinsed in very hot water and thoroughly dried immediately.

Unless equipment of this kind is in a very dirty condition, it is not necessary to wash every time it is used. It is even more beneficial if the surface is 'preserved', which makes it less liable to stick. All that is normally required to preserve it is for the surfaces to be wiped clean while still warm with a clean cloth or paper. Baking trays may require scraping to remove any surplus foods before wiping. This method of preserving a non stick surface is also used for baking tins and moulds.

Omelette and pancake pans may require 'proving' after washing. This is done by spreading a layer of salt in the pans then heating them to a high temperature. The salt is removed and the pan wiped thoroughly with an oily cloth to remove all the salt.

WOOD
Any item made of wood or part wood should never be allowed to soak in water. They should be cleaned immediately after use, washed in hot detergent water, rinsed and dried naturally.

SIEVES
These may require the removal of loose food stuffs from the wire before washing in plenty of water. Give a final rinse under fast running water. To extend the life of a wire sieve do not 'hammer' the mixture through but push it by pressing and rubbing gently bur firmly.

ROLLING PINS
Remove any paste from the rolling pin using a cloth or plastic scraper. Do not use a knife or any other hard instrument as this could life the wood and cause splinters. Wash, rinse and dry naturally. The rolling pin should never be used as a mallet; it is easily dented and would therefore not be any good for smooth rolling.

CHOPPING BOARDS
These should be scrubbed clean while in water, then rinsed, wiped and allowed to stand to air.

MARBLE AND LAMINATED PLASTICS
These are mainly used as working surfaces for rolling out pastes. Clean by scraping off any foods, wash with plenty of hot detergent water, rinse with clean water and wipe dry.

SOFT MATERIALS
The bristles on flour, egg and grease brushes should be rubbed in plenty of water to loosen the particles of foods that are clinging to them, washed well and rinsed. If they have part metal handles they should be well dried to prevent rust. If possible store with the bristles hanging down.

PIPING AND JELLY BAGS
These must be washed immediately after use. Allow them to soak for a while in hot detergent water, then rub them inside and out, making sure that all food is loosened from the seams. Rinse several times and hang to dry. The drying may be speeded up if the bag is rolled inside a clean cloth and wrung out gently. With regard to hygiene, it is advisable to purchase piping bags which can be boiled. Alternatively, cheap plastic disposable types are available.

CHOCOLATE MOULDS

These should be washed in a mild solution of detergent and water, which is luke warm, then rinsed and dried thoroughly. Before using them polish with cotton wool or a very soft flannel cloth. Never use even the mildest form of abrasive or any kind of scraper to remove hardened chocolate, it must only be removed by washing in warm water.

■ SAFETY AT WORK

One must remember that accidents are caused by neglect, insufficient knowledge, inadequate precautions, bad working practices, poor equipment or lack of maintenance.

It is the responsibility of the supervisors and managers to ensure that the equipment and the working environment are safe. They shall provide the required information, supervision and necessary training to the operatives to ensure safety at work, and encourage the staff to check all equipment and report any signs of fault or deterioration.

However, it is the responsibility of all personnel, irrespective of rank or status, to take precautions, and promote and develop working procedures to ensure safe practices.

For their own safety and for the safety of others, everybody should be aware and should recognize possible sources of danger, informing colleagues of potential or real hazards immediately. Employees have a moral responsibility to each other to maintain safe working conditions.

They should ensure that the equipment and the kitchen areas are safe and serviced regularly, that everything is used correctly, and that consideration is given to colleagues when working together to develop and promote safe working practices.

It is important that information regarding safety is extended to all people entering the premises, whether they are employees of the firm or not. It is the responsibility of both management and employees to ensure that their actions and the working environment do not subject others to risks.

For various reasons, natural lighting is not always adequate in kitchens. Many areas of a kitchen, such as above work tables, sinks, near shelves, under canopies, in corners and store rooms shelves, require artificial lighting. To avoid eye strain and, more seriously, accidents, the position of good lighting should always be a priority.

Floors must be soundly constructed of non-slip materials, and it is important that the correct type of cleaning materials are used.

Anything that has spilled on the floor should be cleared, cleaned and dried immediately. Sprinkling a little salt over the wet area will prevent it from being slippery.

Floors should be properly maintained and kept in good repair as damaged floor surfaces can cause accidents.

All passages between working areas must be kept clear from any obstructions and the use of mats of any kind should be avoided.

All machinery, especially those with exposed moving parts or cutting blades, should have effective safety guards.

Never switch on electrical appliances with wet hands. Do not operate a machine if it is not functioning correctly, or if you do not understand how to use it properly.

If a machine develops a fault, switch it off and report it. Request instructions from a responsible person.

Never clean or dismantle electrical apparatus without first ensuring that the machine is switched off and disconnected from the power supply terminal.

It is important that electrical cables are kept as short as possible. They should never be allowed to trail around the floor, hang loosely or be close to the working area.

To protect the user of electrical appliances from electric shocks due to unforseen faults in the wiring or appliances, fit a fuse of the correct size. The electric circuit must also be fitted with a circuit breaker switch. This should be inspected and tested regularly by a competent electrician.

When lighting gas ovens, it is important to observe the basic rules. These are to make sure that the pilot light is lit before turning on the main gas, and that the thermostat is sufficiently high for the pilot flame to ignite the gas.

If no pilot is fitted, always make sure that a lighted taper or match is ready before turning on the gas.

If the gas does not light or blows out, gas will have collected in the oven. Always turn off the gas supply, open the oven doors and allow the gas to escape before relighting. Remember that if gas has accumulated, be it in the oven chamber, or in the top of a solid top stove, even a small spark could cause an explosion.

When a steamer is in use, make sure that the safety valve is free and will release any excessive pressure that could build up within the chamber. Make sure it is not covered or obstructed in any way. Take care when opening the steamer door — to release the high pressure, it is advisable to open it up slowly, up to the safety catch fitted. If a steamer is opened too fast, a large volume of steam could escape quickly, and serious scalding could result.

Deep fat fryers should only be filled to the level mark, about two-thirds full. Take extra care when frying foods which may be wet, and always place the foods slowly into the fryer or the fat will rise fast, spill over and could cause a fire.

If a fire should occur, turn off the appliance and cover the fire with a fire blanket or a thick, damp cloth, or use a foam or dry powder fire extinguisher. Never use water to extinguish a fat fire.

Accidents can be caused by wearing unsuitable footwear. Shoes should be sound, with low heels and non-slip soles. Wearing old and possibly broken shoes is bad practice. Apart from the danger of hot fat or liquids spilling onto the feet, a cook does a lot of standing and walking about during a day's work. Therefore comfortable, well-fitting and sturdy, protective footwear is a good investment.

Always use a board when cutting at a table. Stainless steel and plastic laminate tables are slippery, and will blunt the knife. The knife could also slip and cause an injury.

Always work in a clean and tidy manner, it could prevent accidents. If the table is cluttered, working space will be limited, tools will be difficult to handle properly, and injuries can easily happen.

Always clean and store knives immediately after use. Leaving them in the sink or laying around is detrimental to the tool and could also cause an injury.

Fires are not uncommon in kitchens and all cooks should be on their guard against outbreaks of fire. Gas or electric cookers, heated fats on stoves or in fritures, faulty electrical appliance flexes, cloths and clothing worn by staff, are all fire hazards found in the kitchen. Staff should know where the fire extinguishers are, recognize the various types and understand how to use them if it becomes necessary. Items such as matches and inflammable materials should be safely stored away from any possible danger of being ignited.

Fire exits must be kept clear at all times and as long as there are people on the premises, these should never be locked.

If a fire appears to be spreading throughout the kitchen, and if it is possible to do so, close the doors and windows, so that the fire is confined to that area of the building.

Never use a lift to leave any floor of the building, the power supply could be cut off and the lift would be immobile. Also fumes, smoke and flames can be drawn up the lift shaft.

The chef's jacket or overall should be of a strong material, preferably of the double-breasted type, as this will give extra protection from the heat when working over stoves or in front of ovens. The sleeves are meant to be worn down to the wrists, again to protect the arms from the heat and possible splashes from hot fat or liquids.

The purpose of the apron, which should reach below the knees, is to protect the lower part of the body from being burnt or scalded and to help the clothes stay clean.

Care must be taken with the apron tie tapes: they should be tucked into the top part of the apron to avoid them being caught in moving machinery or any other equipment.

Apart from the point of view of hygiene, jewellery of any kind should never be worn during work. Necklaces, bracelets, chains, or any similar loose type of personal adornments, could get caught in moving machinery or attached to the handles of pots or pans. There is the added danger that without noticing, they could fall into the mixture being prepared.

To be effective, knives should be sharp. A blunt knife will cause a person to exert pressure and, in doing so, the knife can easily slip. It is also a good policy to make sure that the knife handle is free from grease or any other slippery substance so that a good, firm grip is possible.

In all premises there should be notices of procedures to adopt in case of the outbreak of a fire. All employees should read and understand the information given and note the exits to use to evacuate the building and their assembly point.

Even by taking precautions, the possibility of accidents and injuries do occur. Therefore it is important on the part of the management, that provision is made for first aid and that all staff are aware of the facilities. These should include a well-stocked first aid box, within view and easy reach, with the provision to treat minor cuts, scalds and burns. As the title indicates, it is a preliminary treatment only. If the injury is serious or unknown, a qualified opinion and treatment should be sought immediately. Some establishments have members of staff who have undergone a training course in first aid.

All accidents, however minor they may appear, should be reported to the immediate superior. It is required by law that details are then entered in the accident book. Remember that even minor injuries can become infected and the infection passed on to others.

For the professional craftsperson to adopt a safe and correct approach to work, the following points should be considered and used as a guide.

1 Avoid haste and panic; never run in the kitchen.
2 Work methodically and concentrate on the job in hand — distractions can cause accidents.
3 Always use a dry cloth when handling hot trays, pots, etc. — never use an apron or a damp cloth.
4 When removing large trays from the oven, or transferring them from one place to another, use a large, thick, dry cloth and carry each tray by holding the side with one hand and support it by holding the other hand underneath.
5 Do not crowd around stoves, fryers or ovens. Too many people in one place may cause accidents.
6 Give priority to any person carrying hot or heavy things, or taking

things off the stove or out of the oven.

7 Flour sprinkled on trays or handles of pots or pans indicates that they are hot, this is a good practice to follow to make others aware of the danger.

8 Keep handles of pots and pans away from the front of the stove to prevent them being knocked over. Make sure the handles are not situated over direct heat.

9 Before turning on gas taps, always have a taper or match ready alight and always light the gas pilot first.

10 If the oven gas flame should blow out, turn off the gas supply, open the oven doors and allow the gas to escape before relighting.

11 If the fat catches fire, turn off the fuel supply and cover the pan with a metal tray, lid or fire blanket. Never use water.

12 Take extra care when dealing with hot fats, boiling liquids and steamers.

13 Never touch electrical apparatus or switches with wet hands.

14 Never use water to extinguish flames coming from a fire in an electrical applicance. The appliance should be siwtched off at the terminal or, if necessary, at the mains.

15 Always switch off and disconnect the power supply when cleaning machines or working in the mixing bowls with the hands.

16 Keep hands, cloths, clothing and utensils away from machinery while they are in motion.

17 When fitted, always make sure that the safety guards are correctly positioned and locked in place.

18 Knives should always be handled with care, never thrown or waved about and always placed carefully on the table or in the drawer. When walking about with a knife, it should be carried by the handle with the point of the blade towards the floor.

19 If anything is spilt on the floor, clean it up immediately, so that accidents will be avoided.

20 Safe and protective clothing should be worn, eg. a cotton jacket or overall with long sleeves, together with an apron that reaches below the knees to give added protection to the lower part of the body. Good, stout shoes with non-slip soles should be worn to protect the feet.

21 Make sure you know where the fire extinguishers are and that you know how to use them.

22 Check and find out the fire drill procedure, make sure you are acquainted with the exits and assembly points and who to report to after evacuation.

23 Accidents should always be reported to the immediate superior, however slight they may seem.

24 Remember, there is always a reason for an accident to happen.

3 THE METRIC SYSTEM

Length, capacity, weight and temperature are the four main quantities which will meet the basic requirements of the pastry cook. The Système International d'Unités is the modern system of measurement being adopted in Great Britain. The recognized international symbol for the system is SI. In the system all quantity units have basic names, eg metre, litre, and are preceded by a prefix, eg millio, kilo which expresses the value of the unit. The same prefix is used, irrespective of the quantity units to which they apply.

The system is exclusively decimal and the values are in multiples or submultiples in the power of ten. All units and prefixes may be abbreviated in writing by using standardized symbols, eg ml = millilitre, km = kilometre.

Quantity	Unit	Symbol
length	metre	m
capcity	litre	l
weight	kilogram*	kg
	(gram)	g
temperature	Celsius*	
	(centigrade)	°C

* The kilogram (kg) has been chosen as the unit of weight instead of the gram (g), resulting in the irregularity of the system as it has kilo (k) as part of its name.
* In France the term 'grade' is used for 1/100 right angle and centigrade

Prefix	Symbol	Value	
*mega	M	1 000 000	
kilo	k	1 000	
*hecto	h	100	
*deca	da	10	
		1	
*deci	d	0.1	1/10th
*centi	c	0.01	1/100th
milli	m	0.001	1/1 000th

would mean 1/10 000 right angle, to avoid confusion it has been renamed Celsius(°C).

The prefixes marked * are not expected to be in common use, except for centi (c) often used in linear quantity, eg centimetre (cm).

The measurements are written by stating the amount, followed by the prefix and unit name or symbols, eg 1 kg, 1.250 l, 50 mm, 200° C. The prefix should express the whole unit or the number preceding the point denoting part of the unit, eg 1.250 kg means $1\frac{1}{4}$ kilograms, if the figure was written as 12.50 kg it would means $12\frac{1}{2}$ kilograms, or if 0.125 kg this equals 1/8th kilogram.

The following are examples of methods used for writing amounts.

$\frac{1}{4}$ metre	= 0.250 m or 250 mm or 25 cm
$\frac{1}{4}$ kilogram	= 0.75 kg or 750 g
10 grams	= 0.010 kg or 10 g
$1\frac{1}{2}$ litres	= 1.500 l or 1 500 ml
125 mililitres	= 0.125 l or 125 ml

Always leave a space between the amounts and the symbols. To avoid confusion with the litre symbol in printed work, it is best if the whole word litre is written or if script form (*l*) is used. Printing one litre (1 l) looks very much like the number 11.

It should also be noted that the milli symbol is a small m; a capital M must not be used unless intended; for example, if an order was made out for 100 ml of brandy (1/10th or a litre) and it was written as 100 M, this would mean that the order was made for 1 000 000 litres.

Do not use the dot or comma to denote the thousands, but leave a space. If writing 1 500 grams ($1\frac{1}{2}$ kg) it could appear as 1.500 grams which actually means it is $1\frac{1}{2}$ grams.

Only one prefix and unit symbol is required for an amount; for example, for $1\frac{3}{4}$ kg it should be written as 1.75 kg and not 1 kg and 750 g. Some recipe books are giving metric and imperial weights, usually written down side by side. An important point to remember is that the recipe amounts are only approximate and do not convert exactly. While these approximations serve the purpose, they could lead to unbalanced recipes when added or multiplied. It is safe to say that 25 grams equals 1 oz, but if one takes the correct conversion of 10 oz, the true amount would be 283 grams; a difference of 33 grams. 1 pint is often equated to $\frac{1}{2}$ a litre (500 ml); the pint is actually 568 ml, a difference of 68 ml, about 8 per cent.

Conversions should only be used as a guide to amounts. The ideal solution is to think and work using only one or the other system and not attempt to convert.

When measuring it is important to avoid mixing the weights and measures of a recipe. In each case they are balanced in their own rights, eg

1 oz of flour will thicken 1 pt (20 fluid oz) of liquid and 25 g will thicken 500 ml. In each case the proportion of solid to liquid is 1 to 20. If 1 oz were used instead of 25 g, the consistency would be too thick when using 500 ml of liquid, or if 25 g was used instead of 1 oz the consistency would be too thin for 1 pt of liquid.

It is often possible to weigh the liquids required. 1 ml of water is equal to 1 g, 1 litre equal to 1 kg. Other commodities will vary.

1 oz	=	0.028 kg	28.35 g	
8 oz	=	0.226 kg	226.80 g	
1 lb	=	0.453 kg	453.60 g	
$\frac{1}{4}$ pt	=	0.142 l	142.05 ml	
$\frac{1}{2}$ pt	=	0.284 l	284.10 ml	
1 pt	=	0.568 l	568.20 ml	
1 inch	=	0.025 m	25.40 mm	2.54 cm
1 foot	=	0.304 m	304.80 mm	30.48 cm
1 yard	=	914 m	914.40 mm	91.44 cm
32°F	=	0°C	(freezing point)	
212°F	=	100°C	(boiling point)	

Temperature conversion formula:

$$°F - 32 \div 9 \times 5 = °C \qquad °C \div 5 \times 9 + 32 = °F$$

or

$$°F + 40 \div 9 \times 5 - 40 = °C \quad °C + 40 \div 5 \times 9 - 40 = °F$$

■ CONVERSION DIAL

To convert imperial quantities to metric, place a straight edge, starting at the centre on the dial lining up the dot corresponding with the imperial measurement and read off the equivalent metric quantity on the outer scale.

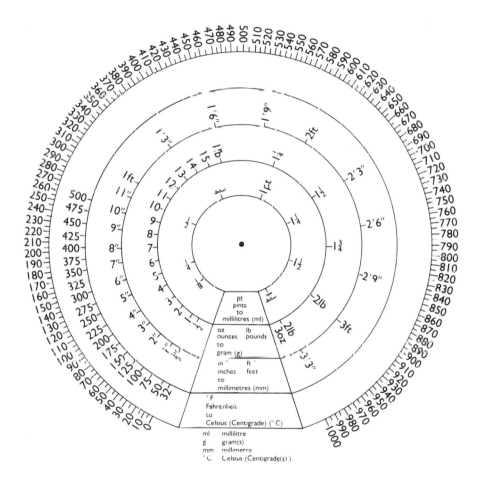

4 EQUIPMENT

Over the years the purposes of basic equipment used in the pastry kitchen have changed very little. If old and modern equipment is compared, it will be noticed that the way they are shaped and the functions that they are meant to perform have not changed.

Greater mechanization and automation has been introduced. Equipment has been improved by the use of different materials and modern techniques in its manufacture. It has become more labour and energy saving, more efficient in use, easier to maintain and, as far as food hygiene is concerned, easier to keep clean.

Ovens, hotplates, bains-maries, fryers and other cooking appliances mostly have an exterior made of stainless steel with removable sections, drip trays, inner oven liners or shelves for ease of cleaning. Most have automatic controls and switches, which (when working correctly) ensure they operate at a constant set temperature, making them more efficient and economical. This assists the pastry cook to avoid errors.

Mixing machines can now be fitted with different sizes of bowls. A variety of attachments can be used to adapt the machine for other useful purposes; for instance, mincing, liquidising, sieving, straining or slicing. Work tables are now made or covered in stainless steel or laminated plastics instead of wood, which made them difficult to clean and developed cracks which harboured germs.

Many small hand-operated utensils and labour-saving devices have been developed to make the work involved in food preparation simpler, and easier, and their use may result in a better quality product being produced in less time. All equipment, large and small, is expensive to purchase and replace. Its usefulness and reliability depends very much on care in use and correct maintenance of individual items. It is the pastry cook's responsibility, and obviously is to his or her advantage, to ensure that all equipment is maintained in good working order.

A regular inspection and checking system is essential for mechanical, electrical and gas appliances. This is often carried out on maintenance contracts or by service engineers on a regular basis. It is of extreme importance that safety devices are in working order and that they are used as per instruction. Any faults in equipment must be reported and repairs carried out by qualified technicians.

Thorough and appropriate cleaning and correct handling will extend the useful life of all equipment. A good craftsperson accepts this as a normal routine in the day's work, as described in the section on cleaning procedures on page 7.

■ TYPES OF EQUIPMENT

Equipment may be classified under three main headings; large and stationery equipment, light equipment and utensils, and personal equipment. The types and sizes required by the catering establishment and the pastry cook will depend on the preparation and production requirements, the type of catering and the output. The following may be considered as basic requirements in a well equipped and busy pastry kitchen.

Large and stationary equipment

It is important that items of equipment which cannot easily be moved are designed or sited so that spillage does not get lodged in inaccessible places. The whole piece of equipment, and all detachable parts, should be easily cleaned. Space should be allowed between walls and the rear of appliances and between one item and another. All items should be designed to either form a perfect joint with the floor or allow sufficient space underneath for cleaning purposes. The design should also be such that sections can be removed to allow cleaning under the covered areas.

OVENS

Special types of ovens, mainly heated by electricity or gas, are used in the pastry kitchen. The cooking chamber is shallow, being only about 150 mm (6″) high, with a floor area of about 800 mm (30″) in depth by between 1000 mm (40″) and 1500 mm (60″) in width, capable of taking four to six baking trays. The heat is retained within by insulating panels.

With the oven being shallow, the door opening is restricted, this results in more heat being retained within the cooking chamber when the door is open. Doors are usually of the up and over or drop down type. At the rear or sides of the chamber a small damper flap is fitted. This may be opened to allow excess steam to escape, or kept closed if steam is required in the oven.

Pastry ovens are available as single units or are built in tiers. The temperature of each unit is independently controlled which enables only the amount of oven space required to be in use. This eliminates the waste of energy by not having to heat a large appliance.

The temperatures are thermostatically controlled by three switches, one which maintains a pre-set temperature and the other two control the top or bottom heat of the chamber. This is a useful feature which enables the operator to bake different items more effectivly, by having more heat or less heat in the area required, eg cream caramels, palmiers and shallow type cakes require more bottom heat. Vol-au-vents, meringue toppings on flans, are best with more top heat. An even temperature throughout the chamber may also be achieved for goods such as cakes and sponges.

The floor of the cooking chamber is usually fitted either with a drip tray or removable section for ease of cleaning.

BOILING TOPS

These could have a solid top of cast iron construction and be heated by either gas or electricity, or they could have an open top with gas flame burners or radiant electric rings. The electric solid top types are usually thermostatically controlled, and are often made with two or four separate plates, each one independently controlled. The gas heated tops concentrate the heat in the centre of the plate, with gradual cooling off towards the edges. This is an economical advantage when the food being cooked requires varying degrees of heat. The open flame or radiant electric rings may be fitted with different sized burners or rings, and the temperature is usually controlled manually. The boiling table must be level and at a reasonable height. Between 750 mm (30″) and 850 mm (34″) is considered a suitable working height. The cook must be able to see inside the pots and be able to lift or manoeuvre the cooking utensils easily.

Solid tops should be kept constantly clean by wiping with a coarse sacking material. When cool at the end of a working session they can be cleaned more thoroughly by brushing with a stiff wire brush and abrasive powders before wiping clean. This should be followed by wiping with an oily cloth to prevent rust forming. Open flame types are fitted with removable drip trays and grids for cleaning.

GRILL (SALAMANDER)

Fierce radiant heat is required for the grill to operate efficiently. The heat may be produced by electricity or gas. The elements or burners are in the top part of the grill. Apart from glazing and fast heating of some items, very little use is made of the grill in the pastry kitchen.

DEEP FAT/OIL FRYERS

These may be floor or table standing models, depending on the size and capacity of the fryer. Most are heated by electricity and fitted with thermostatic controls to maintain the heat of the fat at pre-selected temperatures.

Improved fryers are manufactured to promote a 'cold zone'. The removable heating element is made to fit the size and shape of the frying bowl and is suspended above the bottom. This allows the fat above to get hot, but the layer below the element remains cooler. The result is that particles of food which fall to the bottom will not char and circulate within the fat, thus spoiling the appearance of items being cooked.

To clean the fryer first switch off the power supply, drain the still warm fat through a valve underneath the fryer. The oil will fall through a mesh strainer underneath into a container. The element must be lifted out and cleaned. The frying bowl should be wiped with absorbent paper or cloth to remove food debris. For a more thorough cleaning, half fill the unit with mild detergent water, bring to the boil, drain and reboil with clear water, drain again and dry with a clean cloth.

STEAMERS

This apparatus could be considered as an 'oven' fitted with shelving or trays and which cooks by moist heat. High pressure steam is used to produce the moist heat which may come from a main steam supply boiler, or from water which is heated in a tank situated at the base of the chamber. It may be heated by either gas or electricity and must be thermostatically controlled.

A steam release valve is fitted. This is a safety device which, if the steam pressure increases to a dangerous level, will open to release the excess pressure. This valve and the adjacent areas must be kept clear and not obstructed in any way.

The water tank type of steamer will be damaged if the water supply is not free running as it may otherwise boil dry. The level of water is automatically controlled by a ball valve. This must be checked to see that the operating arm moves freely to allow the water to flow and replenish the tank.

To clean the steamer, turn off the steam or water supply and the fuel supply. Drain the water off. Thoroughly wash the trays and chamber with hot detergent water. Rinse with plenty of hot water and allow it to drain away. Ensure that air will circulate within the chamber by keeping the door slightly open. This will keep the steamer fresh. Remember to turn on the water supply before applying heat.

Take special care when opening the steamer doors when it is in use and when removing items from the shelves. Steam escaping from the chamber when it is opened, and the hot water attached to trays, can cause serious scalding.

HOT CUPBOARD AND BAIN-MARIE

These are available heated either by steam, gas or electricity. The cupboard may have a solid table top or be fitted with a bain-marie section. The type best suited for pastry use is the electrically heated hot cupboard incorporating a bain-marie section on the top, with separate thermostatic controls for each section.

Ideally it should be fitted with wheels or castors so that it is mobile for moving adjacent to the areas where foods are to be served. The electrically heated unit is obviously the most suited as it can be plugged in anywhere.

It should be able to maintain a controlled temperature range between 38° C (100° F) and 94° C (200° F). It can then serve a double purpose. When not required for keeping foods and sauces hot during service, the bain-marie may be used for warming fondant and chocolate and the cupboard can be used for drying meringues. If a tray of water is placed in the bottom of the cupboard, the unit will also serve as a proving cupboard.

The cupboard should have removable sliding doors for ease of opening and to allow room for large trays of food to be accommodated on the shelves within the cabinet. The bain-marie section should be fitted with covered containers in a water-filled or dry heat (waterless) type of well. Gas heated appliances are water-filled. Electrical appliances are normally dry heated.

If a water type bain-marie is used, ensure that there is an adequate supply of water and the well does not dry when the heat is on.

After use, disconnect it from the power supply, drain the water out, wash and wipe dry. Never leave the water in or leave it wet as rust and a build-up of 'fur' may develop. In hard water areas a little soda in the water will help to prevent the furring. (Soda should not be used if aluminium containers are in use.) The cupboard should be wiped clean, including the slide channels for the doors. With removable sliding doors this job is made much easier.

PROVING CUPBOARD

This is a tall cupboard fitted with runners suitably spaced to accept the baking trays used. The moist heat required is provided by a gas or electrically heated water tank situated at the bottom of the cupboard. This provides a moist heat at temperatures in the region of 37° C (100° F) and is used for proving fermented yeast goods. Clean as for a steamer.

Providing the unit is fitted with a removable water tank, the prover could be used as a drying cupboard.

HOT AIR DRYING CUPBOARD

This is virtually the same design as the prover, except that gentle dry heat is produced. It is used for drying out pastillage and royal icing work.

If the temperature is adjustable and it operates at a temperature of 90° C (200° F), it may also be used for drying out meringues.

SUGAR WORK CABINET

Normally this is a glass fronted cabinet used for display and storage of cooked sugar work. The cupboard should be dust and moisture proof, and should be situated away from the working environment. Any internal cleaning must take into account the need for the cupboard to be free of moisture. A dry cleaning method must therefore be used. External surfaces should be cleaned according to the material. To preserve the sugar work in good condition, a tray of silicagel or lime is placed on the bottom of the cabinet to absorb any moisture within the cabinet. The silica-gel or lime must occasionally be dried by heat for it to be continually effective.

BAKING TRAY RACK

This should be situated as near as possible to the oven so that as the trays are brought out from the oven there is a convenient place for them to be rested. The runners on the rack must obviously be of the correct size to accommodate the trays.

As the rack is exposed to the air, baking trays should always be stored upside down to prevent dust settling on the surface on which uncooked foods will be placed.

MIXER

This is the most useful, labour saving, electrically operated appliance available to the pastry cook. The models which are now available feature varying speeds of operation. It is possible to adapt the same machine, using additional attachments, to perform other functions such as liquidizing, puréeing, mincing, chopping, slicing and grating.

The main purpose however is that of a mixer. The size and capacity of the machine will vary according to requirements. It is possible to have two sets of different sized bowls and attachments to fit one machine, to be used according to requirements. The tools for mixing are a hook for heavy doughs, the paddle or beater for creaming mixtures and blending batters and a balloon type whisk for light aerated foam products.

The attachments and tools are made in varying types of metals, eg stainless steel, tinned metal or aluminium. Care must be taken that as they rotate to mix the contents of the bowl, they do not rub against the sides as this would cause the mixture to take on a grey colour from the metals. Some of the smaller machines do have bowls and tools made of toughened plastic, which helps to eradicate problems of poor colour. These tools are usually only employed when producing small quantities.

The machine, for whatever purpose it is used, should never be overloaded; this would place a strain on the motor with eventual failure. Overloading can also be caused by some obstruction in the product or a blockage in the attachments, or by having the motor set at too high a speed.

The machine and its components should be periodically checked and serviced for efficiency and safety. Take care because, after servicing, oil will quite often seep out of the moving parts and drip into the mixture.

When cleaning pay special attention to component parts above and around the mixing bowl as food easily gets splashed and if not removed will dry and possibly fall into the bowl when it is next in use.

WORKING TABLES

These should be fairly heavy construction so that they are stable when worked upon. The pastry cook does require a large table to work on, especially for rolling out pastes. It should be at least 750 mm (30") wide by 1500 mm (60") long and 750 mm (30") high. The correct height for rolling is important so that the pressure may be applied from the shoulders.

The surface of the table should be, if possible, in one piece, free from any cracks or joins. Wooden surfaces do not always come up to this standard and foods become lodged in the grain and cracks in the wood. The ideal surfaces are either marble, stainless steel or plastic laminate. A work top made of a suitable material can be placed on a sturdy table with a poor surface. It must however be of a sufficient dimension to completely cover the top and allow an overhang all round. This is to prevent food debris being caught in the crevice between the two surfaces.

Space must be allowed under any shelves fitted below the table for cleaning the floor, and the table should be mobile to allow cleaning under the table legs.

REFRIGERATORS AND DEEP FREEZERS

Details of these are to be found under their respective heading in the refrigeration and storage section.

■ LIGHT EQUIPMENT AND UTENSILS

The equipment and utensils shown are by no means the comprehensive requirement of the pastry section. The list of items has been compiled by selecting examples of the more specialized pieces of equipment needed for pastry work and to which reference has been made in various sections of the book.

SMALL MOULDS

1 Various sizes of deep rounds suitable for individual egg custard tarts, meat pies and puddings.
2 Cream horn mould.
3 Small ovals for meat pies.
4 Small individual savarin mould, also used for sponges and small cakes.
5 Various sizes of rolled edge tartlets; these may range from 25 mm (1") to 75 mm (3") in diameter.
6 Assorted sizes of fluted moulds; the larger and deeper ones are used for brioche, others for pastries, cakes, sponges and petits fours.
7 Oblong cases for individual sponges or cakes.
8 Three sizes of dariole moulds used for cream caramels, rum babas and madeleines; these are also available in aluminium and tinned copper.
9 Various sizes of boats or barquettes ranging from 50 mm (2") to 100 mm (4") in length, used for marignans, pastries, small cakes, petits fours and savoury cases.

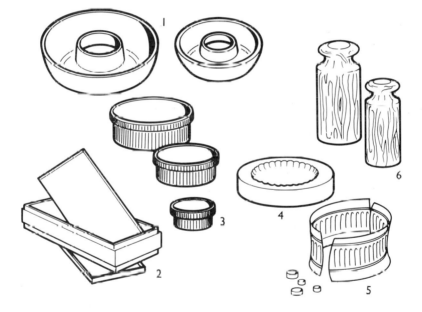

LARGE MOULDS

1 Two sizes of aluminium savarin moulds, 150 mm (6") to 200 mm (8"), also available in tinned metal and tinned copper.
2 Tinned metal case with separate lid and base for biscuit glace.
3 Three sizes of china soufflé cases, sizes available range between 50 mm (2") to 200 mm (8").
4 Wooden block for moulding short-bread. The item shown is to produce a design of 150 mm (6") in diameter but smaller and larger sizes are available.

5 Tinned metal hinged pie mould with clips. Different sizes and patterns are available.
6 Two wooden blocks for moulding of hand raised pies.

PASTRY UTENSILS

1 Baking tray scraper, also useful for smoothing and pressing marzipan onto the side of cakes.
2 Table scraper.
3 Small 'paint' scraper for chocolate and fondant work.
4 Small paste docker.
5 Roller type paste docker.
6 Flour brush.
7 Basket weave pattern rolling pin for marzipan, pastillage and paste decoration.
8 Ribbed pattern rolling pin, used for decorating as weave pattern.
9 Adjustable wheel strip cutters with expanding cutters/blades to cut widths between 12 mm ($\frac{1}{2}$) to 200 mm (8").
10 Ravioli wheel cutter.
11 Paste edge decorating and sealing tweezers.
12 Wood dowellings for shaping brandy snaps and cigarette biscuits.

CONFECTIONERY UTENSILS

1 Cake decorating turntable.
2 Cake section market. Different size and shapes are available.
3 Colour dispensing bottle.
4 Light bulb heating unit for drying royal icing run-outs.
5 Overhead heat lamp approximately 250 watts.
6 Methylated spirit lamp for heating and joining sugar work.
7 Basket weaving frame and metal rods.
8 Wires for sugar basket handle and flower stems.

9 Cut wire whisk for spun sugar.
10 Dipping fork and loop.
11 Plastic leaf maker.
12 Copper sugar boiling pot.
13 Brass sugar boiling thermometer.
14 Saccharometer. This is for the measurement of density.

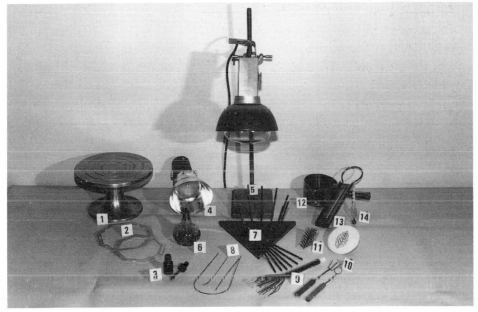

CASTING MOULDS

1 Plastic castles and figure suitable for casting and moulding chocolate, marzipan, pastillage and cold grained sugar.
2 Plaster moulds which are 'home made'. The upper mould was made by using the medallion shown and the lower one from small hard decorations. They are used to cast or mould chocolate, marzipan or pastillage and for casting hot grained sugar.

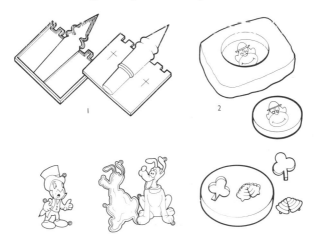

COPPER WARE

The diagram below shows some examples of copper equipment used in pastry work.

1 Two bombe glacé moulds (one showing a screw in top which acts as a stand when filled and inverted to an upright position).
2 Charlotte mould.
3 Whisking bowl.
4 Savarin mould.
5 Two sizes of dariole moulds.
6 Barquette mould.
7 Two sizes of decorative jelly or bavarois moulds.
8 Sugar boiling pan.

■ PERSONAL EQUIPMENT

A range of knives and other small implements are needed by the pastry cook to perform the specialized work required in the pastry kitchen. These are usually their own personal property. Although some items are essential, it is not necessary to have a comprehensive set. When choosing which tools to purchase, each individual must select those which will be best suited to their own personal needs.

Selecting and using the right knife for a task will assist deft manipulation and speed of operation. Craftpersons learn by experience which knife suits them and will often use a particular knife for many purposes because they have become accustomed to it and it suits their style and skill.

Good quality tools are expensive and it is advisable, when selecting items, that the best quality available are obtained. A beginner should choose carefully a few good tools that are a necessity and purchase additional items as required, building up the kit in gradual stages.

Cheap tools may look good but they will not be as effective or as durable as a quality item, and in the long run may prove to be more expensive.

To ensure long life it is necessary to use and look after tools with proper care. The following details will indicate some of the essential points to note when selecting and maintaining tools in good condition.

KNIVES

These are probably the most used tools and should be strong and have well made blades of good quality steel. Those made of stainless steel are easier to keep clean but it will be found that a sharp edge is more easily maintained on an ordinary steel blade.

On a good knife the tang of the blade will be part of the handle. It should be fitted well with a shaped wooden hand grip firmly riveted on. Although it is the blade that does the cutting, it is the hand that controls the action. Not all hands have the same strength and the grip is important. A good, well made knife should be comfortable to grasp and feel balanced as if part of the hand.

Unless the knife is for heavy work, such as chopping, it should have a light spring in the blade. A carver, cake slicer or bread knife, being longer with a flatter blade, will tend to be more flexible. A palette knife must be flexible, but this flexibility should be in the length of the blade and not where it joins the handle.

Small fruit knives, corers, peelers, grooving knives and zesters should be rigid and as they are mainly used for items containing acidic juices, they should preferably be made of stainless steel.

To maintain a sharp cutting edge, cutting should always take place on a board. In pastrywork this is not always possible. Items such as pastes, marzipan and cooked sugar have to be cut on a hard surface, such as a marble slab. It is therefore advisable to set aside one or two knives which are used solely for this purpose.

Immediately after use wash and dry the knives. They should never be left to soak in water as this would cause the wooden handles to swell and eventually crack. At the end of the day's work, clean and polish the blades, using a mild abrasive powder on a damp cloth. Position the cutting edge of the blade on a flat surface and rub gently to remove any stains. Knives which are not used frequently will benefit from lightly coating with oil to prevent rust forming.

When not in use stores the knives in a slotted tool roll or box to protect the cutting edges. Keeping them either bunched up in a cloth, or loosely in a box or drawer, will cause them to rub against each other and they become blunted.

Knives need to be sharp to be effective. With constant use the edges will become blunt. Blunt knives, apart from making the work difficult, will produce bad results and because of the extra pressure that has to be applied, will frequently be the cause of accidents. At least once a year they should be ground and re-set by expert knife grinders. A cook should, however, keep the knife sharp with a steel so that the keen edge is maintained. Avoid using carborundum stone if possible; it quickly wears out the knife and produces a rough uneven edge. Use a well grooved butcher's steel, hold it with the tip pointing away from the body; place the heel of the knife at the top end of the steel, held at an angle of 30°; draw the length of the blade slowly downwards with an even pressure. Place the knife in the same position on the underside of the steel and repeat the process. Wipe the knife clean before using.

PIPING BAGS

These are made of linen, plastic or nylon. They are available in different length sizes ranging from 150 mm (6″) to 500 mm (20″) long.

A beginner is advised to choose in the middle range of sizes. Small ones are very seldom used as most pastry cooks prefer to make paper bags for decorative piping work and unless one has very large and strong hands the larger bags do not serve any useful purpose.

It is important that the bags are made of durable and washable material, with seams that will not come apart when forcing heavy mixtures through.

To keep the bags in good condition and ensure that they do not become contaminated with mould, which could infect the goods, the bags must be kept clean and sterilized. Linen and nylon bags can and should be boiled. Nylon is to be preferred as it is lighter, stronger and non porous. When cleaning the bags wash away foodstuffs with warm water then scrub inside and out in very hot detergent water and rinse. Wring out as much water as possible and hang up to dry before storing away.

Always remove the piping nozzles from the bags as small particles of food will be between the tube and the bag and metal nozzles will rust and cause the bag to stain and rot.

PIPING NOZZLES

There are a wide range of types and sizes of small cake decorating nozzles. These are classified by numbers, each denoting the shape and size produced, such as rosettes, various flower petals, ribbons, ropes and leaves.

To use them correctly requires experience and a beginner does not require all of them. The following are suggested as starters for general decorating work. Numbers 2 and 3 are fine and medium thread for writing and overpiping, numbers 6 and 8 are star pointed for rosettes and scrolls, numbers 5 and 20 have finer points for rope and shells and are suitable for main designs and border decorations. These small nozzles are usually made of stainless steel or brass and are available either with a screw-on or plain top edges. They can be used fitted directly into a piping bag or by screwing onto an adaptor. The adaptor can be metal or plastic. It is shaped like a large nozzle with a screw-on thread at the end. This is fitted into the bag and the tube is either screwed on or, if it is the plain edge type, attached with a threaded collar.

Using the adaptor has the advantage that the piped design may be varied by only having to change the nozzle, without the need to empty the bag or to use another piping bag.

The larger piping nozzles are made of either tinned metal or plastic. They are available in various sizes which are denoted by the size of the hole in a plain tube, or by the number of points on a star nozzle.

The sizes most often used and which will be found to be most useful are the 3 mm ($\frac{1}{8}''$), 6 mm ($\frac{1}{4}''$) and 12 mm ($\frac{1}{2}''$) in the plain type and the 6, 8 or 12 pointed star. To avoid the nozzles becoming blocked after use, they should be soaked in water and washed. Ensure that they are thoroughly dry before storing to avoid rust forming.

The photograph over the page shows a collection of personal tools and implements which the pastry cook should find adequate and suitable for most of the work encountered in the pastry section.

In the top left hand corner is a small thermometer (with case) used to test the low temperatures required when preparing fondant, chocolate and bread doughs. Next to it is an egg wash brush, a ravioli cutter and a scraper useful in chocolate work. Continuing to the right the illustration shows a grapefruit knife, a zesting knife, a peeler, a 3" fruit knife and a 5" knife for rough work.

Shown below the thermometer is a fine wire dipping fork suitable for use in chocolate and dipped sugar work and a pair of scissors useful for cutting pulled sugar.

At the bottom left is displayed a small representative selection of piping nozzles illustrating some of the types and sizes available for use; close by is a sample of cutters.

The set of knives in the lower section shows from left to right an 8″ filleting knife, a 6″ general purpose knife, an 8″ and a 6″ palette knife, a grooved butchers type steel and a 14″ cranked handle palette knife (a useful tool for spreading mixtures in tins that are high sided, for example Swiss roll), a 12″ serrated carving knife used for slicing sponges, cakes and bread is also useful, because of its long straight blade, to level and smooth icing on cakes.

REFRIGERATION AND
5 STORAGE

In all food preparation areas there should be adequate facilities for storing fresh and dry commodities and prepared foods, while they are being prepared, after preparation and after cooking. Not all foods require the same temperature and conditions to preserve them. Basically there are three methods of storing; each having their own specific purposes and requirements.

The deep freeze cabinet or room

These should maintain a constant temperature at or below −18° C (0° F). All prepared foods and commodities which are to be deep frozen must be cold. Any hot foods should be cooled as quickly as possible before freezing.

Food should be packed in moisture proof wrappers or containers, making sure that all the air is excluded from the package in order to retain moisture and flavour. Each item should be individually wrapped for freezing. This makes it easier to select items for defrosting. Each item should be frozen as quickly as possible as this will increase its keeping quality.

It is advantageous if packages are made up in convenient sizes of uniform shape to save space in the deep freeze; for when filling the compartment, packages will stack together closely.

It is advisable to label the packages with details of the contents and date of freezing, so that they may be used in correct rotation. Remember that thawed out foods should never be re-frozen. Bacteria only remains formant in frozen foods. Freezing will not cure any contamination which the food has previously been subjected to prior to freezing.

Do not use containers made of glass, earthenware or similar brittle and fragile materials. Any moisture in the goods being frozen will expand and may break the container.

Ensure that the deep freeze unit is maintained and kept in good working order. When excessive frost builds up within the compartment, allow the stock to run down to a minimum and store temporarily in another unit or wrap well with several layers of thick paper and store temporarily in a normal refrigerator while defrosting and cleaning the freezer. Allow the unit to reach correct working temperature before repacking the goods.

Refrigerators or cold rooms

These should have a working temperature in the region of 5° C (40° F). All foods for storage should be wrapped or placed in covered containers to prevent the food from drying out and from absorbing flavours of other foods which may be stored in the same cabinet.

Do not overload the compartment, but allow room between the goods so that the maximum amount of cold air circulates freely around the items stored.

Bear in mind that refrigerators will not stop bacteria developing but only retard their growth. To maintain its efficiency the refrigeration unit needs to be defrosted regularly. The interior requires thorough cleaning at least once a week.

The larder or cool room

These operate at an average temperature of between 10 to 13° C (50 to 55° F). The room should be dry, well ventilated, vermin proof and be fitted with protective window coverings to keep out flies and insects. It should have adequate, easily cleaned shelving to store containers. Cupboard space is desirable in which to place unwrapped, non perishable foods to protect them from the atmosphere.

These rooms are suitable for storing perishables which are only to be kept for a few days, eg fruits and eggs, and preserved and tinned goods and dry stores such as flour, nuts and chocolate. All foods must be stored well clear of the floor and away from the walls, to allow air to circulate freely.

Some commodities, such as sugars, candied fruits, cocoa, corn flour, do not deteriorate and may be kept at room temperature, between 15° to 18° C (60 to 65° F). It is important to note that a badly ventilated kitchen or pastry room could exceed this temperature and therefore would not be suitable. As with all foods, such commodities should be protected from dust, mould, bacteria and moisture.

It is very important to remember that foods which are not intended for re-heating should be consumed within two hours after removal from chilled storage. Any left overs should be discarded. They should never be re-heated or returned to storage. Cooked foods that are to be served hot are best prepared or heated at the latest possible moment and should be kept, while waiting to be dispensed, at a temperature of not less than 70° C (160° F).

Storage procedures

The following are basic rules to observe when trying to obtain maximum efficiency from the refrigeration unit and cut wastage to a minimum level.

Check food on arrival to make sure it is what has been requested, and in a satisfactory condition for immediate use or is suitable for storage.

Do not use or store food from 'out of code' stock.

Never use badly dented tins or other damaged packages.

Dry goods should be stored at least 45 cm (18") above floor level with sufficient space all round them for ventilation.

Never store near or against damp walls or under water or sewer pipes or close to any area which attracts condensation.

Keep food items well away from non-food items that could contaminate their taste or smell.

Keep food covered or in appropriate containers, which should be labelled and display 'use by' dates.

Store perishables and high-risk foods in refrigerated conditions: chilled foods below 5° C (41° F); frozen foods below −18° C (30° F).

Do not store foods where they might come into contact with water or inedible ice.

Do not store raw and cooked foods in the same refrigerator. If forced to use one refrigerator for both, always place cooked foods above raw food.

Never store any item which may leak and drip on to foods stored below.

Always use clean containers or wrappers and renew or clean the containers after use. Keep soiled containers away from clean food and clean dishes.

While defrosting and cleaning the refrigerator or freezer, foods should be put into another refrigerator.

At no time should the deep freeze or refrigerator be used as a 'dumping ground' for bits and pieces. Nor should they be used as cooling units, this will only reduce the efficiency of the cabinet and possibly spoil other foods already in store.

Cooked foods should always be cooled as quickly as possible to a temperature below 10° C (50° F) before storing. This is best achieved by standing the container on racks or by improvising a method of raising it, so that air can circulate around the base as well as top and sides. Alternatively stand the item in a receptacle in a bowl of cold or iced water, changing the water until the item is chilled sufficiently to store.

Never store foods until they are completely cold as heat will be retained in the centre of large items for some time, even while the exterior is cold. This provides an excellent breeding ground for bacteria.

Cover, wrap or place foods in containers whenever possible to prevent cross contamination and to prevent drying out.

Always place goods in the smallest possible containers, in order not to take up valuable space in the compartment.

Foods must be of good quality and in good condition for storage. It would be a waste of storage space and detrimental to other foods to keep perishables, such as fruits, which are already beginning to deteriorate.

Do not store foods which absorb flavours near any strong smelling foods.

All foods, whether processed or not, are susceptible to deterioration by mould or bacteria. Those which are not deep frozen should be inspected at frequent intervals to determine their condition. If they have become contaminated or in the case of dry goods, infested with mites, flies or weevils, they should be discarded and the containers thoroughly washed clean.

Whenever possible commodities are best kept in the containers as delivered. But if the supplies are packed in paper bags or cases which are easily broken, the contents should be transferred to suitable containers and clearly labelled.

Always use stored supplies in strict rotation, making sure that old stock is used before using the new stock. Most purchases are date marked; this system could also be used on 'home made' products.

Never store cleaning materials anywhere near food.

To avoid wastage from drying out, certain foods which may only be used occasionally, such as fondant and marzipan, are best if purchased or prepared in small quantities. However, if supplied in large quantities it is advisable to divide the batch into smaller amounts and repack in airtight packets or containers. Fresh perishable foods are best ordered or prepared only in the estimated quantity required for immediate use, eg fresh fruits, milk, cream, yeast, custards, bavarois. Items such as spices, flavourings, liquid colourings, baking powder, which tend to lose their characteristic values, are best purchased and stored in small amounts.

Details of storing preparations made from royal icing, gum paste (pastillage), fondant, chocolate and cooked sugar work will be found in the sections dealing specifically with these commodities.

Management Information Sheet now follows - pages 38–41, (HCIMA).

CHILLED AND FROZEN FOOD — AN INTRODUCTION
The aim of pages 38–41 is to help those handling chilled or frozen foods to maintain quality in the storage and use of these foods, whether in a raw or cooked state. These recommendations should be read in conjunction with the relevant food hygiene regulations. Lowering the temperature of food helps to preserve it and prevent *spoilage*. This term *spoilage* is often used to denote deleterious changes which can take place in the food making it unfit to eat. Spoilage can be caused by bacteria, moulds or yeasts which can grow in food if the temperature is suitable for them. Such microbial spilage causes changes in colour, flavour, odour and appearance eg souring of milk and mould growth on fruit. Spoilage caused by the growth of microbes makes the food unfit for consumption. If certain types of microbe, such as some of the bacteria like salmonella, are allowed to grow in good then a food poisoning hazard exists.

Another type of spoilage is caused by chemical changes in the food. Chemical spoilage can result in rancidity in fats. Enzymes (chemical catalysts which increase the rate of chemical change) can also cause spoilage by reacting with food constituents in a disorganised manner and may cause flavour and colour changes.

The speed at which all these types of spoilage takes place is influenced by the temperature at which food is stored. The lower the temperature the slower these changes will be and the longer the food will be preserved. Hence, chilled food can normally be stored for only a few days whereas frozen foods can be stored for many months without spoilage taking place.

Food can be chilled or frozen in either the uncooked or the cooked state. For many years we have been used to storing raw food in refrigerators prior to cooking. Similarly for frozen foods – deep freezers are commonplace in our kitchens for the storage of raw food. More recently the cook-chill and cook-freeze methods of catering have been developed. In both cases the food is cooked before storage either chilled or frozen.

It is clear that low temperature storage of food either raw or cooked is a very useful tool for the caterer to use. But like all tools they must be used properly in order to get the desired result.

CHILLED FOODS

Foods are chilled to slow down the rate of spoilage. Chilled foods are foods which are normally handled at temperatures just above the freezing point of the food ie − 1° to + 8° C (30° – 44° F). The lower the temperature in this range, the slower the growth of micro-organisms and the biochemical changes which spoil the flavour, colour, texture and nutritional value of foods. At temperatures just above the freezing point of the food, the growth of spoilage bacteria is not entirely stopped, so food may be kept for up to 4 days (96 hours) after it has been cooked and chilled (5 days including the day of production).

FROZEN FOODS

Foods are frozen to stop the growth of micro-organisms. The normal storage temperature for frozen foods is − 18° (0° F) or below and no microbial growth can occur at this temperature. Although food may be stored for some months at this temperature with no microbial spoilage there may be some loss of quality because of enzymic or other biochemical changes eg rancidity development in fatty fish or pork. Each food will have its own storage life before appreciable deterioration sets in. The freezing process may be applied to almost all foods either in the raw or cooked state. The freezing process does not kill all the bacteria in the food, thus when it is thawed, bacteria will begin to grow again and it is therefore important to control the storage temperature. Once food has thawed, it should be eaten within a short time or be discarded.

LOWERING TEMPERATURE TO REDUCE FOOD POISONING HAZARDS

Avoiding contamination of food by microbes, chilling and/or freezing rapidly and storage at the correct temperature is the best way of ensuring the quality of perishable foodstuffs. Microbes growing on one foodstuff can contaminate another foodstuff hence care in handling is required to avoid such cross-contamination.

The growth of food poisoning bacteria may produce no change in the food's appearance or flavour, and hence no indication of the hazard. However, food poisoning bacteris – the more important ones are listed in the diagram rarely multiply in foods below + 7° C (42° F) so that chilling and holding below 5° C (38° F) is normally an effective safeguard. Various raw foods may contain such organisms in low numbers, while contamination may be caused during handling or processing by a human carrier or by cross-contamination from one food to another. Any food poisoning bacteria which are present will grow if chilled food products are allowed to rise in temperature so it is very important to observe the right temperatures to avoid health hazards.

HYGIENE

Staff must know and carry out the rules of hygiene. Full details of the legal requirements are given in the *Food Hygiene (General Regulations 1970. SI No. 1172*. An excellent booklet on this subject is published by HMSO called *Clean Catering*. Responsible persons within catering establishments, a wide range of perishable goods shall not be stored between the temperatures of 63° C (145° F) and 10° C (50° F) because microbes multiply very fast in this temperature range. Recommended temperatures for all food products stored in catering establishments will be given in the subsequent information sheets. It should be noted that

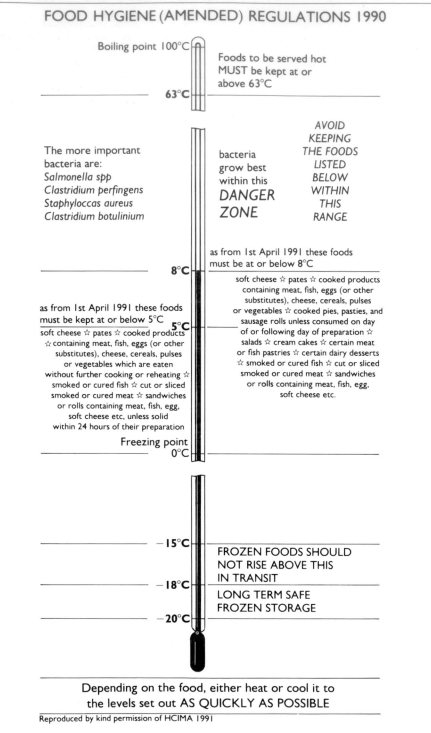

FOOD HYGIENE (AMENDED) REGULATIONS 1990

Boiling point 100°C

63°C

Foods to be served hot MUST be kept at or above 63°C

The more important bacteria are:
Salmonella spp
Clastridium perfingens
Staphyloccas aureus
Clastridium botulinium

bacteria grow best within this
DANGER ZONE

AVOID KEEPING THE FOODS LISTED BELOW WITHIN THIS RANGE

as from 1st April 1991 these foods must be at or below 8°C

8°C

soft cheese ☆ pates ☆ cooked products containing meat, fish, eggs (or other substitutes), cheese, cereals, pulses or vegetables ☆ cooked pies, pasties, and sausage rolls unless consumed on day of or following day of preparation ☆ salads ☆ cream cakes ☆ certain meat or fish pastries ☆ certain dairy desserts ☆ smoked or cured fish ☆ cut or sliced smoked or cured meat ☆ sandwiches or rolls containing meat, fish, egg, soft cheese etc.

as from 1st April 1991 these foods must be kept at or below 5°C
5°C
soft cheese ☆ pates ☆ cooked products ☆ containing meat, fish, eggs (or other substitutes), cheese, cereals, pulses or vegetables which are eaten without further cooking or reheating ☆ smoked or cured fish ☆ cut or sliced smoked or cured meat ☆ sandwiches or rolls containing meat, fish, egg, soft cheese etc, unless solid within 24 hours of their preparation

Freezing point
0°C

−15°C

−18°C

−20°C

FROZEN FOODS SHOULD NOT RISE ABOVE THIS IN TRANSIT

LONG TERM SAFE FROZEN STORAGE

Depending on the food, either heat or cool it to the levels set out AS QUICKLY AS POSSIBLE

Reproduced by kind permission of HCIMA 1991

different products may have different optimum temperatures for chill storage, although all frozen food should be kept below − 18° C (0° F) to assure the minimum deterioration in quality.

COOK-CHILL AND COOK-FREEZE CATERING

Pre-cooked chilled or frozen food may be produced either by the food manufacturing industry or by the caterer himself *Cook-chill* food may undergo the following sequence of operations: Raw food is prepared, cooked and chilled to below 10° C, stored for not more than 96 hours between 0° and +3° C (32° F – 36° F) before finishing and service. The food may require reheating to 80° C if it is to be served hot, or it may be served cold.

Cook-freeze food may undergo the following sequence of operations: Raw food prepared, cooked, packed frozen and stored at − 18° C (0° F); It may be transported in the frozen state before regeneration, which may involve thawing and reheating to about 80° C if it is to be served hot.

It is important to remember that once the food has been removed from either the chill store or the frozen store and thawed, it is as susceptible as any food to the growth of food spoilage or poisoning organisms.

Further details on recommendations for chilled and frozen foods including information on cook-chill and cook-freeze systems will be given in subsequent Management Information Sheets.

6 BASIC WORKING TERMINOLOGY AND TECHNIQUES

To achieve success, develop speed and gain experience, a worker must have knowledge of the correct procedures and be able to select and handle commodities, equipment and utensils. Knowledge and understanding of the reasons for using particular methods of work are essential to avoid repetitive mistakes. Once the basic principles are understood, confidence is gained and it enables the development of personal skills and acquisition of craft techniques to take place.

It would be impractical to describe methods in detail for all the various products, so terms which explain a general process or sequence of operations, together with the type of utensils to use, are explained under the following headings. Further craft skills will be included in their respective sections.

■ METHODS OF WORK

Kneading

This is the process of mixing and stretching a dough or paste to develop the gluten, which is the protein content in the flour. This can be performed manually or mechanically and the action should produce a smooth, elasticated product. It is an important process that will allow the dough to hold the increasing and expanding air, gas or steam cells, that develop within the mixture.

The flour and other ingredients are placed into a suitable bowl; the correct amount of liquids are added; mixed until clear, ie until the mixture leaves the side of the bowl. At this point the gluten begins to develop. If kneading manually, transfer the mixture to a lightly floured table. Work the dough with the hands until it is formed into a ball. Using the heel of the hand, push the top section of the dough away from oneself until the mixture is elongated, then fold it back over to make a ball shape once more. Give the ball of dough a quarter turn and repeat the stretching process until the mixture takes on a smooth silky texture.

If mixed by machine, this texture is achieved at low speeds using a dough hook.

Creaming

This is a method of mixing used when the product contains a high proportion of fat. Creaming incorporates air cells into a fat and sugar mixture by beating. The bowl used should be large enough to allow room for fast movement of spoon or hand. A suitable bowl of stainless steel, china or plastic and a wooden spoon or spatula are required. Sugar will act as an abrasive in a creamed mixture so aluminium bowls should not be selected for use, otherwise a grey coloured mixture will result.

Using the spoon or hands, mix and press the soft fats and sugar (fine for preference), against the sides of the bowl. This is to break down any lumps. Stir and beat vigorously to incorporate as much air as possible, producing a mixture which is light in texture and colour. The lightness of colour is due to the fact that as air is incorporated into the mixture and the volume increases, the colour in the ingredients spreads throughout the mixture.

If the creaming is done by a machine, a beater or paddle is used. Care should be taken with certain items not to overbeat the mixture. The fats used must be soft, but not oily. If the mixture curdles, a little warmth on the outside of the bowl, or a small addition of the measured flour, should smooth it and return it to an even texture. Adding further ingredients when the mixture is curdled, will result in a heavy, greasy product of poor quality.

Care is important when adding any kind of liquid. This should be added gradually and the mixture well beaten with each addition. If the ingredients used are all at the same temperature, there will be less risk of curdling the mixture. Special attention is required when adding further ingredients. They should be cut or folded in gently, or the air incorporated will be forced out and the lightness of the product lost.

Whisking

This is slightly different to the creaming method although, as in creaming, the action imparts the maximum quantity of air into the mixture, the difference is in the ingredients. Whereas creaming relies mainly on solids, in whisking, liquid ingredients are used to produce a foam.

A clean, grease-free bowl made of stainless steel, china or copper and a good, fine hardened wire balloon whisk must be used. The bowl should be large enough to take the increased volume of mixture.

A machine, which can vary in size and capacity, is normally used in production kitchens. It beats air into the mixture by fast rotation of the wires on the whisk. This is simplicity itself and will give greater volume. The pastry cook has only to observe the mixture until it reaches the required stage and then switch off. For smaller quantities generation can be achieved by means of a hand whisk. To avoid getting tired quickly, the whisk should be activated by use of the hand and wrist only, not by movement of the whole arm.

Place liquid and other ingredients required into the bowl. Commence by beating slowly, turning the bowl and lifting the mixture upwards with the whisk. This traps air as the mixture is drawn from the side and then falls back into the bowl. As the mixture thickens and gains volume, continue to whisk, but increase the speed until the foam is at the required stage for use.

The term 'ribbon stage' means that the mixture has attained a thick flowing consistency, which when dropped from the whisk, will retain its impression on the surface of the mixture for a moment. The term 'whisked to a peak' denotes that the mixture is a firm mass of foam.

Do not use aluminium bowls as these cause the mixture to take on a grey colour. When whisking egg whites, avoid using plastic, it has the tendency to feel 'greasy'; consequently the egg does not adhere to the sides of the bowl and is therefore harder to whisk and does not collect and retain air.

Rubbing in

As a rule, when a recipe uses a proportion of half or less fat to flour, the rubbing in method is used. The purpose of rubbing in is to reduce the fat to small particles. At the same time the fat will coat the flour grains, stopping water penetrating directly into the flour, thus reducing or eliminating the formation of gluten within the mixture. The fat particles will melt during cooking and give off moisture. During the cooking process the moisture is converted to small pockets of steam, which expand and raise the mixture. When the mixture is fully cooked it will aerate as air enters the vacated steam pockets.

Place the flour into a bowl, add the firm fats cut into small pieces. Using the tips of the fingers rub flour and fats together, lifting the ingredients and allowing them to fall back into the bowl. In this way the mixture is kept cool and air is incorporated.

Do not overrub or the mixture will form into a paste. The appearance of the mixture should resemble breadcrumbs.

The liquid to be added should be measured accurately and incorporated all at once. After adding liquids do not overmix as this will toughen the mixture. Combine just sufficiently to bind all ingredients together. Prepared correctly the finished product will retain its shape and have a melt-in-the-mouth texture.

Folding in

This is a method which follows naturally from the previous section on whisking. This term is used to describe the combining of other ingredients into the aerated mixture so that there is little or no reduction in lightness or volume. It consists of turning the preparation over gently, while other ingredients are added gradually.

For best possible results, use a large metal spoon and turning the mixture bowl at the same time, lift the mixture and fold over, ensuring that the spoon reaches the bottom of the bowl with each stroke.

A very important point to remember is that every time the spoon cuts through, the motion causes a reduction in the number of air pockets, therefore care must be taken not to overwork the mixture. When mixtures of different consistencies are used, it is advisable to add lighter mixtures to heavier ones. When adding flour or sugar, this should be streamed in gradually. When producing large amounts, providing it is done with care, the hand may be used for folding in.

Cutting in

This applies to the creamed mixes. Because of the denser consistency, the folding action is almost impossible. The spoon's movement in cutting in is to incorporate other ingredients without stirring or beating.

Paste rolling

Rolling out pastes is a very important process in pastry work. Best results are achieved when pinned (rolled) out on a smooth, cool surface; the ideal one being a marble slab. Only a light dusting of flour, sugar or cornflour is required, depending on which paste is being used and for what purpose.

When the pre-prepared paste is ready for use, it is rolled flat to the required shape and size by using a rolling pin. Avoid overhandling and prepare the paste into the shape required, eg for a round, a round ball of paste, for a square or rectangular shape the paste should be formed into a square or rectangle. It is advisable to roll out only the quantity of paste required for immediate use as certain pastes will toughen with additional handling.

Avoid unnecessary trimmings. Flour-based pastes are tougher when rolled out more than once.

Starting from the centre of the paste, using even pressure on the pin with the palms of the hands, roll and press the pin over the paste. Roll upwards, then return to the centre. Roll downwards. Turn the paste a quarter turn. Repeat the rolling process on the paste in the opposite direction, taking care to keep the same thickness throughout. Repeat this process until the desired thickness is achieved. Occasionally dust lightly, turning the paste around and over to avoid it sticking and help retain its shape. Adjust the pressure applied, to suit the type of paste. Never stretch the paste, as this causes it to shrink and lose the shape required during cooking.

Some pastes, because of the texture and bulk, lend themselves to be rolled by mechanical aids, namely a pastry brake; a roller type machine, turned by hand or electric motor.

It is best if some pastes, like short and puff, are allowed to rest before rolling and after being moulded, preferably in the refrigerator, to avoid shrinking and distortion during cooking.

Piping

Piping is the term used for shaping various mixtures by forcing them through a piping bag fitted with a piping tube (nozzle). All kinds of designs and ornamentation can be made by varying the direction of the piping and the amount of pressure used to force the mixture through, and by selecting the appropriate nozzle.

To fill the bag, fit the chosen nozzle and fold the top of the bag back to form a cuff. This ensures that the mixture will not spill on the outside of the bag. If the mixture used is of a runny consistency, it can be retained in the bag by twisting the part of the bag immediately above the nozzle, then pushing it firmly into the nozzle. With one hand, hold the inside of the cuff, half fill the bag with a spoon, scraping the surplus mixture over the cuff, and ease the mixture to the bottom of the bag without trapping air inside. Do not overfill as this will cause difficulty when applying pressure.

To pipe, hold the top of the bag tightly between the index finger and thumb, then force out the mixture by applying even pressure with the palm of the hand and the other fingers. Use the other hand only as a guide. An important point to note is that it is not always the size of the nozzle that denotes the size of the finished item, but the pressure applied to the bag. Do not attempt to 'write' with the bag, but allow the mixture to be dropped or pressed into position.

When using melted chocolate, royal icing and butter cream to pipe fine lines, intricate designs and writing, the normal piping bag if too heavy and bulky to control. A cone, made of strong, non porous paper, is more suitable. Good quality greaseproof, which will not break under pressure, is ideal for this.

The most suitable size for work of this nature is a cone made from a triangle measuring 300 mm (10″) on each side.

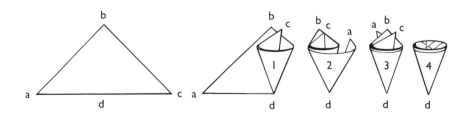

1 Take the right hand corner marked c and bring it up to meet the corner marked b, curling it so it forms a cone shape with its point at d.
2 Hold this in position with the left hand, while wrapping the remaining paper around the cone.
3 Bring all three corners, a b and c, together. If there is a hole formed at point d, put fingers of left hand into cone and twist the paper round until the gap has closed.
4 Fold the three corners, a b and c over, inside the opening of the cone to hold it in position.

The cone should hold together firmly and the point d cut off clean and straight to the required aperture for use. If a small piping nozzle is to be used, cut the point so that the nozzle when fitted will project about 5 mm ($\frac{1}{4}$") out of the point. A left handed person would have to work in reverse.

Uniform piping of shapes, length, size and thickness, requires skill. This skill can be assisted by correct manipulation of the bag in conjunction with the pattern of breathing. It will be found that the action of pressing and moving the bag is concurrent with the rhythm of breathing. Any form of distraction which interrupts the pattern of breathing consequently interrupts the piping.

The resulting piping may not be as even and neat as desired. It is noticeable that skilled persons never talk or allow themselves to be distracted while piping.

■ THICKENING LIQUIDS

Liquids must be thickened in order to use them as the basis for certain sweets, eg for the production of milk puddings, blancmanges, custards, sauces, glazes, or as a base to take further ingredients. Thickening is achieved in many ways, by using one or a combination of commodities, mixing and cooking methods. The type and quantity of thickening agent and length of cooking time, determines the finished consistency of the product.

Thick bottom pots or pans should be used to cook in as there is a danger of the mixture sticking and burning if the metal is too thin. Tinned copper or stainless steel are ideal. Aluminium is suitable, but care should be taken, otherwise during continued stirring and whisking, the mixture may turn grey or discolour, especially if acidic ingredients are used. The vessel should be large enough to allow stirring or whisking to take place quickly and easily, without the mixture spilling over the top.

Points to remember are that an unpleasant taste of raw flour is noticed if starch thickeners are not well cooked, but that an extended cooking time will reduce the mixture by evaporation and give a thicker consistency.

Using different types of commodities, the following have been set out as general guidelines. In each case the appropriate approach to methods, examples of ingredients and end products are given.

Starches (powders)

Flour, cornflour, custard powder, arrowroot, fécule and ground rice are the main ingredients used to thicken. These milled powders should first be blended with part of the measured liquid to form a thin cream. The remaining liquid is then brought to the boil and poured onto the blended mix and whisked fast. It must then be transferred to a clean pan to continue the cooking process and should be stirred continually with a wooden spoon or spatula until the mixture has thickened fully.

Cornflour is used for sauces and blancmanges. Custard powder is cornflour with additions of flavour and colour. Rice flour is suitable for milk puddings. Arrowroot is used mainly for sauces and glazes as it will clear and become transparent when cooked. Fécule (potato flour) is used to adjust the consistency of mixtures if further thickening is needed. It should be noted that liquids thickened with fécule and arrowroot will thin out if cooked too long. It is advisable that both arrowroot and fécule are added at the final stage of preparation.

Kneaded butter (beurre manié)

Prepare by mixing together equal quantities of butter and flour. This is sometimes called a cold roux. Small amounts are added gradually to the boiling liquid, whisks briskly with each addition and as the butter melts, the flour is dispersed evenly and slowly throughout the liquid, preventing the formation of lumps. Continue adding until the liquid reaches the required thickness. Cook out the flour by simmering gently for a short while, stirring continuously with a wooden spoon or spatula. This method is used for panada base and for adjusting the consistency of creamy sauces.

Granules

Rice, semolina, sago and tapioca come under this heading. They are used mainly for milk puddings and base mixes, eg rice for Condés and for Semolina moulds.

Using a whisk to stir, slowly rain the correct amount of grain into the pan containing the measured quantity of boiling liquid. Reduce the heat to simmering point and stir occasionally with a wooden spoon or spatula until cooked. Do not continue whisking as the mixture may discolour, and in the case of rice, it would break the grain.

Egg yolks

These will thicken a liquid by their coagulation. Yolks and sugar are beaten together in a bowl, hot liquid is poured on and the mixture is then whisked briskly. The mixture must be transferred into a clean pan for cooking over a gentle heat. Stir all the time with a wooden spoon or spatula. When the mixture thickens, the consistency should coat the spoon. The mixture will curdle if it is allowed to overcook or boil. Strain immediately into a cold container to prevent further cooking. Used for egg custard sauce (sauce anglaise) and as a base to take further ingredients, eg bavarois.

Reduction

This is a means of achieving the required thickened consistency, by evaporating the liquid during extended cooking. A good example of this method would be the preparation of glaze. The jam and liquids are brought to a boil, then allowed to simmer until the required thickness has been reached. A point to bear in mind is that if sugar is added to a hot mixture, it will thin the consistency while hot, but it will thicken again as it cools down.

Although not thickening agents, gelatine will set a liquid when cooled, and whole eggs will set a liquid when cooked.

7 PREPARING FOR PRODUCTION

In all areas of food preparation success depends on planning. All aspects should be considered; the staff, equipment, commodities, cost and time available.

To make full use of the time available a programme is essential. The flow of work is of great importance. For example: if a yeast product is being made, the free time during the proving and cooking periods could be used for other work. In the case of an apple pie being produced, the paste should be made first. While it rests, preparation of the apples should be undertaken. If fruit salad were to appear on the same menu, it would be prepared while other items were cooking.

Many basic preparations can be used for other items or dishes; for example if choux paste was being made to produce soufflé fritters, extra paste could be used to prepare profiteroles or éclairs, which could be stored and used later, saving time and energy.

Planned 'mise en place' is an essential factor in the system of work adopted. Basic preparations such as fillings, pastes, creams, sauces etc can be pre-prepared and suitable amounts kept available. Many items such as meringue shells, sponges, biscuits, flans, tartlets and puff pastry cases, may be prepared in part for finishing when required.

Ingredients required for production should be of the correct texture and temperature for mixing. They should be allowed to stand in the warm or at room temperature, or placed in the refrigerator, depending on the method of production: ie if they are to be creamed, the fats should be of a soft texture; for rubbing in, the fats are best if cold and firm. Have at hand the correct ingredients and equipment that will be needed. Prepare the necessary tins, moulds, trays, etc by greasing, lining, flouring or sugaring as required.

Measure ingredients correctly; always check that the scales are accurate. This is especially important when working with small quantities. Many recipe books use imperial and metric measurements; they must not be interchanged, otherwise the recipe will not work!

With regard to use of cookers, one should plan the work so that top cooking areas as well as ovens are utilized, avoiding the use of only one or the other. Bear in mind that the heat of cookers will affect the room temperature, and remember also the time required for ovens to reach the required cooking temperature. Shelves should be arranged in the appropriate positions, while the ovens are still cold.

'Clean and clear as you go' and 'everything has a place and there is a place for everything' are good policies to follow. If equipment is easily found the kitchen can be kept in a clean and tidy condition and standards of hygiene will be easily maintained. A tidy working area will promote speed and efficiency during work procedures.

■ THE MISE EN PLACE SYSTEM

The term 'mise en place' means to put in place. As far as the pastry cook is concerned it means to have the basic preparations required ready for the production and service of sweet and savoury dishes.

The system is an integral part of planning for production so that effective co-ordination of work flow is achieved. The function of mise en place is to have equipment and materials ready for use in a prepared or semi-prepared form, so that dishes may be made with the minimum of time and effort and without delay and interruptions. The aim obviously is to maintain quality of product, while ensuring success and speed of service.

Work flow which allows items to be prepared easily, and ready for service at the time required, depends very much on adequate preparations of basic mixtures, commodities and materials. Mise en place is not only having the required ingredients in stock, but the necessary preparations such as pastes and sauces, cooked or partly cooked items, eg creams, fillings and ingredients which may require some form of processing or finishing before use.

The preparation of trays, moulds which may need to be greased, lined or prepared in one form or another, would also come under the heading of mise en place.

The types, variety and quantity of basic preparations that have to be pre-prepared are determined by the type of catering establishment, menu, output and the availability of suitable storage facilities. The way in which they are used and incorporated into the working system is dependent on the personal preferences of the chef in charge. Details regarding specific methods of storage are explained later in the section and also in the section dealing with refrigeration and storage.

Certain mixtures can be made and used immediately, while others require lengthy preparation or may have to stand for a period of time before they are ready for use, eg puff paste. Others may have to cool before use, eg pastry cream and some may have to set, eg bavarois, jellies or moulded ice-creams. The factors must be taken into account when planning the flow of work.

Many items of mise en place in pastry work, such as pastes, sauces, fillings, creams, sponges, are required regularly, while others have to be made according to specific menu requirements.

It is possible to use some preparations for other purposes, thus saving time, energy and labour. For example, if praline was being made for petits fours or to use in a gâteaux, extra sugar could be caramelized and used to preparing moulds for cream caramels, or if sponge fingers were being made for charlottes, any extras could be stored and used at a later date for pastries and trifles. If éclairs were being made, some of the paste could be used to produce profiteroles for sweets or, if piped small, as garnish for consommé.

No benefit is achieved if the mise en place product requires much time and manipulation to reconstitute. The item may just as well be made as and when required. For example, hot custard sauce is quickly and easily made, to reheat it would take just as long and the result would not be so good. The same applies to butter cream, if made and kept in the refrigerator it would become hard, and when required for use it would have to be softened and rebeaten to achieve the smooth texture required.

Items which have keeping qualities, or may be stored successfully, may be produced in large amounts, while others have to be made in smaller quantities as and when required. Unless the mise en place can be successfully stored, it is not advisable to produce more than the estimated required amount. Apart from wastage, there is the danger of food becoming contaminated by bacteria. Always store foods in suitable containers. Tins can affect flavour and colour and cause harmful effects to the consumer. Fruit from an open tin, for example, should be transferred to stainless steel, china or plastic containers.

It is never advisable to pre-mould paste on trays or in moulds too far in advance of baking; it would cause the metal to stain the paste and is detrimental to the product. If paste is pre-prepared rolled or cut out, it should be laid on greaseproof paper and transferred to the baking tray when cooking is required.

All items that are stored require some form of covering to protect the products from the atmosphere, to retain freshness and to prevent them drying out.

All hot items which are to be kept in refrigerated storage must be chilled before storing. Apart from reducing the efficiency of the cold compart-ment, they could affect other goods already in store. Do not use containers larger than necessary, this will only take up valuable space in the refrigeration cabinet.

Items that are to be kept in the deep freeze are best wrapped individually or in small quantities and dated. This makes it more convenient to select only the required amount and easier to keep the stock in rotation of age.

Some items which have been pre-prepared in portions or small sizes, may be baked from the frozen state. It must be noted that this will cause the oven to drop in temperature, so allowances must be made if the product is to bake successfully.

The 'à la carte' menu especially requires that basic preparations and commodities are always kept in stock to enable speedy production and service of dishes ordered from the menu. For example, Italian meringue, ice-cream, sponge and fruits that would be required to complete an order for a soufflé surprise, would be ready for assembly when the order was received. The same would apply to fruits and sauces for completing coupes and other ice-cream dishes. Meringue shells and vacherins will be ready for filling as required. Fresh fruits, such as oranges, pineapple and grapes, which are not affected by storage, may be pre-cut for adding to other fruits like apples, pears and bananas when the order for fruit salad is received.

The mise en place system is essential in catering establishments which cater for large numbers of chance customers, or which have an extensive variety of dishes on the menu. Different types of catering require varying types and amounts of mise en place. There is no set rule to give with regard to the actual type of amount of mise en place that is to be produced. As already stated, this would depend on the type of catering and the facilities available.

Menus should be studied in advance and used as a blueprint to order the required commodities and plan the necessary mise en place. The requirements of the kitchen and larder sections must also be considered.

The following examples give some indication of the usual range of mise en place which is standard to catering establishments which have an extensive selection of dishes on the menu. Brief details regarding suggested methods of storage and suitable length of time for storage without spoiling are given. Specific recipes and methods have been omitted. There are many recipe books in which they may be found and they are so variable. Many pastry cooks favour their own ideas and recipes.

■ PASTES

PUFF PASTES

The two most popular methods for production of puff paste are the French and Scotch methods. Each is normally given 'six turns'. While the pastes are being produced, and after they have been made, it is difficult to tell how many turns have been given and which type is which. To avoid confusion, pastry cooks have adopted the following methods of marking the pastes to denote the number of turns given and the type of paste made.

To indicate the number of turns given to a paste made by the French method, make a corresponding number of indentations on the paste with the tip of the finger (fig. 1 below). The same is done with the Scotch method, but a trellis is also marked on the surface with the back of a knife (fig. 2 below). Any left over trimmings are layered together and given one more turn, marked by numerous indentations (fig. 3 below).

It is recommended that the final two turns are given about half an hour before the paste is to be used.

When produced by hand it is easier to make small amounts of puff paste. The most that can be manipulated successfully is a quantity of 2 kg (4 lbs) of flour.

at 4 turns   at 6 turns

Puff pastes are best when made the day before required. They may be kept for up to three days in a normal refrigerator and should be wrapped in a damp cloth or plastic sheeting to prevent a skin forming. They may be stored in a deep freeze when wrapped in plastic for up to three months. It must be noted that frozen puff paste must be allowed to thaw out slowly in a cool room, alternatively the required amount can be transferred into a refrigerator the day before use.

SHORT PASTE
Once made, this only requires about half an hour in a cool place or in the refrigerator to be ready for use. If it is to be stored, wrap in greaseproof paper and keep in the refrigerator. It is best if only the immediate requirement is made as after twenty four hours the paste starts to deteriorate and takes on a dull grey colour.

SUGAR PASTE
It is necessary that this paste is allowed to become firm in the refrigerator before use. Store wrapped in a cloth or greaseproof paper. Immediately before use it may need a little further mixing to make it pliable for rolling and moulding. It keeps successfully for up to a week in the refrigerator. It is used for flans, tartlets and fruit tarts.

SHORTBREAD PASTE
The method of storage is as for sugar paste. It is suitable for biscuits and bases for sweets and gâteaux. The mixture may be flavoured by adding grated zest of lemon and oranges, chocolate, cocoa, ground almonds, essences. The piped variety and Viennese are best if piped when the mixture is freshly made.

CHOUX PASTE

Store in a china, plastic or stainless steel bowl, covered with an air tight lid or piece of wet greaseproof paper. This can be kept for up to twenty four hours but it may be necessary to beat in a little egg to reconstitute the mixture before using. This stored paste is used for beignets soufflés, when featured on an à la carte menu, or by the kitchen for the production of potato dishes. These is no advantage in making it in advance for use in pastries and gâteaux.

NOODLES, RAVIOLIS AND STRUDEL PASTES

It is necessary that these are allowed to rest in a cool place before attempting to roll or stretch out. They should be well wrapped in a damp cloth or plastic to avoid a skin forming. When about to use do not re-knead as this will make them very elastic and difficult to produce the thin layer required. Providing they are wrapped to prevent air getting in, they may be kept for up to three days in a refrigerator. Green noodle paste is made by using sieved spinach as part of the liquid. (See also savoury section for dried noodles.)

DANISH PASTE

It is best prepared the day before required but ensure that the liquid used is ice cold. Store wrapped in plastic sheeting or very damp cloth. As with puff paste, give the final turn half an hour before using. Used for Danish pastries and croissants.

BRIOCHE PASTE

This paste is also best if made the day before and by adding cold liquids. Store in a suitable size of covered container, allowing for extra volume as it proves. The paste must be kept in the refrigerator, where slow proving occurs and it becomes firm as the fat content solidifies. When moulding, work quickly to avoid the mixture becoming soft. The paste is used for brioche rolls and various buns. Sugarless brioche is also used for specific savoury dishes.

LINZER PASTE

Two kinds of this paste can be made, one using the rubbing in method and the other the creaming method. For the rubbing in method it is necessary to chill the mixture in the refrigerator as it has to be rolled for moulding. If the paste is to be piped the creaming method is required and it should be used as soon as it is made.

■ FILLINGS

ALMOND CREAM/FRANGIPANE, BUTTER CREAM, LEMON CURD, APPLE PURÉE

Cover with wet greaseproof paper and store in a cool place for one day or up to three days in the refrigerator.

PASTRY CREAM, COOKED RICE FOR CONDÉS AND CROQUETTES
Cover with a buttered or oiled paper. Use as soon as possible and within twenty four hours.

WHIPPED CREAM
(fresh and synthetic)   Keep constantly in the refrigerator and use the same day.

SIEVED JAMS, MINCEMEAT
Store in non-corrosive containers with tight fitting lids. In a cool place it will keep for up to two months.

APPLE FILLINGS FOR TARTS AND STRUDELS
Prepare only the required amounts and keep in a cool place or in the refrigerator. Use the same day. For strudel it is necessary to allow the filling to stand for about an hour to macerate the fruit.

■ SAUCES AND LIQUIDS

COLD MILK SAUCES
(eg chocolate, coffee, almond, vanilla, custards)   These must be cooled, covered with wet greaseproof paper and kept in the refrigerator. Use the same day. If any cream is to be added this should be done just before serving or using.

ALL HOT SAUCES
(eg egg custard, custards, jam, fruit, thickened syrups and fruit juices) They are best made just before they are required for service and kept in covered containers in a bain-marie of hot water. The non-milk sauces may be retained for future re-heating. Allowances must be made for sauces that will thicken due to evaporation of the liquids.

COLD JAM, FRUIT AND THICKENED SAUCES
(eg apricot, melba, chocolate and thickened syrups and fruit juices) Keep covered with wet greaseproof paper or sprinkle with sugar to prevent a skin forming on the surface. May be stored for up to two weeks in the refrigerator, using a non-corrosive container.

STOCK SYRUPS AND BUN WASH
Store in covered containers. These will keep indefinitely in a cool place. If gelatine or other additives are added to bun wash, store for only one week in the refrigerator.

EGGWASH
Prepare only the required amount for use. Store under refrigeration if not used immediately.

MERINGUE

Italian meringue When cold, cover with damp greaseproof paper or plastic sheeting. Press the layer well on the surface to exclude any air. It is best if used up immediately as it tends to become softer when stored for longer periods.

Ordinary meringue This can only be made when about to be used as it very quickly softens. The sugar content dissolves rapidly and the meringue becomes syrupy.

■ BAKED GOODS

DRIED OR COOKED MERINGUES

(eg meringue shells, vacherins, petits fours) Provided they are well dried out, these may be stored in dustproof cardboard boxes. To avoid breaking arrange in layers with sheets of kitchen or greaseproof paper between each layer. Store in a dry area at room temperature. These will keep for up to two months. Japonaise may also be stored in the same way, but only for two weeks as it tends to soften after that time.

SPONGES

(eg Genoese, fatless, Swiss roll, sponge fingers) Wrap in plastic or store in airtight containers up to one day in a cool area, three days in the refrigerator or up to three months in the deep freeze.

COOKED YEAST GOODS

(eg savarins, babas, marignans, pomponettes, croûtes) Keep in dustproof containers for up to one day in a cool area. Wrapped in plastic or greaseproof for up the the three months in the deep freeze. Allow to thaw out completely before soaking, otherwise they will not soak up sufficient liquid or will break up.

CHOUX PASTE CASES

(eg éclairs, buns, profiteroles, gâteaux St. Honoré and polka bases) Keep in air tight containers for up to one day in a cool area, three days in the refrigerator and up to one month in the deep freeze. Small profiteroles which are to be used as garnish for consommé may be left in a covered container in a dry cupboard, as they are to be moistened when they are served, it does not matter if they dry out.

TYPES OF SWEET CASES AND BASES

(eg tartlets, barquettes, flans, macaroons, friands, frangipane filled tartlets and barquettes) They may be kept in air tight containers for up to one week in a cool area, ready for filling, finishing and decorating as and when required.

Short paste cases are not suitable for keeping. They tend to dry out and crack.

COOKED PUFF PASTE

(eg baked sheets for mille-feuilles, cream horn cases or made up bande cooked blind) These should be placed on wire cooling racks and stored in a dry cupboard ready for finishing the following day.

Other examples of puff pastry items which may be made, cooked and stored are palmiers, galettes, allumettes, sacristans, and langues de boeuf. Providing they are kept in a dry dustproof cupboard they will retain their freshness for up to a week, ready for serving or finishing as required.

CAKES

(eg small plain and fruit cakes or large cakes for slicing into portions) They should be wrapped in plastic or foil or kept in airtight containers. These will keep for up to one week in a cool area. Deep freezing is not recommended as when thawed out the moisture content spoils the appearance and flavour of the product.

Rich fruit cakes and Christmas puddings should be well wrapped in foil or kept in air tight containers. They should keep for six months. These cakes and puddings do improve with age, but recipes vary so it is advisable to occasionally check the condition as some recipes may not produce the same keeping qualities as others.

■ FRUITS

POACHED FRESH FRUITS

(eg apples, pears, apricots, peaches)   Once they are cooked they are best stored in shallow containers. This makes it easier to lift pieces out for service without breaking the fruit.

Soft fruits, such as raspberries and blackberries, only require boiling sugar syrup to be poured over them and they can then be left to cool without any further cooking. Only prepare sufficient for two days and store in the refrigerator in a covered container.

POACHED DRIED FRUITS

(eg figs, prunes, apricots, apples)   Dried fruits are normally required to be pre-soaked in cold water for at least twelve hours before cooking. Cooked and allowed to cool in the same liquid, they can be stored as fresh poached fruits.

SMALL DRIED FRUITS

(eg currants, sultanas, raisins) These fruits must be cleaned before storage. To remove the stalks and other small foreign bodies, rub them over a coarse breadcrumb sieve, the small particles will fall through the sieve, any large pieces will be seen and can be removed by hand. They should then be washed, drained and spread on a cloth for at least one day to dry out. Best stored in covered china or glass containers. Do not seal air-tight but allow the fruit to 'breathe' or fermentation may occur. Store in a dry cool cupboard.

CANDIED OR CRYSTALLIZED FRUITS, PEELS AND STEMS
If they are to be used in cakes it is advisable to wash off some of the sugar and syrup and allow to dry as above. Angelica is usually coated with dry hardened sugar. This should be washed off before using for decoration or any other purpose. Do not, however, allow to steep too long in water or they will lose their colour and flavour. Keep candied and crystallized fruits in airtight containers to avoid them drying out and to prevent the candied fruits from re-crystallizing.

■ PETITS FOURS

FONDANTS
(eg fondant creams or coconut kisses) These may be flavoured and coloured to choice (vanilla, strawberry, rum, mint, orange, lemon, liquers and spirits). Once dry, they are packed in layers in air-tight containers with a sheet of waxed or silicone paper between each layer. They will keep indefinitely in a cool dry cupboard. The fondant cream may be decorated by overpiping when required for service.

COOKED SWEETMEATS
(eg toffee, fudge, nougat or praline, which may have various additions such as chocolate, nuts, candied fruits) These are usually moulded in shallow trays, eg a Swiss roll tin and cut into pieces when required. Store wrapped in waxed paper in a cool dry cupboard and they will keep indefinitely.

TURKISH DELIGHT
Once set they are cut into cubes and heavily coated with the following mixture: one part powdered magnesia and six parts icing sugar. Packed loosely in a dry cardboard or wooden container they will keep for about one month in a dry area.

BISCUITS 'PETITS FOURS SECS'
(eg shortbreads, macaroons, ratafias, wine biscuits, tuiles, English and Parisian rout biscuits, friandes meringues, petits palmiers, brandy snaps, langues de chat, cornets, cigarettes and copeaux) These should be stored in containers lined and covered with absorbent paper. They will keep for up to two weeks. Do not mix the varieties as some contain more moisture than others.

FONDANT CENTRES
These centres are laid out on wire grills ready to be coated with fondant or chocolate the following day. Most of the above mentioned petits fours are suitable for coating. Sponge and biscuit shapes should be dipped in or brushed with boiling apricot glaze or covered with marzipan to seal the

surfaces before coating. Butter cream, ganache and/or dry fruits can be arranged on top and chilled in the refrigerator before coating with fondant. It will be easier to coat and eventually decorate if the pieces are arranged in straight lines on the wire grills.

GLAZED FRUITS

The fruits used must be firm, absolutely dry and have unbroken skins. If they are only slight moist the sugar coating will quickly melt. They are best prepared the day before being required and should be laid out on wire grids covered with absorbent paper. Keep in a well ventilated area. If required immediately, accelerate drying with an electric fan. The following are some of the fruits used and methods of preparation.

Oranges, satsumas, mandarins etc Carefully remove the peel and pith. Separate the segments without breaking the skin. Smaller fruits may be separated with two segments together.

Grapes – black and white Using small scissors remove in pairs. Small grapes may be removed in threes or fours. Leave on a stem as long as possible to allow for holding when dipping, this may be cut off after dipping.

Fresh cherries Leave these on their stalks and keep in twos.

Redcurrants Select small bunches. Remove any soft or blemished berries and leave a long stem if possible for holding.

Strawberries Leave these on the stalk. If washing is required they should be dried immediately and gently on a cloth or blown dry with an air drier. Do not prepare or dip strawberries too far in advance. Ensure that they are good and firm for use. Strawberries may also be dipped in fondant.

Cape gooseberries (physalis) Open the leaves and twist them together upright to form a stem. They may also be dipped in fondant or chocolate.

Dates, glacé cherries, soft prunes If syrupy, wash and dry the dates and cherries. The prunes and dates are split to remove the stone and then filled with marzipan. Cherries are cut in half and marzipan is sandwiched between them.

Fresh dates Using a wooden skewer, push out the stone and fill the cavity with butter cream or fondant. These cannot be dipped in cooked sugar if butter cream is used.

■ MISCELLANEOUS

NUTS

(eg almonds, hazel, pistachio, coconut and walnuts) Most nuts are supplied prepared ready for use, skinned, whole, sliced or nibbed. If they do require skinning, plunge them into boiling water for about fifteen seconds then immediately cool in cold water. Drain and rub them together inside a cloth, the skins should fall off easily. Remove the debris and spread out on a dry cloth to dry at room temperature.

If nibbed almonds have to be made, chop the nuts and remove the fine powder by passing through a medium sieve. Sieve the remainder through a coarse sieve to allow the nibs of uniform size to go through, leaving the rough chopped pieces in the sieve. These may be re-chopped and re-sieved.

To roast the nuts, spread a shallow layer on a baking tray and leave in a moderate oven until brown. To colour nuts, place them in a mixing bowl, spinkle on the required liquid colouring and immediately rub together to spread the colour evenly. Dry in a cool oven at 60° C (140° F). Coconut is susceptible to contamination by bacteria and must be heat treated by placing it on a tray and heating in the oven at a temperature of 75° C (170° F) for at least fifteen minutes.

Make sure that all nuts are cold and dry before storing. Store in airtight containers and only stock sufficient for one month's supply. Prolonged storage promotes rancidity and infestation by weevils and moths.

BREADCRUMBS

Stale bread should be used, so that it will crumble easily. Fresh bread placed in the refrigerator for one or two days will become suitable for crumbling.

When making large amounts, half fill the bowl of a dough mixer with bread cut into pieces, fit the paddle or cake beater and operate the mixer at low speed for about twenty minutes. Pass through a coarse sieve to remove the crust and any large pieces. If only small amounts are required rub a suitable size piece of bread on a cheese grater. Store in a covered container for one day in a cool room, or up to one week in the refrigerator.

The following sweets are some examples of dishes which may be partly prepared and kept for finishing as necessary.

SAVARINS, BABAS ETC

These may be made and soaked with syrup, kept in the refrigerator ready for glazing and filled as required the following day.

TRIFLES

The sponge, jam and fruit may be soaked and placed in the service dishes and stored in the refrigerator. The custard, cream and other finishing required may be completed on the following day.

FLANS

Only the drier type of flans may be prepared in advance, eg Bakewell tart, lemon curd and flans with a pastry cream base. Any milk type fillings must be kept in the refrigerator. Others may be left in a cool cupboard.

GÂTEAUX

Genoese sponges may be split, soaked and filled as required, wrapped or covered and kept in the refrigerator, ready to be decorated the following day. Butter cream and jam filled sponges will successfully freeze and will keep in good condition for at least one month.

SPONGE SLICES

Sponges which are to be coated in some way for use as pastries may be prepared, cut and coated with hot apricot jam or marzipan, then laid out on wire grills ready to be covered with fondant or chocolate. Remember to allow the pastries to achieve room temperature before coating.

CREAM CARAMEL, DIPLOMATE PUDDING, CRÈME BEAU RIVAGE

It is usual for these to be prepared in advance. Store in the refrigerator but use within twenty four hours of making.

PANCAKES

A limited number of ready cooked pancakes may be kept in the refrigerator for up to twelve hours. Keep them well wrapped up to avoid drying out. To prevent them sticking together, spread out on to a cool surface as soon as they are made and sprinkle a little sugar between each one before piling together. Alternatively, so that they are suitable for savoury items, they may be interleaved with greaseproof paper.

■ FRESH FRUIT CASES

Several types of fruits lend themselves to be used as cases for the presentation of sweet dishes, eg melons, oranges and pineapples.

MELONS

These can be cut lengthways, or the top removed and the flesh scooped out using a spoon or a 'parisienne' scoop. Smaller melons may be cut in half, scooped out and used for individual portions.

ORANGES

These are emptied by cutting off the tops and removing the flesh by either using a grapefruit knife or by scooping out with a spoon.

PINEAPPLE

This may be cut in half lengthways, leaving the fresh looking leaves attached. Scoop or cut out the flesh.

An alternative method is to cut off the top leaving the leaves attached. This part is later used as the lid. The flesh is removed from the thick skin of the pineapple, using a sharp filleting knife. A cut is made around the inside of the fruit close to the layer of skin, taking care not to cut through it. The cut should almost reach the base. The body of the fruit now contains a cut 'core' of flesh held only at the base. To release this core insert the knife into the fruit near the base. Move the knife from side to side inside the fruit to cut the core from the base. During this operation the part of the blade passing through the skin must be kept in the same position to prevent an increase in the size of the incision in the skin.

Pineapple cases may be washed out after use, dried and stored in the deep freeze for future use.

The empty fruit cases may be used as presentation containers for various fillings such as fruits, bavarois, creams, ice-creams, and rice for Condé and Creole dishes.

■ LIAISON WITH THE KITCHEN AND LARDER

Because of the specialized staff, equipment and cooking facilities available in the pastry section, a close liaison should exist with the kitchen and larder. This is necessary in order to provide the kitchen with the required types of savoury mise en place which are more ably and conveniently made in the pastry section.

Some items are prepared and cooked in pastry and sent to the appropriate party for their completion and service. To avoid contamination of savoury flavours in the pastry area, ingredients, or basic compositions, are made by the kitchen or larder and sent to the pastry for preparation and, in some cases, cooking. These items are then returned to the kitchen or larder for service.

The following is the accepted procedure used between co-operating areas, although the system can vary between one establishment and another.

The following items are prepared and cooked in pastry then sent to the appropriate party for completion and service.

1 Vol-au-vents for entrées, bouchées for fish or starter courses, fleurons as garnish for fish dishes, pancakes for savoury fillings.
2 Small profiteroles, crème royale, pancakes, cheese straws, bread sticks (flutes), required as garnish for soups.
3 Small bouchées, tartlets, barquettes, profiteroles, savoury biscuits, to be completed with savoury fillings by the larder as part of a selection for canapes.
4 Cheese palmiers, cheese straws, salted almonds, crêpinettes, for service with cocktails at the reception or bar areas.

For the following dishes, the filling or savoury preparations are sent into the pastry section by either the kitchen or larder. It is then the pastry cook's responsibility to prepare the necessary pastes, assemble and cook the dishes, then return them to the kitchen or larder for finishing and service.

Hot pies, eg chicken pie; steamed puddings, eg steak and kidney; jambon en croûte, filet de boeuf Wellington, dartois, hand raised pies, sausage rolls, cornish pasties, pizzas, quiches and ramequins (for the last two the pastry cook would also prepare the egg mixture).

Basic compositions which are prepared in the pastry and sent to the kitchen for final processing, would include the following:

Choux paste for potato dishes and gnocchi parisienne, noodles, lasagne and cannelloni squares, ravioli, gnocchi piémontaise and romaine.

These are prepared and sent to the kitchen for cooking, finishing and serving. The filling for ravioli and the cooked sieved potatoes for gnocchi piémontaise would come from the kitchen. The pastry cook would cook the mixture for gnocchi romaine, spread it out on a greased tray to cool and send it to the kitchen for cutting and serving.

Noodles, lasagne and cannelloni squares, may be made in advance. They must then be dried by spreading or hanging in a dry, clean, ventilated area until hard. They will keep for one month stored in a dustproof box or bag.

For savoury soufflés and omelettes soufflés the pastry cook would be expected to whip the egg whites and pass them on to the kitchen for incorporating into the mixes.

8 PREPARING MOULDS AND TRAYS

Many cakes, pastries and sweets are prepared, baked, or set in moulds. In order that these items can easily be removed without losing shape or breaking, thorough preparation by greasing, lining or coating is needed. What is used and how it is done depends on the type of mixture, filling or finished appearance. There are many different shapes and sizes of moulds, made of various materials. Depending on the end product, the moulds could be greased, lined with paper, floured or sugared. For specific products a lining of paste, biscuits, sponge, bread, jelly or caramel would be used.

Trays and moulds that are to be used for baking tend to stick when they are new. To help overcome this problem, they are 'proved' or 'burnt out'. This is done by greasing heavily with lard, spinkling with salt and placing in a hot oven to heat thoroughly until the fat begins to smoke. Remove with care, wash in hot water and wipe clean then dry. If tins are in daily use all that is necessary to keep them clean is a good rubbing with a clean cloth, to remove foodstuffs and surplus grease as soon as they have been emptied and while they are still hot. They must then be kept in a ventilated, dustproof place. Providing that they are kept clean, they will become almost non-stick, requiring an occasional wash only when grease starts to accumulate.

Clarified butter, margarine, oil or lard are used for greasing. For a light coating, melt and use in liquid form. For a heavier layer, brush with fats of a soft consistency.

Tins and trays can be lined with greaseproof or silicone paper. Because of the process used in its manufacture, silicone paper has advantages over greaseproof. It does not shrink, or require greasing and if clean, can be used more than once.

■ PREPARATION OF DIFFERENT CONTAINERS

Sponge and cake tins
Brush the inside of the tin with an even coating of soft fat. Line the bottom with greaseproof paper cut to the same size and shape as the base; grease this also with a light coating of fat. Sprinkle in some flour; turn the tin to spread the flour evenly over the base and sides and than tap out the

surplus. An additional lining of greaseproof paper may also be used around the sides. This should be fitted before flouring. Paper tends to shrink with heat and may distort the shape of the cake. To overcome this, use two overlapping strips. Never have the paper higher than the moulds as it may burn and may prevent the top of the cake from cooking. For large, rich, and fruit cakes, which take a long time to cook, it is advisable to pre-line with several layers of thick paper before lining with greaseproof.

Swiss roll tins

Grease the inside of the tin. Place over it a piece of greaseproof paper large enough to cover it. To cut the paper to size, draw the back of the knife along the edge of the tin using sufficient pressure to sever the paper to the shape required to fit the tin. Brush on a thin coating of fat, then press the paper into the base of the tin and lightly flour. It is not necessary to line the sides as the sponge has to be trimmed before rolling. To remove the cooked sponge use the point of a knife and loosen the sides.

Baking trays

The method of preparing a baking tray depends on the items being made. It is important however that they are never greased or floured heavily.

Using melted fats, brush lightly, wiping the surplus off with absorbent paper. Too much grease would cause the items to spread or slip on the tray. If it requires flouring, allow the fat to set and only give a very light even dusting. Excessive flour would burn and spoil the appearance of the finished article.

For some purposes, instead of greasing, trays are lined with paper. Greaseproof, silicone or rice paper are used depending on the product. Take care to see that the paper is cut or folded to fit the tray. It should not overlap the sides.

The following examples illustrate the method of preparing trays for specific uses.

Greased only puff or other pastes, scones, bread rolls.
Greased and floured choux pastries, Viennese biscuits.
Grease-proof or silicone paper meringue shells, sponge fingers.
Rice paper macaroons, florentines.

Savarin, baba and marignan moulds

These should be greased by brushing with a heavy coating of soft fats. As no lining is used and because the shape of the moulds will not allow the use of a knife to loosen the cooked filling, it is essential that the moulds are thoroughly and evenly greased, including the top of the edges. They may be coated with flour, which gives a smooth finish, or with castor sugar to give a deeper colour and a hard crust.

Soufflé cases and pudding soufflé moulds

Using warm melted clarified butter, coat liberally the insides of the cases or moulds. Allow some of the surplus to drain out. Turn upside down on a flat surface, allow to cool and set. This will leave a rim of butter around the top edge which allows the filling to slip and rise evenly up the sides. The inside is coated with sugar for sweet soufflés and with finely grated dry cheese or breadcrumbs for savoury varieties.

Charlotte moulds

For cold sweets, moulds are lined with either sponge fingers, swiss roll or jelly, or a combination of any two. Bread is used for hot sweets.

The following are examples of popular types which require lining in this manner.

CHARLOTTE RUSSE

Cover the bottom with sponge fingers cut into wedge shapes, or with a round of sponge prepared to the size of the base of the mould. Arrange sponge fingers around the sides, ensuring there are no gaps between the pieces. A tight fit is essential to retain the mixture.

CHARLOTTE MOSCOVITE

Set red jelly on the bottom of the mould about 6 mm ($\frac{1}{4}$") thick. Arrange sponge fingers around the sides as for charlotte russe.

CHARLOTTE ROYALE

Line the bottom and sides with thin slices of small swiss roll 40 mm ($1\frac{1}{2}$") diameter. If gaps are showing do not plug with sponge. This will spoil the finished appearance. Cover the gaps internally with thin slices of sponge. The moulds may be prelined with jelly as detailed under chartreuse.

CHARTREUSE

This involves lining a circular mould with jelly and fruit. The jelly must be made slightly stronger than normal. First set a layer of jelly on the bottom of the mould about 6 mm ($\frac{1}{4}$") thick, when set, stand a second mould inside, of the same shape but 12 mm ($\frac{1}{2}$") smaller, filled with iced water. Fill the gap between the moulds with jelly that is cold and on setting point (warm jelly will melt the bottom layer). Allow to set firm. To loosen the inner mould, pour out the cold water and replace with hot water. Leave this only long enough to allow the inner mould to be detached from the jelly without melting it; then pour it away immediately. Carefully remove the inner mould by easing it out gently. Take care not to break the jelly. The fruit intended for use should have been prepared, ie sliced and dried. This must then be dipped into jelly and arranged attractively inside the jelly mould and allowed to set before filling.

APPLE CHARLOTTE (HOT)

Using trimmed slices of bread about 6 mm ($\frac{1}{4}''$) thick, cut out three rounds (discs), one about 40 mm ($1\frac{1}{2}''$) in diameter and two to the size of the base of the mould. Cut each of the large rounds into six triangular sections. Cut also sufficient finger shapes about 25 mm (1") wide, and as high as the mould, to line the sides, allowing extra pieces for overlapping. Dip all the pieces into melted butter then press each piece firmly into the mould, starting with the small round in the centre of the base. Then place the triangular sections (points to centre), and arrange them in a circular overlapping pattern to completely cover the base. Lastly, stand the fingers around the sides, again overlapping them. The overlapping is important as the bread shrinks slightly during cooking and the mixture may seep out.

■ LINING WITH PASTES

There are a variety of products which require the lining of moulds, flan rings or basins with a paste to hold further fillings. Care should be taken that the thickness of the paste is correct; if too thick it may not cook sufficiently; if too thick it may break and the filling seep out. The thickness required will depend on the paste used and the purpose for which the case is made.

All pastes are best used chilled. When using short or puff, it is easier to mould if the pastes are allowed to rest after rolling. To avoid shrinkage and distortion while they are being cooked, the pastes should be rested after moulding as well.

For flan cases that have to be baked empty (blind), it is necessary to line the inside of the pastry with a round of greaseproof paper to prevent the sides of the pastry collapsing. Dry beans, or something similar, are used to hold the paper in place and to support the sides. Do not have the paper higher than the rim of paste. When the paste has set remove the beans and paper and replace flan case back in over to finish cooking.

To assist in moulding, it is helpful if the moulds are greased and chilled in the refrigerator; the fat will set and become tacky, making it easier to hold the paste in position while lining the mould. After lining, dock the paste (perforate base of pastry using fork or docker) to release steam and air from under the paste, allowing it to bake flat.

The following examples will give an understanding of the different methods employed for lining moulds with paste.

Flans

Grease the flan ring with soft fat then chill. Roll out a round of paste 3 mm ($\frac{1}{8}''$) thick, slightly larger than the diameter of the flan ring, sufficient to cover the sides and the base. Do not have the piece too large, as this will make it difficult to handle. Fold the paste into quarters and unfold over the flan ring, or roll on to the pin and lay over the ring. Ease the paste evenly into the base and on to the sides, allowing the surplus to overlap the rim. This process can be made easier by using a small piece of surplus paste to press into the angle of the flan ring where it meets the tray, ensuring a good fit without stretching or puncturing the paste. When the paste has been fitted in, cut the surplus away by rolling a pin across the top of the ring. Using the thumb, press the paste against the inside of the ring, making sure that all the air has been excluded from the base. It is important to press evenly, taking care not to thin the paste by pressing too hard. Raise the paste slightly above the top of the ring, pressing the edge between index finger and thumb so that it is forced inwards. This ensures that the ring can be removed easily after baking. Do not allow paste to remain on top of the rim. The edge may be pinched with fingers or pastry tweezers. Dock the base.

Tartlets
Have ready the moulds lightly greased. Roll out the paste 3 mm ($\frac{1}{8}''$) thick. Cut out rounds of paste slightly smaller than the moulds, using a plain or fluted cutter, and place in the centre of the mould. Using the tip of the thumb, press the paste in at the base of the curved edge; the shape will spoil if the pressure is applied to the sides or centre. Raise the edge of the paste level with the rim; this is known as 'thumbing up'. Dock the base. As the moulds have slanting sides, it is not necessary to line with paper and beans. If desired plain paper cases filled with beans or empty moulds may be used to hold the paste.

Barquettes
Arrange close together on the table the required number of lightly greased barquettes (boat shape) moulds. Roll out the paste 3 mm ($\frac{1}{8}''$) thick and roll it up on to the pin, then unroll to cover the moulds. Using a piece of paste, press down the layer of pastry into the moulds, so that it takes their shape. Using two rolling pins together, roll over the paste to cut it off on the edges of the moulds. If adjustment to shape is required, this may be done with the fingers. Dock the base. This method of lining is also suitable for tartlets, providing they are of the sharp edge, not the rolled or curved rims type.

Pudding bowls and patty moulds
This method is used with products that are steamed or baked; the filling being encased in paste. The moulds could be bowls, patty tins or small pie dishes. The paste is rolled out to a thickness between 3 mm ($\frac{1}{8}''$) and 6 mm

($\frac{1}{4}''$); the larger the mould the thicker the paste. Grease the bowl well with soft fat. Roll out the paste into a round approximately twice the diameter of the bowl all to the required thickness. Lightly dust with flour and fold in half to obtain a semi-circular piece of paste. Gather the open edges up and draw together to form a pocket. Lift the paste and place in the bottom of the bowl with the edges uppermost. Open the pocket, press around the sides, allowing the paste to overlap the top of the bowl. This overlapping is necessary so that after filling the edge may be sealed to the paste top.

When lining small shallow moulds press the paste in to expel the air. Moisten the edges. After filling, place a round of paste on top large enough to seal to the overlapping edge. If the moulds have sharp edges the rolling pin may be used to seal and cut; if not, press to seal and trim with a knife.

Cream horns

Roll out the puff paste to 2 mm ($\frac{1}{12}''$) thick and 300 mm (12") wide. Cut into strips 20 mm($\frac{3}{4}''$) wide and lightly brush with milk or eggwash.

Press one end of the paste strip on to the tip of the cornet mould and firmly wind the strip up to cover the mould, overlapping each layer by 5 mm ($\frac{1}{4}''$). Make sure that the moist side of the paste is on the outside and not against the mould. Do not stretch the paste when winding on as during cooking it shrinks and may break or force itself off the mould.

If the tip of the mould is left uncovered when starting to wind the paste, it will make it easier to remove the cooked paste after baking by making it possible to give the top of the mould a sharp tap on a hard surface to loosen the mould from the paste.

Flan and cake rings

It is sometimes necessary to mould or bake a mixture inside a bottomless ring-type mould. If the mixture is of a soft nature, or of a type that may become soft during cooking, there is a danger that it may seep out of the base. To overcome this, place the ring in the centre of a round of greased and wet greaseproof paper, which should be at least 50 mm (2") larger than the ring being used, twist and tuck the paper up to and around the bottom edge of the ring to form a raised border, which will hold together and prevent the mixture seeping out.

Hand raised pies

This method of moulding is associated with savoury meat pies, using hot water paste. Special wooden blocks of different sizes are available for this purpose, or alternatively a suitably straight-sided glass jar may be used. For this method of moulding the paste must be used while it is still hot. It may be kept in a covered bowl standing in a bain-marie of hot water.

Judge the amount of paste required for the size of pie being made and form it into a ball on the work table. Press the base of the block hard into the centre of the ball. Raise the paste at the edges of the block up and around the sides by pressing firmly but evenly with the palms of the hands, rotating the block as the pressure is applied. Aim to achieve an even thickness of 5 to 6 mm ($\frac{1}{4}''$) around the sides and at the base.

Allow the paste to cool, then remove the block and fill as required. Moisten the top edges and cover with a piece of paste. Pinch to seal the edges and decorate with cut out patterns of thin rolled out paste. Finish by brushing with eggwash before baking.

Special metal moulds are also used for hot water paste savoury pies, usually fluted or impressed to form a pattern on the sides of the paste. They are made in two parts, hinged on one end with a retaining clip at the other to hold it closed. Only a light greasing of the mould is required. The method of lining is to roll out the paste and press it over the base and around the sides. After filling, the top is covered, sealed and decorated. To remove the mould after cooking, allow to cool slightly, unfasten the clips and ease the mould away from the paste.

It is usual when making these pies to leave a hole in the top so that after they are cooked and cooled, aspic jelly may be poured into the pies.

Other mould preparations

COLD SOUFFLÉ
The desired finished appearance of this sweet is that of a mixture which has risen in a soufflé case. To obtain this effect, it is necessary to line the outside of the mould so that the mixture sets in a raised position. Using a double thickness of greaseproof or silicone paper, wrap firmly around the outside of the case so that the paper is at least 25 mm (1") above the rim. Secure by tying or taping.

CARAMEL
Pour hot caramel on to the bottom of the moulds. The caramel may be left on the bottom, or the mould may be turned around so that the sides also become coated. Care must be taken as the caramel is hot – approximately 160° C (320° F).

PAPER CASES
These are often used for producing small cakes. They do not require greasing. It is advisable that they are stood inside a firm mould or they may collapse out of shape while being filled or during cooking.

MACHINE MOULDING
This method is used for large scale production. It has the advantage of speed and producing items of uniform size and shape.

9 CONVENIENCE FOODS

For a long time many foods have been available in semi-prepared forms and although they have not been thought of as such, they are in a sense convenience, or ready-to-use foods. Jams, tinned and candied fruits, jellies, marzipan, fondant, chocolate and ice-cream come into this category. Even butter, margarine, milk and cream may be considered forms of convenience foods.

Basically convenience foods are ready-to-use products which require the minimum of time, effort, energy and skill to reconstitute or to prepare. They yield roughly the same product that pastry cooks would normally make from basic 'raw' commodities.

Convenience foods are expected to withstand the difficulties of transport. They must be of a suitable nature to be stored. Some form of processing is required to preserve them. Usually preservation is achieved by one of the following methods: quick (blast) freezing, freeze drying, dehydration or canning. Suitable facilities must therefore be available to the user to maintain the products in their respective conditions until required for use. Basic essential requirements are: suitable deep freeze and dry storage facilities, mixing and cooking equipment, and suitable systems for retaining the prepared foods either hot or chilled as required for service.

Much research has gone into the development of convenience foods. The standard and quality of most products is exceptionally good. The processing of products is performed under strict quality and hygiene control and the basic commodities used for production are selected for quality and suitability.

The type and quantities of convenience foods used depends on the nature of the catering operation, its size and facilities available in food preparation rooms. The skill of the staff and the number employed, as well as the amount of equipment available, will also determine how much is incorporated into the menu.

There is a wide choice of convenience foods which range from simple mixes and dishes to the more exotic and classical varieties. The following are examples of the most popular products available.

1 Fruits and fillings for pies, tarts, tartlets and flans. These may be
   obtained canned, frozen or dehydrated and only require opening,

thawing or reconstituting by soaking in water to be ready for use.

2 Pre-mixes for pastes, sponges, cakes, biscuits and puddings are produced which only need the addition of liquid with a recommended amount of mixing. Some mixes require the liquid to be eggs and milk, others may specify water only. Many cakes and sponge mixes have the advantage that the same product can be used for various preparations. for example a cake mix could also be used for a steamed spong. By adding other ingredients such as sultanas, currants and glacé cherries, a plain cake mix would produce a fruit cake.

3 Thickened products such as blancmange, whipped and flavoured creams, cream caramel (caramel often included), custard and other sauces are all available, using instant or easy to prepare methods.

4 Many made-up dishes are obtainable either as large items or as individual portions. These are usually frozen goods and will require defrosting, eg gâteaux, trifles and pastries. Pies, tarts and puddings are available and may require cooking or reheating.

It is important that instructions given with the products are strictly adhered to. The products have been tried and tested and unless the specified details for preparation and cooking are followed, the results may not be as good as they should be. This is especially important with frozen foods. There is a danger of food poisoning if the products are not thawed out and reheated, if required, in the correct manner.

Freshly prepared foods are naturally far better in flavour, colour, texture and, almost always, in nutritional value. They do, however, take longer to prepare and require skilled staff to process them. A selection of ingredients is required to produce a fresh food item, whereas many convenience foods are complete in themselves.

Convenience foods can still be attractive and tasty but they lack the full fresh flavour and colour of well prepared fresh foods. The emphasis in on 'well prepared', otherwise it is possible that convenience foods could be an improvement over poorly prepared fresh food.

The main points to consider have been summed up under specific headings which compare the advantages and disadvantages of their use.

EASE OF PREPARATION
Convenience foods are complete, or almost complete, within themselves. The processing only requires following simple instructions, whereas freshley prepared foods do require more basic preparations of raw materials.

RELIABILITY
The ranges of convenience foods available have been developed and tested, using top quality ingredients. Providing the manufacturers' instructions are followed, consistently good results should be achieved.

TIME SAVING

Very little time is required to prepare dishes from convenience or ready to use foods. The basic preparation and processing of fresh foods does require much more time and labour.

WASTE CONTROL

With convenience foods, except for mistakes in storing or preparing, there is no waste. With fresh foods there is likely to be more wastage due to the type of commodity being used or the lack of understanding by the operator.

AVAILABILITY OF SUPPLIES

Providing the planning of orders for supplies is correct and suitable storage facilities are available, there is no problem with convenience and ready to use foods.

The availability of fresh foods is affected by seasons and suppliers. Certain commodities are only available for a limited season. Suppliers may be restricted by weather, traffic, price or strike problems, which can affect delivery of orders.

STORAGE

Most convenience foods are in pre-packed or concentrated form. Less space is required for storage and because of their keeping qualities it is possible to store large quantities and more varieties for longer periods.

A variety of ingredients may be required to produce a particular dish made from freshly prepared foods and all of these items require storage space. To avoid unnecessary wastage many fresh foods will only be ordered in limited quantities as they are not yet processed.

COSTS

Convenience foods do cost more, but this could be offset by the economy achieved in preparation time and labour costs. Freshly prepared foods are normally cheaper but are more time consuming in the preparation. The extra labour costs can be recovered when certain fresh foods are in season and are much cheaper.

PORTION AND COST CONTROL

Convenience foods are easily controlled. The same yield is achieved every time from a specific quantity of production. Portion control is still possible with freshly prepared foods, but costs and profits will vary. In many cases such variations, when using fresh commodities, can occur from day to day.

VARIETY ON THE MENUS

A combination of convenience and ready prepared foods, together with a selection of freshly prepared foods, is the best course to take when planning menus. With careful planning a variety of dishes, both for small and for large menus, can be produced, having the extra advantage that a supplementary supply of dishes is always available if convenience and ready prepared foods are in stock.

The caterer must carefully consider the inclusion of convenience foods in the menus. The decision to use them will naturally be affected by customer expectation, demands and spending power.

10 ICE-CREAM

Ice-cream is a mise en place commodity which gives scope to the pastry cook to prepare a wide range of dishes, suitable for table d'hôte, à la carte and banquet menus.

■ TYPES OF ICES

SINGLE FLAVOURED ICES
Milk or water-base ices may be served on their own as a sweet in their own right.

SORBETS
These are light water ices, flavoured with wines, spirits, liqueurs or fruits. They are traditionally served at banquets, following the fish, or in between the entrée and roasts or relevée courses.

FRUIT DISHES
Ice-cream is combined with fruits and sauces for coupes, eg Andalouse, Edna May, or Jacques. It is used in composition dishes, such as Poire Hélène, Pêche Melba, Cerise Jubilée and Fraise Sarah Bernardt.

SOUFFLÉ SURPRISE
These are especially suitable for banquet and à la carte service. A combination of sponge, fruit and ice-cream is covered and decorated with meringue and flashed through a hot oven to lightly colour, eg Milord, Nòrvegienne, or Grand succèss. To hold after preparation and before cooking, they may be kept for up to fifteen minutes in a normal refrigerator, or up to one hour in the deep freeze. Do not store a prepared soufflé surprise for more than one hour in the deep freeze as the fruit will ice up and will not thaw out sufficiently when finished in the oven.

The following are moulded enriched ice-cream mixtures.

BOMBE GLACÉ
These are prepared by lining the mould with one flavour of ice-cream then filling with a bombe preparation of a different flavour, eg Aida, Brésilienne, or Grand Duc.

BISCUIT GLACÉ

This is a preparation similar to the bombe mixture but it is moulded in an oblong shaped mould. It may be of a single flavour, eg praline, or in layers of several flavours, eg neapolitain.

A bombe or biscuit mixture can also be used in moulds shaped as large fruits, eg pineapples or melons. These are filled with a mixture that has the flavour corresponding to the shape. The mould may also be pre-lined with a different coloured ice-cream, to represent the skin of the fruit, eg green for melon, with a pale yellow, green or red filling.

SOUFFLÉ GLACÉ

These are moulded in the same way as for cold soufflés, eg milanaise. The difference is that instead of using gelatine to make them set, they are frozen. They can be made in a variety of flavours, eg rum, orange, lemon, or coffee, or can be flavoured with spirits and liqueurs.

OTHER MOULDED ICE-CREAMS

Cassata is an Italian ice-cream containing candied fruits and nuts. It should be composed of at least three coloured and flavoured ices, eg white vanilla, green pistachio, red strawberry.

For some other dishes, the ice-cream mixture is made by using the flesh of the fruit. This is then used to refill the 'shell' of the fruit, eg pineapples, oranges, and melons.

■ STORAGE OF ICE-CREAM

Correct storage facilities are important. It is necessary for long term storage (up to six months) to keep the ice-cream at $-20°$ C ($-4°$ F). It is obvious that a cabinet which is used often, with continual opening and closing, will be less efficient. So a deep freeze cabinet which is used only for long term storage is advisable.

Ice-cream that is required for service must be of a softer texture and should preferably be kept in a separate cabinet. The temperature within the cabinet must be maintained at a constant temperature of $-18°$ C ($0°$ F). Under these conditions it is advisable to keep only the required amount for daily use.

Never keep ice-cream in a normal refrigerator or in an open area for more than ten minutes; it will very quickly thaw. It is illegal to sell ice-cream that is above $-2°$ C ($28°$ F). Ice-cream that has gone above this temperature or has melted should never be re-frozen and must be discarded because of the possible contamination by harmful bacteria.

Sorbets and other water-base ices should only be held for a few days in a cabinet with a temperature of $-18°$ C ($0°$ F), eg a service type cabinet. Once frozen hard they do not thaw out to a creamy texture but to a runny, syrupy consistency, therefore large stocks should not be stored. Only the amount required for immediate use should be purchased or made.

■ TRANSPORTING ICE-CREAMS

To preserve the condition of ice-cream which has to be served some distance away from the storage cabinet, as may be required for a buffet or outside catering function, the ice-cream may be held in a firm state by placing it in a water tight container, which in turn is packed into a large vessel containing ice. The ice should be tightly packed broken ice, mixed with salt. This lowers the freezing point of the ice (approximately one part salt to eight parts broken ice) and it will retain the ice-cream in a suitable condition for about an hour. If it is to be kept longer, drain off any melted ice water and repack. The recommended period of time depends on the climate and environment. The ice-cream must maintain a temperature of −15° C (4° F) and a regular check must be made to ascertain the condition.

■ ICE-CREAM MANUFACTURING REGULATIONS

For the majority of catering establishments it is not economical, nor is it possible, to produce ice-cream so that it conforms to the 'Ice-cream heat treatment' regulation 1959. Because of this and for the sake of convenience, most establishments obtain ready prepared ice-creams from manufacturers.

The regulations make the following points.

1 Prepared mixtures must not be kept more than one hour at a temperature exceeding 7° C (45° F) before being heated.
2 To pasteurize the mixture it must be heated at a temperature of not less then 69° C (150° F) for a period of thirty minutes, or 71° C (160° F) for ten minutes, or 80° C (175° F) for fifteen seconds, or 150° C (300° F) for two seconds.
3 The Environmental Health Department requires that a 'recording thermometer' is used. This instrument will record the temperature, time and date of a batch of ice-cream mixture that has been subjected to the heat treatment. It is a legal requirement that these recorded details are available to the health officer inspecting the establishment producing the ice-cream.
4 It must then be cooled to 7° C (45° F) within ninety minutes of heating and kept at this temperature until frozen, which should take place as soon as possible.
5 Once frozen, ice-cream must be kept at a temperature of −2° C (28° F).

Ice-cream regulations 1967

These regulations state the following minimum food requirements: 5 per cent fat content, 10 per cent sugar content, $7\frac{1}{2}$ per cent milk solids except fats. These standards apply only to all products named 'ice-cream'. They do not apply to water ices.

If using raw shell eggs, it is important that reference be made to the food poisoning precautions stated on page 105.

11 AERATION

The appearance and eating qualities of cakes, pastries, puddings and pastes, depend very much on the lightness of the products. There are several ways of achieving a good result. Natural, chemical and biological actions, used singly or in combination, will, in various ways, incorporate steam, gas or air cells into mixtures.

The combination of raw ingredients must be such that, during the process of manufacture and cooking, the mixture will stretch and trap the cells. Eggs and fats have properties that hold air cells which are produced when whisking or beating. Flour contains gluten, a protein subsance that develops on elastic texture capable of holding the increasing and expanding cells within the structure of the item being cooked.

The appearance of the end product should be considered when selecting the appropriate flour. If the product is expected to develop large gaps or spaces within the structure, eg yeast dough, puff or choux paste, a strong flour with a high gluten content is required. For sponge-like textures, with a network of small cells, a weaker flour, with low gluten content, should be used.

Be it in major or minor amounts, the development of steam or air pockets within the mix will always take place owing to the fact that a certain amount of air and moisture is present in all mixings.

Bread and other yeast goods are raised by gas cells produced by yeast fermentation; light sponges and soufflés by whisking air into eggs. Other products may depend on gas cells obtained by using baking powders, aerated fats, rubbed in fats, or a combination of fats and baking powder.

When subjected to heat during the cooking process, the steam, air or gas cells incorporated will expand and increase the volume of the mixture. This action continues until the heat coagulates the proteins and starches that are present, giving a multi-cell like appearance to the products.

The cooking speed must, therefore, be controlled by temperature adjustments to allow the expanding action to develop correctly. If the outside surfaces set too early, the inner parts will still continue to expand, erupting on the top surface, causing the product to peak or crack. if, on the other hand, the expansion takes place too quickly before the mixture coagulates, the air or gas cells will escape and the product collapse.

Except for yeast products the mixture should be as cool as possible when placed in the oven to cook. The gas and air in a cold mixture will remain in suspension longer than in a warm mixture.

■ FORMULA BALANCE

If using the rule of 'equal weights all round', then the amounts of sugar, fat, eggs and flour used must be equal to each other in weight. The baking powder required to lift this mixture would be 15 g ($\frac{1}{2}$ oz) to each 500 g (1 lb) of flour used.

In products using the creaming method much air is incorporated by beating. This acts as a raising agent, therefore the amount of baking powder included would have to be reduced. When the rubbing method is used there is less air introduced, consequently the amount of baking powder required must be increased. No baking powder is needed when the product is made by whisking eggs and sugar and using little or no fat. Sufficient air is incorporated into the mixture which, by itself, will raise and lighten the cake.

■ RECIPE BALANCE

It is always advisable to follow a given recipe. Each is tried and tested and is known to give satisfactory results. There are times, however, when a recipe may be altered, either to improve the product, or to make it more economical.

Care must be taken when altering the quantity of one ingredient to adjust the proportions of other ingredients. All quantities would have to be adjusted to balance the whole for good results.

If the fat content, which is a shortening agent, is reduced, then the amount of egg, which is a toughening factor, would also have to be reduced, otherwise the resulting product will be of a hard texture. The same principle applies if extra fats are used to make the mixture short and crumbly; then extra eggs would be needed to prevent it being heavy and greasy.

Aerated fats and eggs having a lifting effect. Any reduction in their quantities must be counter balanced by an increase of baking powder. If they are increased, the amount of baking powder must be reduced. When the amount of egg used in a mixture is a high proportion of the ingredients, the amount of baking powder is reduced. For items such as a Genoese sponge or Swiss roll, baking powder is not required at all. If the amount of egg used is reduced, a small amount of baking powder would have to be added to rebalance the aeration of the mixture. Sugar, as well as being a sweetener and giving colour to a crust, has an opening effect and promotes aeration within the mixture. If the mixture being made has a high sugar content, and the goods are intended to have a close texture, eg biscuits or pastes, the quantity of baking powder should be reduced or omitted altogether.

When some of the egg is replaced with milk, which is non-aerating agent, an increase of baking powder will be necessary.

■ NATURAL RAISING AGENTS

Air and steam are incorporated into mixtures by what is known as a mechanical method. This does not mean that a machine must be used, but the mixture is handled in a specific way, involving physical action.

STEAM

As already mentioned, steam is a raising agent found in all products. In some cases, methods are used that will introduce more steam into a mixture to produce predetermined results.

In puff paste, fat is incorporated into the paste in layers. During the cooking process vapour is produced from the paste and the melting fat, lifting the layers of paste which are kept separated and set by the heat in the oven.

In choux paste more than one third of the mixture is water. During the cooking the water turns to steam and blows out the protein and starch mixture which eventually sets into a hard empty shell.

When using the rubbing-in method of mixing, the small particles of fat will melt, producing steam cells which expand, raising and lightening the mixture. The same principle applies to puddings and pastes using chopped suet. Baking powder is added when the recipes using this method have a low fat content.

AIR

Air is incorporated into mixtures using a combination of methods. Sieving the flour will introduce air. Creaming and beating fats and sugar will incorporate air cells into the mixture. The whisking of eggs and sugar will suspend air bubbles in the mixture, thus producing a foam. If the mixture is warmed over gentle heat the process is accelerated and air cells are more easily retained in the foam due to the slight coagulation of the eggs.

■ CHEMICAL RAISING AGENT

Baking powder is a chemical raising agent composed of one part alkali and two parts acid. When moistened and heated it will react to produce carbon dioxide gas (CO_2).

Baking powder can be bought ready made, or it may be prepared by mixing thoroughly one part bicarbonate of soda (alkali) with two parts cream of tartar (acid). The addition of one part of rice or corn flour will retard any deterioration by moisture during storage.

It is the CO_2 produced which assists aeration in mixtures. To ensure even distribution of the baking powder, it is recommended that it is sieved several times with the flour.

Once the cake mixture is made it should be cooked immediately or the gases will start to develop and break out of the mixture. Some toughened mixes, such as scones, will benefit from the reaction and yield a better product if allowed to stand for a short while before baking.

It is possible to combine bicarbonate of soda with another form of acid which will react in the same way as cream of tartar and give the finished product its individual appearance, colour and flavour. An example is for 500 g (1 lb) of flour add one rounded teaspoon of bicarbonate of soda with 50 g (2 oz) of treacle. This is used in steamed sponges and puddings.

When working in small amounts, the use of a pre-tested measuring spoon will measure an accurate quantity of baking powder and is preferable to using scales.

Baking powder, whether bought or home made, should always be stored in an air-tight container. Any form of moisture will make it react and render it useless.

To ensure effective results, baking powder should only be purchased and stored in small quantities. Its condition may be tested by stirring a teaspoon of the powder in a small glass of warm water. If it gives off bubbles freely it is still active, if not, it should be disposed of.

■ BIOLOGICAL RAISING AGENT

Yeast is a living single-celled organism, belonging to a group of minute fungi. The individual cells are so small that they can only be seen with the aid of a microscope. If 4 000 were placed side by side they would measure about 25 mm (1").

Yeast requires moisture, food and warmth to be active. A flour dough meets these requirements. Moisture is provided by the liquids used in mixing. Food, in the form of simple sugar solutions, is derived from the starch in the flour. The warmth is controlled by the working conditions, equipment, ingredients and liquids used. The ideal temperature for yeast fermentation is between 25° C (80° F) and 32° C (90° F).

In ideal conditions, the yeast cells will grow by a continual reproduction process called budding as described in the sequence at the top of page 84.

During the process fermentation occurs and it produces carbon dioxide (CO_2) and ethyl alcohol. The gas cells increase the volume of the dough and the alcohol, which is evaporated during cooking, imparts a characteristic flavour to the product. This process is termed proving.

Single yeast cell

Initial formation of bud

Growth of bud

Separation of cells

Each cell repeating the reproduction process

The fermentation continues throughout the period of preparation and proving of the dough. When prepared items are cooking, the fermentation will continue until the temperature goes above 52° C (127° F) when the heat kills the yeast and the fermentation ceases. The gas cells contained in the dough will continue to expand and raise the mixture until the proteins and starches are set by the heat.

Large quantities of CO_2 gas cells contained within the dough produce a lighter product with greater volume.

Besides having the necessary nutrients for yeast action, a strong flour with a high gluten content is required to produce an elasticated dough that will hold the increasing and expanding gases during the fermentation, proving and baking. It must be noted that excessive quantities of yeast or prolonged proving of the dough, has a softening effect on the gluten strand and will reduce the dough's elasticity.

To distribute the yeast evenly with other ingredients and to develop the gluten, a yeast dough should be well mixed and thoroughly kneaded. Proving is done in gentle heat, at about 35° C (95° F), in a moist atmosphere, either by using a proving cupboard or by improvising and using a tray of warm water underneath the items, while devising a method of covering to retain the humidity and present a skin forming. When the dough has risen to double its size, it is rekneaded (knocked back). This will expel the gases and reintroduce fresh oxygen which stimulates the yeast and ensures a more even texture. It is then allowed to prove once more before being moulded into shape and finally proved before baking.

Fresh bakers' compressed yeast is best for producing fermented goods and is commercially available in 500 g (1 lb) packs. Providing it is kept well wrapped and stored in a refrigerator or cool place, it will keep fresh for several days.

Compressed yeast will work better if used at room temperature 20° C or (67° F). It must be fresh, with a good fawn colour, have a pleasant smell and should crumble easily. If the yeast is soft and sticky, or has brown dried stains, it is best discarded.

Yeast is also obtainable in dried granule or flake form. By taking appropriate precautions to keep it clean and dry, it can be stored for up to one year. In some cases reconstitution, by soaking in warm water, is necessary for it to become active. However, some dried yeasts are available which must be sprinkled directly into the flour and must not be pre-mixed with liquid. It is important to note that compared to fresh yeast, only half the weight of dried yeast is needed to ferment any recipe.

■ SPECIAL POINTS

Salt is necessary in a yeast mixture. Without it the product would lack flavour. It controls the yeast action and also strengthens the dough by acting upon the gluten in the flour. However, care must be taken that the salt never comes into direct contact with the yeast. This would kill it. Also, if too much salt were used, the fermentation would be retarded and, if excessive, stop altogether.

Although sugar is food for yeast, too much sugar can kill some of the yeast cells. Precautions against this must be taken when following recipes and methods that suggest creaming yeast and sugar together. It is not advisable to mix them and let them stand. The mix should be diluted and used immediately.

The action of yeast will be much slower in enriched yeast doughs. The eggs in these types of mixtures have a binding effect and the fats are shortening agents which tend to soften the gluten strands in the mixtures. This weakens the structure of a dough and it would not then be sufficiently elastic to hold large gas cells. This results in a denser end product than ordinary bread doughs.

If at any stage during the preparation of yeast goods, whether adding liquid, mixing, moulding or proving, the temperature of the mixture exceeds 52° C (127° F), then the yeast and its action will be destroyed.

The following are points to remember.

1 Use a strong flour of high gluten content and knead thoroughly to get an elastic dough.
2 Use the correct amount of liquid and ensure it is the correct temperature.
3 Keep the dough warm, moist and covered to avoid a crust forming on the surface.
4 Do not prove in a dry or high heat.
5 Do not overprove or the product will puncture and collapse.
6 Use only the correct quantity of salt.
7 Do not mix salt and yeast.
8 Make sure the yeast is fresh.
9 Do not mix yeast and sugar and allow it to stand undiluted.

12 FLOURS

To achieve reliable results in flour confectionery, it is important to choose the correct type of flour; one which has the ability to produce the item required. Using an unsuitable flour often results in poor products.

Millers produce flours from selected wheats which are then balanced and blended to give a variety of grades, strengths and qualities, each being suitable for a specific purpose.

Patent is a high grade quality flour, containing hardly any bran. It is very white in colour and gives the best results for all types of work. 'Bakers' grade is a general purpose flour, not so refined. It gives satisfactory results and is cheaper to use.

■ THE STRENGTH OF THE FLOUR

The strength of the flour is governed by the quality and quantity of the proteins it contains.

Flour is a composition of between 70 and 76 per cent starch, 7 and 13 per cent proteins, 13 per cent moisture, $2\frac{1}{2}$ per cent sugar, 1 per cent fat and $\frac{1}{2}$ per cent mineral salts.

Pastry cooks often refer to flours as being strong or weak. These terms refer to the strength indicating the content of non-soluble proteins contained in the flours which, when mixed with water, will form an elastic substance called gluten. This elastic property in a mixture is very important from the pastry cook's point of view. Without it, the air or gas incorporated would escape and the product collapse. During the process of cooking, the gluten and other proteins in the mixture, coagulate and form the framework supporting the bulk of the products.

Wheat grown in countries that have extreme winter climates, such as Canada and Eastern Europe, will yield strong flours with a high gluten content. Weaker flours are milled from wheats grown in milder climates such as England, Western Europe and Australia.

STRONG FLOUR
These are also known as hard or bread flours and will contain between 70 and 73 per cent starch and 10 to 13 per cent gluten-forming proteins. They can absorb more water than weaker flours and are used for products which will have a high rise, eg yeast goods, choux and puff pastes.

WEAK FLOURS

These are also referred to as soft or cake flours and will have between 73 and 76 per cent starch and 7 to 10 per cent gluten-forming proteins. These are more suitable for producing items of a shorter and denser texture, such as cakes, sponges, biscuits, short and sweet pastes. Heavy fruit cakes, however, will benefit if part of the flour used is of the strong type, as the extra gluten will give a better structure to support the extra weight of the fruit.

The gluten strength in a mixture can be altered by using different methods of manipulation, or by adding certain ingredients, which will either develop or soften the gluten.

Gluten is toughened by salt, by long contact with water (as when a dough is left to stand) and also by kneading and rolling the dough. Yeast has a softening effect on the dough which must therefore be kneaded well to develop the gluten.

Acids, such as lemon juice, vinegar and cream of tartar, will act on the gluten strands, making them more pliable and less likely to contract.

Fats, milk, eggs, sugar and yeast also have a softening effect on the gluten, which weaken its structure, forming keeping properties. For this reason, puff paste should be rolled carefully to obtain even layers of fat and the paste and fat should not be allowed to mix.

The addition of either corn or rice flour increases the amount of starch, making a flour softer; a practice often used when making biscuits and shortbreads.

Understanding the effect these additions and alterations have on flours will clarify many points of production where different textures of finished products are involved, and suggest where adjustments may be made when products develop faults.

The strength of flour can be tested by pressing the flour firmly in the hand, opening the hand and shaking gently. If the flour becomes loose, it shows that it is of the stronger type. A weaker flour will tend to cling together in a lump.

To check the gluten content of flour, the following method will give a good guide. Mix some flour with sufficient water to form a dough. Place in a bowl of cold water and allow to stand for about twenty minutes. Gently knead while in the water to release the starch. Occasionally change the water. Continue kneading and changing water until all the starch is washed out and the water is clear. The result will be a brown-grey elastic gluten ball, a third of this is pure gluten, and two-thirds is water. To check the percentage of gluten use, for example, 250 g (10 ozs) of flour, if the finished wet gluten ball weighs 75 g (3 ozs), this equals 50 g (2 ozs) water and 25 g (1 oz) gluten. The result will show that the gluten content of the 250 g (10 ozs) of flour is 10 per cent.

It is also of interest to bake the gluten ball to see the effect of the expansion of steam and air. As it has no starch it will blow up into a large bubble. With further baking it will set crisp and firm. This is the key to the framework and volume of bread or any baked flour product.

■ DIFFERENT TYPES OF FLOUR

HIGH RATIO FLOUR
This kind of flour is specially processed. The name is given because of its ability to absorb higher proportions of liquids, fats and sugars than normal flours. It will produce a batter unlike the mixtures generally known. Its uses are limited. It is not suitable for use in standard recipes. The manufacturers normally supply special recipes and methods to use which must be followed if successful results are to be achieved.

SELF RAISING FLOURS
These are prepared flours and have a controlled amount of raising agent. Using this type of flour can eliminate errors, but is not always suitable for particular products which may require more or less raising power. Pastry cooks mostly use plain flour and add the required amount of raising agent to suit the product being made.

WHOLEMEAL FLOUR
This is milled from the whole of the grain. No bran or wheatgerm has been removed. Because the bran is absorbant, extra liquid may be required for recipes using this type of flour.

WHEATMEAL
This is a mixture of white flour and most of the bran and wheatgerm. Regulations state that it cannot be supplied on the market under this name. Instead, it is sold under the name 'brown'. It can be made by combining white and wholemeal flours.

SEMOLINA
This is a coarsely ground product from the starchy part of the wheat. It does not have any bran or wheat germ. It is used mainly for puddings and savoury gnocchi (gnocchi romaine).

CORNFLOUR
This is finely milled from maize corn. It contains no gluten and is mostly starch. It is used mainly to thicken liquids and becomes thicker and firmer on cooling. It is used mainly for puddings and sauces. Cornflour is often added to other flours when, for specific purposes, they are required to be softer.

RICE FLOUR

This is finely ground rice used mainly as a dusting medium and for milk puddings and thickening sauces. It is sometimes added to biscuits, shortbreads and macaroons to give a drier and crisper product.

ARROWROOT

This is a pure starch obtained from the root of the maranta plant in the West Indies. It is easily digested and will thicken liquids. In clear liquids it remains almost transparent.

FÉCULE

This is the name given to potato and chestnut flours, mostly used as thickening agents for liquids, but which cannot withstand prolonged boiling periods.

■ STORAGE OF FLOURS

Flours should be stored in dry, clean bins with close fitting lids. Old flour should be removed and the bins brushed out before refilling with fresh supplies. It is advisable to have the containers clearly labelled with their content to avoid mistakes when selecting the correct flour for use.

13 FATS AND OILS

Fats and oils may be termed as creamy or fluid substances. The main difference between them is in the melting point (the temperature at which they start to melt). Fats will turn oily when warmed; remain fairly firm at room temperature and become quite hard when chilled. It must be understood that different kinds of fats have varying melting points.

Oils are fluid at room temperature, change very little when warmed and become slightly thicker and cloudy when very cold.

Milk and animal fats are derived from natural sources. Other fats are made by processing oils, or fat and oils, with emulsifying agents to produce various blends of compounds suitable as substitutes for natural fats.

Different kinds of fats are used for pastry work, each having its own particular flavour, colour, purpose and function in the preparation of the required end product. The main purpose of using fats is to enrich a product and make it more palatable and digestable by softening the gluten strands in a flour mixture. The combination of colour, flavour and shortness in a product depends largely on the amount and type of fat used. The structural appearance is determined by the method of mixing and incorporating suitable kinds of fats with other ingredients to make the mixture function in a predetermined manner.

■ FUNCTIONS OF FATS

As well as imparting their own particular flavour and colour to the product, different types of fats are selected to perform a particular function.

The main objective for incorporating fat into a mixture is to shorten it and soften the gluten strands. This will produce a more tender product.

All fats have the ability to promote varying amounts of aeration in a mixture. By rubbing in and by laminating the fat into a paste, steam aeration is produced during the cooking.

Most fats, when beaten on their own or combined with other ingredients, have 'plastic' properties that will hold air. This promotes lightness during the baking.

The creaming of fats will incorporate air cells which will increase the volume and lighten the mixture.

In all these cases, the aeration and rise of a product is achieved by the air or steam or a combination of both, which expands within the product during baking.

To a lesser extent, a rubbed-in mixture also incorporates air.

Fats are used extensively in many ways to produce items of a specific appearance, quality and texture. The various fats have their own individual properties and qualities which when incorporated into the mixture largely determine the type, quality and flavour of the end product.

All kinds of fats produce energy, and when incorporated into any product will naturally increase the nutritional value of the food.

Fats are a stable, moist part of a product that will enrich and enhance its eating qualities, improve the keeping properties and prevent the product drying out too quickly, thus prolonging its shelf life. If a slice of cake and a slice of bread are compared, even after a short time it will be obvious that the cake, which contains more fat, will be moist, while the bread will be much drier.

All types of flour mixtures are tenderized by fat. The higher the proportion of fat used, the softer will be the gluten strands, thus giving the baked product a lighter, richer, or denser texture. The proportion of fat and the method of production used, determines the structure and appearance of the goods.

White fats and lard may be used for deep frying, but oil is more suitable for sweet items as it has a neutral flavour. Unless kept for a long period of time, fat compounds and oils do not need refrigeration. Providing they are stored in a cool, dry place, they keep satisfactorily for a long time (two months).

■ MILK AND ANIMAL FATS

BUTTER

With regard to taste and quality in products, butter is always used for high quality goods because of its flavour and purity. So much so, that an association of French pastry cooks (Maître Pâtissier de France) stipulate in their membership rules that members will maintain the standard by using only pure butter, cream, and fresh eggs in their products.

A pure butter is almost white. Colour is added by the manufacturers for appearance. It should have a smooth, firm, plastic texture, without trace of grain or oiliness. A strong odour indicates the start of rancidity and although not harmful it must be remembered that any flavour, good or bad, will be imparted to the products, therefore it affects the taste of the finished goods.

Butter is available salted or unsalted; the salt being added to enhance the flavour and preserve it. Butter has excellent creaming properties and when used for this purpose it should be soft, but not oily. For butter creams, unsalted butter is best as salt could spoil the flavour. When making puff or Danish pastes, or rubbed in mixtures, the butter must be cool and firm.

For certain requirements melted, clarified butter is required. This is prepared by melting butter in a pan over a gentle heat. When it is completely melted, allow it to stand for a short while. Remove any scum from the surface and gently strain through a tammy cloth, making sure that the sediment is left in the pan. Alternatively, melt the butter then allow to cool and set hard in a bowl. Lift out the hardened piece of butter and scrape the sediment off the bottom. Re-melt for use as and when required. A large amount may be prepared this way and stored for future use.

A concentrated butter is available, from which the liquid has been extracted, leaving the product with a fat content of approximately 99.5%. When used in recipes, allowance must be made for this lack of liquid, or the fat content will be too high. This butter is ideal for making puff paste: less than the usual amount is required, it is firm and imparts the richness and good flavour of butter.

LARD

A refined lard is rendered from pork fat. It has a particularly agreeable flavour and is almost neutral in colour. It has hardly any moisture; this gives it the shortening properties which makes it a suitable medium for making hot water and rubbed-in pastes for savoury products. To tone down the flavour and still retain the shortening qualities for sweet items, it should be mixed with equal proportions of butter or margarine as in short paste. Lard lacks the creaming properties that most other fats have.

SUET

This is a hard, white fat found around the kidney regions of animals. Beef suet is the type used for pastry work, mainly for steamed puddings, suet paste and mincemeat. The fat should be fresh, firm and dry, with no unpleasant smells or blood clots.

To prepare the suet, break down into small lumps and remove all the skin and blood spots. Chop with a large knife, or grate using a coarse grater. Keep the fat coated with some of the measured flour to prevent it becoming sticky or sticking, to the knife, board or grater. Convenience packs of shredded suet are available. This must be used cold and care taken when mixing the paste not to crush the granules of fat. This product has the same properties as fresh suet, but not the same flavour. Vegetarian 'suets', made from vegetable oils, are available.

All natural fats should be stored in refrigerated conditions. This is especially important with milk and animal fats, as they very easily turn rancid in warm weather and in the hot temperatures found in kitchens. They should only be brought out when needed to allow them to adjust to the consistency and temperature required.

■ FAT COMPOUNDS

MARGARINE
This is a butter substitute available in varying quality grades. It can be creamed and used as butter and has the ability to retain more air in its structure, thus giving greater volume to a product. In many ways, margarine gives a better developed product than butter, but lacks its good flavour.

WHITE FAT
This is smooth, neutral flavoured fat, having the same shortening properties as lard. It can be creamed and has a longer storage life than lard.

PASTRY FATS AND MARGARINES
These are special types of prepared, toughened fats, with a high melting point for making puff pastry. They are able to withstand the treatment entailed in the making of puff pastes and have the ability to be rolled and manipulated to produce the build up of layers of paste and fat which is what promotes the flaky texture of cooked puff pastries.

To achieve an even lamination (layers of fat and dough) in puff pastry it is important that the fat is kneaded and brought to the same consistency as the paste. A soft fat will roll out or blend in with the paste, but if the fat is too hard it will break through or not roll evenly and appear as large pieces in the paste, instead of layers.

As these special blends give extra lift to puff paste, less fat is required to achieve the same effect. Again it must be stated that the appearance required will be achieved in the end product, but the paste will lack the flavour given by butter.

SPECIAL CAKE FATS
These are high grade shortenings; sometimes termed as high ratio fats. They have the ability to hold higher proportions of sugar and liquids and should be used with special flours to produce very light cakes and sponges. Special methods of production are required when using these products, and special recipes are provided by the manufacturers and suppliers.

OILS
Edible oils are derived from vegetable sources which include fruits, seeds,

and nuts. Olive oil is a high grade oil, but rather expensive to use in pastry products. Very little benefit is achieved from its delicate flavour. Other refined oils have the same properties and suitability, but are of inferior grade regarding colour and flavour.

Oils have a limited purpose in pastry work. They do enrich and flavour mixtures, but do not have the ability to hold air. They are used mainly in mixtures where shortening and aeration are not essential, eg batters, noodles and strudel pastes. Because of the high temperature oils can be heated to, before decomposing and becoming dark in colour, their major uses in the pastry kitchen are for deep and shallow frying and for the greasing of trays and moulds.

Other forms of oils are extracted from aromatic plants, seeds and fruits and prepared in concentrated form for essences and flavourings, eg lemon, orange, peppermint, almond.

■ KOSHER FATS

Fats that require a special mention are the particular blends of Kosher margarines and shortenings, which must be used by caterers when preparing food for consumers who are of the Jewish faith. Their religion imposes certain traditional dietary laws. One is the forbidding of eating milk and meat products during the same meal. This means that the type of fat used must meet these dietary requirements, eg butter and cream should not be used if meat is served at the same meal. Lard is never used as this is a product of pork, a meat that is forbidden by their laws.

14 SUGARS (SUCROSE)

Sugar is a carbohydrate constituent of most plants and is one of the purest and most readily available energy giving foods. The two main sources of sugar are from the sugar-cane, which is grown in tropical and sub-tropical countries, and from sugar-beet, a root crop cultivated in areas with temperate climates. After extraction and refinement both these sugars, technically known as sucrose, are similar in appearance, flavour, food value and chemical composition. Both possess the same abilities to sweeten and the other functional properties needed for all manner of bakery and confectionery work.

Sugar is processed in varying degrees of refinement. It is produced in many forms for specific purposes and is available in fine white powder, small and large crystals, lumps, brown sugars and syrups, all of which have their own distinctive flavour and uses.

■ TYPES OF SUGAR

ICING SUGAR
High quality granulated sugar is ground and sieved through fine mesh to produce a fine, white powdered sugar. Small quantities of calcium phosphate or starch are added to absorb moisture and assist the powdered sugar to retain its free flowing qualities.

It is used mainly for decorative purposes; for royal and water icing, butter creams, modelling pastes and marzipans, as a dusting medium and also in certain types of biscuits.

Coating a baked paste with a layer of icing sugar and caramelizing it under the grill, or in a hot oven will give a clear, glass-like surface glaze.

CASTOR SUGAR
This is a white, fine, evenly graded crystallized sugar. It dissolves quickly and easily when mixed with other ingredients. It gives a smooth texture to rubbed in pastes, shortbreads and aerated goods that use the creaming or whisking method of preparation, eg cakes, sponges and biscuits.

GRANULATED SUGAR
This is an all purpose white sugar, composed of larger sized crystals. It is used for sweetening when liquids are present and for biscuits which require a hard, crunchy texture. If used in cakes and pastes, the crystals

may not dissolve completely, resulting in a speckled surface and a grained texture in the cooked product. Granulated sugar is usually considered unsuitable for a creamed mixture as it does not give a fully aerated product. However, it is ideal for boiled sugar work.

LOAF SUGAR
This is made from large, compressed blocks of granulated sugar which are then cut into cubes. This method of manufacture produces the sugar most suited for sugar boiling because of its purity.

CUBE SUGAR
This is a moulded form of granulated sugar, mostly used for the service of beverages. Extra care must be taken if it is used for sugar boiling as the cubes tend to retain a residue on the surface from the moulds used in their production.

NIB SUGAR
This is broken sugar which has been sieved to standardize the grain size. It is used mainly for decorating the tops of cakes and buns.

BROWN CANE SUGARS
Demerara sugar is a partially refined, fairly dry, light brown sugar. Barbados sugar is a less refined, smaller grained, dark brown, moist sugar. Both give a dark colour and characteristic flavour to puddings, rich cakes and biscuits, but they may need partially dissolving before adding to mixtures. These sugars are also very popular served with coffee.

TREACLE
This is a dark coloured, thick syrup with a slightly 'burned' flavour. It is made from the concentrated, filtered liquid molasses after the sugar has been extracted from sugar-cane. Mainly used for rich fruit cakes, ginger cakes, puddings and biscuits.

GOLDEN SYRUP
As the name suggests, it is a golden coloured heavy syrup; it could also be termed a purified, inverted by-product of sugar refining. It is used for steamed and baked puddings, tartlets, flans and sauces. It may be used as a sweetening agent, but does have its own characteristic flavour which must be taken into account when using it.

HONEY
This is a natural product mainly for table use. It can be obtained in clear or cloudy crystallized form and is used for cakes, biscuits, brandy snaps and nougat.

GLUCOSE
This is available as a clear syrup or in powder form. It is produced from starch, grapes or sucrose with the addition of a weak acid to invert the

sugars. It can be used with chocolate to make a pliable modelling paste, added to fondant to give a smoother and shinier finish, boiled with sugar to prevent crystallization, and incorporated into cake mixtures to produce a moist product with a longer 'shelf life'.

When using these syrups in mixtures, the proportion of sugar in the recipes should be reduced and the mixture should be cooked at lower temperatures as syrups caramelize at lower temperatures than sugar.

Providing sugar is kept dry and clean it will last indefinitely if stored in suitable containers, or left in the original packaging. It is advisable to use separate scoops and clean pans when weighing or measuring sugar to avoid contamination from other commodities which could spoil the product beind made, eg when boiling sugar or whisking egg whites.

■ FUNCTIONS OF SUGAR

Sugar is one of the most versatile commodities used in pastry work. As with most other ingredients, selecting the right type and using it in the correct manner for the purpose required is very important. Apart from being used as a sweetening agent, sugar has other essential functions in pastry work. During the mixing and cooking it will promote aeration and colour in baked products. It should be noted, however, that although it imparts flavour into products, it does have a softening effect on the gluten, resulting in a denser product and a smaller rise than would have occurred had the sugar been reduced or omitted. When added to sauces and glazes it stabilizes the textures, enabling them to retain fluidity and shine. A little fine sugar added when whisking egg whites will give the proteins an adhesive strength, enabling them to retain a higher proportion of air.

Sugar that is added in baked egg custard mixtures delays the coagulation of the proteins in eggs, resulting in a smoother and firmer product. Used correctly, and in sufficient amounts, sugar has the power to preserve foods, as in crystallized and preserved fruits and hams. Sugar lowers the freezing point in ice-creams, keeping the mixture soft, smooth and free from ice grain. The same action applies when preparing fruits for freezing, they will benefit if they are first rolled in sugar, or soaked in a sugar syrup.

Crystal or powdered sugars can be processed on their own, or combined with other ingredients to produce various pastes, icings and decorative speciality sugar confectionery such as marzipans, royal icing and gum paste (pastillage).

Crystal sugar may be coloured to decorate the rims of glasses when serving creamy type sweets and for decorating iced cakes and pastries.

Sugar is also cooked and used in preparations and incorporated into other mixtures, for example, Italian meringue, fondant, fudge, petits fours, pulled sugar work, candied and crystallized fruits. With extended cooking, sugar will change colour from clear to light brown and then almost to black. The darker colours are used for toffees, caramel and praline, and also for flavours and colourings.

15 EGGS

It could be said that the egg is the original convenience food. It is almost a pre-packed meal in itself. It contains energy and body building nutrients, including minerals, carbohydrates, fat and a high proportion of proteins.

Hen eggs are the most versatile and indispensable raw commodity available to the pastry cook. They have coagulating and air retaining properties without which many products could not be made.

Various methods of manipulation and preparation are employed to utilize the egg. Used in the right proportion to other ingredients, eggs have qualities which can be used to produce goods of different texture, appearance, composition, richness and flavour. These qualities will be lost if skill and understanding in use is lacking and if the correct procedures are not adopted. An important point to note is that coagulation (hardening) of the white starts at 60° C (140° F) and yolks at 65° C (150° F).

■ FUNCTIONS OF EGGS

To understand and appreciate the functional qualities and useful purposes of eggs, the following details are best read and practised in conjunction with the sections dealing with mixing methods, aeration, equipment and recipes using these methods of production.

Eggs possess filming properties; when whisked they will produce a foam structure holding large quantities of air cells which are used as raising and lightening agents in baked goods such as sponges and biscuits. More reliable results are achieved if whole eggs are whisked over a gentle heat, such as in a warm bain marie, or if warmed sugar is used. Because of the partial coagulation started, the eggs form the network of air cells more easily and the foam will have stronger stability to withstand the additional mixing of other ingredients without losing air and collapsing.

When whisking egg whites it is very important that no grease or even traces of the yolk are present either in the ingredients or on the equipment being used. Grease shortens the elastic properties of the albumen and no amount of whisking will aerate or stiffen the mixture. Only fresh eggs should be used as stale eggs tend to be watery. Plastic utensils tend to feel greasy so they should not be used for ingredients that require to be whisked to a foam.

To make sure that eggs are fresh and that no grease is present, it is best to break each egg separately in a bowl before adding to the rest. The easiest way to separate the yolks from the whites is to crack the egg and, with the thumbs, pull the shells apart and tip the yolk from one half of the shell to the other. Alternatively break the egg into a small funnel or onto the hand, allowing the white to fall away.

If the whites are placed in a bowl covered with a dry cloth and allowed to stand in a cool ventilated place for several hours some of the moisture will evaporate. This strengthens the albumen and yields a firmer and more stable mixture.

The addition of a little sugar, or a few drops of lemon juice, or a pinch of cream of tartar, on commencement of whisking will stabilize the proteins in the whites and allow them to be beaten longer, so incorporating more air, giving a firmer mixture with greater volume. Do not use all three additives or use too much, as this would reduce the strength of the whites.

If during the whisking the mixture appears to go grainy or watery, which may happen if the eggs are stale and weak, add a little sugar or salt, followed by a brisk whisking. This should smooth out the mixture. A mixture which appears grainy or watery should never be used as it lacks air and stability and would spoil any product.

Stiffly beaten whites of eggs will incorporate vast amounts of air, allowing much sugar to be incorporated to make meringue which can be used for pastries, coatings, toppings or fillings. As aerated foam they are added to cooked flour-based preparations which will, upon baking, make very light puddings such as soufflés and sponge fingers. Added to creams, custards and purées, they give lightness and volume, as in bavarois, cold soufflés, mousses and ice-creams.

Whites of eggs are used in the preparation of royal icing; a mixture of icing sugar and whites which is used as a decorating medium for cakes. White of egg may be used as a binder for marzipan and for the making of biscuits, which are required to be hard and brittle, eg macaroons and japonaise mixtures which are used for pastries, gâteaux and tortens.

A mixture of whole eggs and milk, moulded, and cooked slowly, using the 'bain-marie method', will set by coagulation into a firm custard cream, eg cream caramel and baked egg custard. Egg yolks, used on their own, will thicken a liquid when heated to produce a smooth rich sauce. With both of these mixtures care must be taken to ensure that the cooking temperature does not go above 80° C (180° F) or the proteins in the eggs and milk will coagulate too much causing solids to separate from the liquids (curdle). It is advisable to remove the mixture from the bain-marie or pot to stop further cooking taking place once the mixture has reached the above temperature.

A sweet or sauce known as sabayon or zabaglione is made by whisking equal quantities of yolks, sugar and wine, over gentle heat. The effect of coagulation and aeration achieved will give a rich, warm, creamy mixture. A heavy wine, eg marsala is used for sweets and a light wine for sauces.

Yolks and whites may be beaten separately, then blended together. This method is used for omelette soufflés and as a base for sponge fingers. It is not advisable to prepare too much of these mixtures because on standing, they will soften and give flat results.

Cloudy liquids, such as jellies or syrups, may be clarified by using egg whites. The whites are whisked into the warm liquids and allowed to stand for a short while. By coagulation, they will collect any sediment, bring it to the surface where it may be skimmed off, and leave the liquid clear.

By brushing a paste or a dough product with egg, or a mixture of egg, milk or water, it will bake to a smooth golden colour. Care must be taken when producing goods which are expected to rise, such as vol-au-vents or scones, that the egg-wash is not allowed to run down the sides. During baking the effect of the egg coagulating would prevent any rise taking place on the egg-washed sides, with the possibility of the unwashed sides rising even higher than expected.

Eggs are used as moistening agents when mixing together dry ingredients during the production of pastes, cakes, puddings and biscuits. They may be beaten with other ingredients to promote aeration, as in creaming or batter methods.

■ COMPOSITION AND SIZE OF EGGS

Eggs are composed of three main parts. Approximately twelve per cent shell, thirty per cent yolk and fifty eight per cent white. It is not a good practice to follow a recipe where it states 'use four eggs', unless the eggs are known to be of a standard size. The eggs available may be small, extra large or of unequal sizes, in which case the proportion of other ingredients to the amount of liquid egg may not be correct. It is very important that a balanced recipe is used. To this end it would be advisable to measure the eggs for use. Taking the 'standard' egg as a basis, the following may serve as a guide.

Whole eggs 10 to $\frac{1}{2}$ litre (12 to 1 pt)
Whites   17 to $\frac{1}{2}$ litre (20 to 1 pt)
Yolks   28 to $\frac{1}{2}$ litre (32 to 1 pt)

■ QUALITY AND CLASSIFICATION OF EGGS

The external appearance of the egg does not indicate its quality or freshness. It is always advisable to break the eggs separately for it requires only one bad egg mixed into the rest to spoil the whole bunch.

The colour of the shell or yolk, or the size of an egg, do not in any way affect the quality, except for the colour it imparts to the product. Weight for weight, all sizes have the same food value.

An egg should feel heavy for its size. A light egg means that it contains air and is not fresh. When the egg is broken the yolk should be firm, well rounded and of even colour, positioned in the centre of the white. The white should have a high proportion to thick white which goes slightly thinner at the edges. As eggs deteriorate, the yolk appears flat with faint blemishes on the surface and the white becomes watery and spreads.

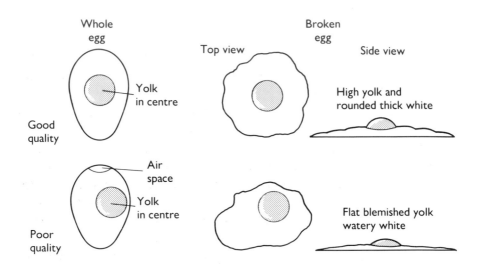

A simple check may be made by placing the whole eggs in cold salted water, approximately 100 g salt to the litre (4 oz to 2 pt). A fresh egg will sink and stay at the bottom. The older and staler the egg, the more bouyant it will be. The reason for this is that as the egg deteriorates, the air inside increases, giving more bouyancy. The yolk becomes displaced from the centre during deterioration and settles against the top part of the shell. Blood spots are sometimes found in the white and although as such they are not harmful, they will in a short time decompose and start to smell.

The quality standard for eggs are in three classes.

Class A First quality: fresh, clean and intact.
Class B Second quality: may be preserved, have dirty shells or could have been washed.
Class C Could be cracked, washed, preserved. Mostly used by large scale food processors.

Unclassified eggs are not suitable for human consumption.

■ GRADING AND SIZING OF EGGS

Fresh hen eggs are inspected for quality and graded into sizes at packing stations under strict hygiene and quality controls. Since January 1978 eggs

Size grade	Weight in grams	Approximate weight in ounces	Termed as:
1	70 or over	$2\frac{1}{2}$ or over	Extra large
2	65–70	2	Large
3	60–65	2	Standard
4	55–60	2	Standard
5	50–55	$1\frac{3}{4}$	Medium
6	45–50	$1\frac{1}{2}$	Small
7	under 45	under $1\frac{1}{2}$	Extra small

have been graded and grouped by weight into seven size bands to conform with EEC regulations.

Prices vary depending on the time of the year. This is most noticeable in he late summer and autumn when there are more smaller eggs produced in relation to larger ones. For a large consumer of eggs, the size grade, weight and price should be compared to obtain the best value. Using the scale band figures as a guide, and noting that on average between eight to ten large eggs, ten to twelve standard, twelve to fourteen medium and fourteen to sixteen small eggs will equal half a litre (one pint), it is possible to select and purchase the most economical size for production work. For example it may work out cheaper, while still obtaining the amount of liquid egg, to use thirteen number 5 eggs instead of ten number 2.

■ STORAGE OF EGGS

Eggs that are to be stored for a period of time should not be washed until required. This would remove the natural coating on the shell which, to some extent, protects and preserves the eggs. The shell is porous and a certain amount of the moisture is lost by evaporation. If moisture can come out, air can enter. This will also allow penetration of any flavours from the surrounding atmosphere. Eggs must not be stored near strong smelling foods, such as cheese, onions or fish.

Fresh eggs which have been removed from the shell may be stored under refrigeration and kept for several days if the yolks of whole eggs are covered and are below the surface of the whites. Yolks stored on their own should have a layer of water poured on top to prevent a skin forming. Whites must be kept in tightly covered containers.

Eggs in their shells are best kept in their original trays, boxes or on racks, with the rounded side upwards. The yolk is anchored in the centre of the white by connecting membranes and if the eggs are stored pointed side up, these membranes break, allowing the yolk to rise and come into contact with the shell. As the shell is porous, air, and therefore bacteria, can penetrate the shell and cause the yolk in contact with the shell to deteriorate. In time the natural gap of air develops in the egg at the rounded end, but a membrane between the shell and the white of egg cushions the yolk preventing it from rising and contacting the shell when it is correctly stored. For this reason it is not advisable to store loose eggs in a dish or bowl. There is an added danger of them getting broken.

■ MAINTAINING THE QUALITY OF EGGS

Only the amount of eggs required for immediate use should be kept in the kitchen. It is bad practice to keep cases of eggs in warm food-preparation areas. Storage temperature is the main factor in maintaining egg quality. For example, eggs stored at 38° C (100° F) will begin to deteriorate after three days, at 27° C (80° F) after eight days. They may be kept up to three months if stored at 5° C (40° F). As a point of interest a fertile egg will only take twenty one days at a temperature of 37° C (99° F) to become a live chick.

■ PRESERVING EGGS

Shelled whole eggs, yolks or white may be frozen for use at a later date. It is best if they are frozen in small quantities as this will allow only the amount required to be thawed for use. It is important that frozen eggs are allowed to defrost slowly, without any applied heat, as this would partly coagulate them and they would lose the properties required of them. Once defrosted they deteriorate quickly and should be used as soon as possible.

Eggs may be preserved by coating the shell with special varnishes, or by dipping in paraffin wax. Both of these will seal the shell and prevent evaporation of the moisture and stop penetration of bacteria. If dirty, eggs should be wiped clean (but not washed) before being stored. Eggs which are more than three days old, cracked or dirty should not be preserved as bacteria may already have entered.

■ PROCESSED EGGS

Eggs which are available in bulk are especially suitable for large-scale catering and can be obtained in frozen or dried forms. They have the advantage of being cheaper than fresh eggs and it is possible to hold a large supply in stock.

FROZEN EGGS

These are obtainable as whole eggs, yolks or whites. They are supplied in sealed cans or plastic containers and must be kept frozen until required. They must defrost slowly and completely. The ideal way is to place the unopened containers in cold water at a temperature of 15° C (60° F) and leave them overnight. Once defrosted they should be used as soon as possible and, as with all frozen foods, must not be refrozen.

DRIED EGGS

These have the advantage that they are easily stored in any dry area and are a useful standby in case of emergencies. Once the bag is opened, the contents should be used up as quickly as possible. If there is any surplus it should be kept in an airtight container. To reconstitute dried egg powder, stir one part powder to three parts water and leave to stand for about ten minutes before use. The mixture lacks the aerating properties of liquid eggs so some form of raising agent is required in the product, eg baking powder.

DRIED ALBUMEN

This is obtainable in powder or flake form and is reconstituted by stirring 75 g (3 ozs) of albumen into $\frac{1}{2}$ l (1 pt) of water. Leave to stand for at least three hours before using. It then has the same properties as normal egg white and may be used as such.

SUBSTITUTE EGG WHITE

This may be used as egg whites for royal icing and meringue. It lacks the stability of whites and is not recommended for use as aeration in soufflés and bavarois. There are several of these synthetic whites, under different brand names, on the market.

■ RAW SHELL EGGS – SALMONELLA FOOD POISONING

Following a number of outbreaks of salmonella food poisoning, raw shell eggs are considered to be a possible source of infection. Although not a major risk, precautions must be taken. For most caterers, this has presented some problems in the production of certain types of sweet and other dishes using eggs.

The duty of Environmental Health Departments is to ensure that everyone is made aware of the risks associated with the consumption of products containing raw or lightly-cooked eggs.

It is recommended that shell eggs should be cooked at a high temperature and for a prolonged cooking time in order to kill the salmonella bacteria.

Caterers are advised that recipes using raw shell eggs that require little or no cooking should be changed to specify the use of pasteurized eggs —

frozen, liquid or dried.

By all indications, the use of raw shell eggs in foods such as sabayons, mousses, omelets, bavarois, uncooked meringue, royal icing, egg custard sauces, ice-creams and other items which only receive minimum cooking, should cease.

Recommendations on a number of hygiene rules for storage, handling and preparation of eggs are as follows:

1 Eggs should be stored in a cool, dry place, preferably in a refrigerator.
2 Eggs should be stored separately to avoid possible contamination of such foods as raw and cooked meats and cheese.
3 Egg stocks should be limited to amounts required and should be used on the basis of first in, first out.
4 Hands must be washed before and after handling eggs.
5 Cracked eggs should not be used.
6 Storage and food preparation areas and equipment and tools should be cleaned between the preparation of raw and cooked foods and other commodities.
7 Egg products that are to be eaten cold should be consumed as soon as possible after preparation. They can be served up to 24 hours after preparation if they have been stored at a temperature below 5° C (45° F).
8 Egg products that are to be eaten hot, should be served immediately or kept at temperatures at or above 63° C (145° F). If they are left over they must be discarded.

To protect their customers, their business and themselves, it is strongly advised that caterers keep up to date with information, advice and assistance, which may be obtained from the local Environmental Health Departments of District and Borough Councils.

16 FLAVOURINGS AND COLOURINGS

All prepared foods depend on ingredients and methods of production to obtain their own individual flavour and colour.

As much as is economically possible, natural ingredients should be used as they are obviously superior. Products containing natural ingredients are more palatable and are therefore appreciated more. If, for example, butter is used instead of margarine, or fresh lemon juice is used in place of essence, then the product will be superior in quality and taste. Fresh oranges and lemons, liqueurs, spirits, wines, cocoa, almonds should always be used in preference to artificial concentrated colourings and flavourings. However, it is a fact that to produce a wider variety of confectionery goods more economically, colourings, essences and extracts, both artificial and natural, are used to compensate for the natural flavours and colours lacking when more expensive ingredients are not used.

Food additives are available in an extensive range to suit many purposes. Many compounds are produced which are ready blended as flavourings and colourings.

There are two main sources of concentrated flavourings. One that is prepared from fruits and plants and the other which is chemically produced to stimulate flavours. The main sources of natural flavourings are different parts of plants. These include fruits, seeds, roots, stems, bark, leaves, buds and flowers. They may be classified under four main headings: herbs, spices, natural extracts and essences.

All flavourings should be used in moderation and the amounts carefully measured. They are intended to enhance the flavour of foods. Using too much or adding too many varieties to a product could spoil a good basic recipe.

Always store flavourings in a metal or glass non-corrosive container, eg an airtight glass jar or bottle. Store in a cool, dry and dark place. This is to enable them to keep their colour and any aromatic fragrance. They deteriorate with time so are best purchased in small quantities.

Flavourings, essences and colours produced as food additives must be harmless to meet legal requirements. A point to note however is that various countries issue different permitted lists of standards required. What may be permitted in one country may be banned in another. The user need not worry unduly, providing the goods have been purchased from reputable suppliers. Artificial colourings are made from inorganic pigments. There are an unlimited variety of these colours. As with flavourings, all colourings must meet legal requirements being non toxic and harmless.

■ NATURAL INGREDIENTS FOR FLAVOUR AND COLOUR

Natural ingredients have the advantages of being more palatable and more nutritious. The following are examples of natural commodities that may be incorporated into mixtures to give flavour and colour to products.

Oranges and lemons
The zest may be grated and added to cakes and other mixings. The thinly peeled zest can be steeped in liquid to produce syrups. The whole rind may be candied and used cut up in cakes, puddings and other sweets. The juices may be added to mixtures when producing jellies, bavarois, sauces and ice creams.

Cocoa, chocolate powder and ground almonds
These can be added to flour for use in cakes and puddings. Cocoa and chocolate can be combined with liquids for use in sweets and sauces and also for flavouring in butter cream. Cocoa has a strong, dark, bitter flavour; chocolate is more delicate and paler in colour, and as it contains more fat and sugar, the recipe may have to be adjusted to maintain a correct balance.

Coffee
Coffee beans, crushed or ground, may be infused in milk and other liquids for flavouring sauces and egg custards. Concentrated coffee syrup for colouring can be made by adding ground coffee to a strong sugar syrup which is heated almost to boiling point, allowed to stand until cold, and then strained. Coffee extract is available in liquid form. Instant (dried) coffee may be used, but it is advisable to reconstitute it in a little hot water to form a thick cream before adding it to the liquid in the recipe.

Wines, liqueurs and spirits
These are used as flavourings, either by being added to the mixture or for moistening the finished product.

Flavoured sugars, syrups and alcohol
Sugar, as well as being part of the bulk of a product because it sweetens, could be considered a natural flavouring. It is practice of many pastry cooks to flavour batches of dry sugars with natural substances. These

sugars are then used instead of pure sugar when mixing ingredients for products requiring a particular flavour. Vanilla pods, cinnamon sticks, cloves, zest of oranges or lemons, ginger, any spicy seeds and crushed coffee beans are suitable substances to use.

When the flavoured sugar is used up it should be replaced immediately with a fresh supply. This procedure should continue until the flavours contained within the substances are exhausted. The containers for these sugars should be airtight to retain the flavours. Before using, it is necessary to sieve the sugars to remove the substances. The same procedure would apply when the substances are added to alcohol or sugar syrups to use as liquid flavourings. These should be stored in bottles with a tight fitting screw-top or cork to retain the flavours.

Herbs
The flavours derived from herbs lend themselves more to savoury dishes and have only a limited use in confectionery work: angelica and bay leaves being the main exceptions.

Angelica is obtained from a plant with a thick but hollow stem. It is prepared crystallized. It does not have a very strong flavour and is mainly cut up and used in sweet dishes and cakes and for decorative purposes.

Bay leaves are from an evergreen plant. They have a powerful sweet flavour and are used, dried or fresh, in liquids for syrups, milk puddings and sauces.

Spices
Spices in seed or powdered form are used for confectionery work. The term 'spices' covers a wide range of aromatic flavours. The following are most often used in sweet products.

All spice or mixed spice is a term given to a blend of sweet spices: a combination of powdered cinnamon, nutmeg and cloves. It is used in cakes, yeast buns, fruit loaves and in pies and tarts when apples are the main ingredient

Aniseed, from the small seed of the anise plant, has an unmistakable licorice flavour. It is occasionally used to flavour cakes, fruits and syrups.

Caraway seeds are small, black seeds, slightly tapered at one end. They have a sharp flavour which slightly resembles aniseed. They are used mostly for breads and cakes.

Cinnamon is the inner part of the bark of a small tree. It has a sweet, pungent flavour. When whole, it resembles a thin roll, about the size of a pencil (cinnamon stick), and is used to flavour liquids for cooking fruit compôtes and syrups. In powder form it is used for cakes and yeast buns.

Cloves are dried, unopened flower buds. They resemble a small black nail and give a strong pungent taste which blends well with most dishes containing cooked apples.

Coriander seeds are small dried fruits, very similar in appearance to white pepper corns, except that they have faint lines and are hollow. They have a mild, sweet, delicate flavour and are mostly used in syrups.

Ginger is part of the root of a plant. It resembles a small, badly shaped potato. It has a hot, spicy flavour and is available preserved in syrup in crystallized or powdered forms. It is used for cakes, biscuits, puddings and petits fours.

Nutmeg is the kernel of a fruit similar to the peach. It has a sweet, spicy flavour and is available in nut or powdered form. The whole nut retains its flavour for a longer period of time. It is preferable to use the nut whole and grate it only when required to obtain maximum flavour. Nutmeg is used for cakes, junkets, hot and cold milk puddings and custards.

Poppy seeds are small seeds about the size of a pin head, from the poppy plant. They have a pleasant nutty flavour and are mostly used for continental and special types of breads.

Essential oils and essences

These liquid flavourings are processed in a concentrated liquid form from the essential oils extracted from plants and fruits. This is done either by pressing, or by distilling the parts which contain the flavours and then diluting with alcohol. Not all products lend themselves to this process and consequently the variety of natural essences is limited.

Almond essence is obtained from almonds by pressing and distillation. A cheaper variety is obtained by using peach or apricot kernels.

Fruit essences are mainly produced from oranges and lemons. Most other fruits do not contain the oils to produce natural essences. The essential oils are pressed from the rinds of the fruits.

Peppermint essence is obtained by distilling a mint plant. Because of its very strong flavour, care is required with the quantity used.

The vanilla pod, the fruit of a climbing orchid, resembles a long, thin black bean. Vanilla essence is produced by macerating the vanilla pod in alcohol and afterwards filtering it. It is allowed to ferment. This produces crystals which flavour the alcohol. The vanilla pod may also be added to liquid products. After use it can be washed, dried and used again until the flavour is exhausted.

Orange and rose waters These flowers contain essential oils which are extracted by steeping petals in hot water which is then distilled. This produces a delicate flavour. It is used for light sponge biscuits and marzipan.

Manufactured essences are composed of various chemical compounds. They are cheap to produce and resemble natural flavours fairly closely, but lack the true natural aromas. They are available in an extensive range. Simulated flavours of fruits, spices, liqueurs and spirits are produced. Seldom do these essences contain natural oils.

■ COLOURINGS

If the appearance of food has a good colour which suggests its true flavour it will be more attractive to the eye. All colours should be used with care and moderation. More colouring can be added to a mixture, but if too much is used it cannot always be removed.

As with flavourings, the colour of the product should, as much as possible, be achieved by using natural ingredients. This is not always possible as some ingredients are unsuitable when combined, eg chocolate which is greasy and therefore cannot be used to colour royal icing or meringue. Artificial colouring may be added to enhance the appearance or give eye appeal in these cases.

A wide range of colours, natural and artificial, are available as concentrated liquids and pastes. Powders that require mixing with a liquid before use are also available.

Good quality colourings should be used which blend easily with other ingredients and will not be affected by the acidic content of foods such as gelatine and fruit juices. They should be able to withstand high cooking temperatures and low refrigeration temperatures.

Natural colourings

Natural colours are produced from plants and animals. These are limited in the variety available but by careful mixing, other shades of colour may be achieved.

Green colours are produced by extracting the colour from plants such as spinach and nettles. Orange is obtained from the fermented pulp and seeds of a West Indies plant, usually supplied in a paste form, it is easily diluted with spirits and alcohol. Red colour, cochineal, is prepared from a small South African insect. The colouring is obtained from the female after it has been killed, dried and ground to a powder. Water is added and the mixture is boiled for prolonged periods and reduced to a bright red colour. It is not often used because of its high price and scarcity. Yellow is obtained from two main sources: saffron, which is the dried stigma of the crocus and from turmeric which is the root from a plant of the ginger family.

Natural colouring ingredients

A brown colour is obtained by cooking sugar to a dark caramel colour, then diluting it with water to a density of 30° (measured with a saccharometer). Upon cooling it will have the consistency of a thick syrup.

Brown sugars and treacles are used in cakes and puddings, giving the products flavour as well as their corresponding colours.

Block chocolate, cocoa and chocolate powders are used in many mixings. If they are mixed with flour products, the cocoa or chocolate powder should be sieved with the flour. To flavour hot liquids the powders, or cut up chocolate, may be added to the liquids while they are heating. When using melted block chocolate with cold mixtures, it must be remembered that melted chocolate will set hard when in contact with cold surfaces. The addition must take place quickly to avoid lumps and to ensure even dispersion. When adding cocoa or chocolate powders to creams, thick or cold mixtures, the powders should first be dissolved fully with very hot water to form a creamy consistency. Powders do not dissolve easily when incorporated into cold mixtures.

Artificial colourings

These are made from inorganic pigments of which there are an unlimited variety. As with flavourings, all colourings must meet legal requirements being non toxic and harmless.

17 EDIBLE GUMS

Edible gums or gelling agents are substances used in confectionery. They have properties that will gel and set liquids to varying degrees of viscosity and into soft or semi-rigid forms. The main types used for confectionery work are gelatine, agar-agar, gum tragacanth and gum arabic. Various commercially produced jellying agents are also available under branded names. Correctly used, and in the right proportions for the consistency required, these gums give scope to the pastry cook to prepare a variety of good products which are attractive, economical and artistic in shape and composition.

All gelling agents should be stored in dust-proof containers and kept absolutely dry. Any contact with moisture converts the gums into suitable media for growth of bacteria.

■ GELATINE

Gelatine is a concentrated and refined product obtained by boiling the proteins 'collagen', contained in the bones and tissues of animals. It is processed and marketed in granulated, flaked or sheet forms and in varying grades of gelling strengths.

It is used as a stiffening agent for sweet dishes such as clear and whipped jellies, bavarois, cold soufflés and mousses and for the preparation of marshmallows and Turkish delight. In the manufacture of ice-creams it will prevent the formation of large ice crystals and retain the smooth creamy texture. Aspic gelatine is a savoury flavoured type used for cold soups, savoury mousses, filling for meat pies and for decorative cold larder work.

A good quality gelatine should not have any unpleasant odour. It will be clear when dissolved and have only a faint yellow colour. Lower grades tend to be darker in colour and have a slight smell of glue.

Isinglass is of high quality and is a more expensive gelatine. It is obtained from the swimming bladder of the sturgeon and is produced in fine sheet form. It is considered to be the purest of gelatines and to have greater stiffening powers.

It is a false economy to use the cheaper quality gelatines; in many cases they could spoil the delicate flavours, textures, and presentation of otherwise good products.

The characteristics of gelatines are such that a fluid is formed when they are mixed with hot liquids and upon cooling the mixture will gel and set. 50 g (2 oz) of gelatine will set 1 *l* (2 pts) of liquid. For creamy consistencies, such as bavarois and mousses, less gelatine is required. Gelatine also has foaming abilities, achieved by whisking a jelly mixture when almost on setting point. Gelatine is insoluble in cold water but it will swell and absorb up to five parts of cold water.

To ensure that it dissolves completely and evenly, gelatine should be soaked in cold water and then dissolved by moist heat, eg over a bain-marie or by adding hot liquid. Granulated or flaked gelatine should be stirred into a bowl containing cold water (approximately one part gelatine to six parts water). Leaf gelatine is soaked in plenty of cold water until soft and flabby, when the surplus water is squeezed out. In both cases allow at least fifteen minutes soaking time. Thick leaf gelatine may take longer. To dissolve, stand the bowl containing the soaked gelatine in a tray or pot of hot water, cover with a lid or wet greaseproof paper and leave without stirring until clear. Prolonged heating and high temperatures (above 60° C (140° F)) should be avoided as these can affect the gelling properties of the gelatine and as the liquid evaporates it leaves the solution thick, making it difficult to combine easily with other ingredients. Never use dry heat to dissolve gelatine; it will easily dry out and burn. If a skin should form on top of the solution or it becomes thick, a little hot water poured on top and gently stirred in will disperse it.

For certain recipes and methods, the soaked gelatine may be dissolved by adding directly to hot mixtures. Care should be taken when adding to milk base preparations that they are not too hot, as the acid used for refining the gelatine may curdle the mixture. It is best to mention at this stage that fruits, like fresh pineapple and figs, contain an enzyme which has a chemical reaction and prevents the gelatine from setting. These fruits should be boiled before using.

Clear jellies
Clear jellies can be made with most clear liquids including wines, tinned fruit syrups, fruit juices, sweetened flavoured liquids or a combination of these.

Sweetened liquids may be flavoured by adding the juices and thinly peeled or grated zest of lemons and oranges plus, if desired, cinnamon sticks, coriander seeds, bay leaves and cloves. The liquid and other ingredients are brought to the boil and allowed to simmer for about half an hour to infuse the flavours. The mixture is then cooled and strained.

To prepare the jellies, use clean and grease free equipment. The pot should be of a deep type and at least twice the size of the volume of the mixture being made.

Place the required amount of liquid and gelatine in the pot: 50 g (2 oz) of gelatine to each litre (2 pts) of liquid. Whisk in two egg whites. Place over a gentle heat, whisking all the while. If whisking is insufficient, or the heating up is too fast, the egg albumen is not broken up and will quickly coagulate. The action of the whites is to produce a froth, which carries the impurities to the surface, thus clarifying the jelly. Just before simmering point is reached, stop the whisking, remove from the heat and allow to stand for about ten minutes. To strain the jelly, lift off the froth into a warm jelly bag or cloth (thick felt material), gently and slowly ladle the jelly through and allow to drain into a warm bowl. The froth will act as an extra straining medium. Depending on the resulting clarity, it may be necessary to repeat the straining process.

As far as possible do this work in a warm draught-free area to prevent the mixture from cooling and possibly setting during the operation. Any colouring should be added while the mixture is still warm. The prepared mixture is then ready for moulding as required. Better results are obtained if the jelly is allowed to cool before pouring into moulds. If chilled while still hot the jelly is apt to be cloudy.

A point to remember is that jellies will be stiffer and rubbery in texture if allowed to stand too long in the refrigerator. After a period of time they may split and crack upon being turned out of the mould. Clear jellies should never be placed in the deep freeze to set. This will form crystals of ice and the jelly will break up when thawed.

To remove the set jelly from the mould, warm the outside of the mould by dipping the bowl in a container of hot water. Make sure that the hot water reaches all parts of the outside of the mould. Also make sure that the process does not allow the jelly to melt; just give it sufficient time to become loose. Wipe the water off the mould and immediately invert on to the serving dish and gently jerk forward and backwards to loosen the jelly and allow it to drop down.

The ideal moulds to use are either aluminium or tinned copper as these are thin and allow quick penetration of heat. Plastic moulds, because of their pliability, are useful. Thick glass or china are not good conductors of heat, making it difficult to unmould the jelly easily.

The following are some examples of sweets and preparations using clear jellies.

PLAIN JELLY
Any single flavour which after being turned out may be decorated using fruit or whipped cream or both.

RIBBON JELLY
Differently flavoured and coloured jellies are moulded in layers. Each layer should be set before pouring on the second and subsequent layers.

As each layer is built up, make sure that the jelly mixture being added is cold and on setting point. If even slightly warm it would melt the previous layer and spoil the effect.

FRUIT JELLY

Layers are built up as for ribbon jelly, using only one or a combination of flavours. With each layer arrange the fruit and allow to set. The fruit may be of a single type or may be a selection of different fruits. Points to remember are that grapes may cause the jelly to go cloudy; bananas and apples may discolour and pineapple must be pre-cooked.

WHIPPED JELLY

This is known as 'gelée moscovite' and requires a stronger then normal jelly. When it is on setting point (thick and syrupy in appearance and consistency), it is whisked briskly until a foam is achieved. It must then be quickly poured into a cold mould and chilled immediately.

MARBLED JELLY

Prepare whipped jelly and some plain jelly. As the whipped jelly is poured into the moulds, the plain jelly is added in a thin stream to form streaks throughout the mixture. The plain jelly should be on setting point. Another method of preparing marbled jelly, which gives a different effect, is to have a light coloured clear jelly in the mould which is just on setting point, gently stir in some preset jellies of different colours cut into thin strips or small dice.

JELLIES FOR DECORATION

For these purposes, prepare the jellies stronger than normal.

DICED JELLY

Mould the jelly in a shallow tray. When set, cut into dice or press through a cake cooling wire rack. This is useful for decorating the tops and around the sides of sweet dishes.

MASKING JELLY

When the jelly is on setting point it may be used for coating fruits, flans and for lining moulds. Make sure the fruit is dry before coating with jelly.

JELLY CUT-OUTS

Prepare an extra firm jelly. Pour onto a lightly oiled sheet of greaseproof paper and allow to set firm. Using a knife, or small fancy cutters, cut into the required shapes and sizes. This is used for decorating sweet dishes, ice creams, pastries, etc. A variety of colours and flavours may be used, including chocolate, which are added to the warm jelly before setting.

Opaque jellies

The preparation is the same as for clear jellies, except that the use of egg whites for clarification is not required as the finished product is not expected to be transparent. Unclear liquids may be used, or other ingredients added to the clear jellies to produce the opaque varieties. These types can be made to look very attractive; are full of flavour and very nutritious because of the extra concentration of goods added. The following are some examples:

Milk is used as the basis, instead of water, and it may be flavoured by infusing coffee or chocolate or zest of lemons and oranges while it is warming. Do not use the juices of the citrus fruits and make sure that the milk is not too hot when adding the gelatine, otherwise the milk may curdle.

Harlequin jelly is produced by adding to a cold milk jelly dice of premade chocolate and strawberry jellies.

Eggs may be added to jellies; the amount used will vary according to the richness required.

Using egg yolks only, whisk into a clear jelly and return to a gentle heat, stirring all the while until the mixture begins to thicken. On no account must the mixture be allowed to reach boiling point. Cool rapidly, if possible on ice, and pour into lightly oiled moulds to set. Another method is to fold stiffly beaten egg whites into a cold jelly, which is just on setting point.

Whipped or unwhipped cream may be stirred into a cold, clear jelly and allowed to set. It is very important in this case that the jelly is cold, otherwise the cream would curdle and separate out. The amount of cream used should be measured and considered as part of the total liquid.

Another type of jelly is one which uses approximately equal amounts of strained fruit purée and water. Add the prepared gelatine to hot water. When dissolved, sweeten and colour if required. As the fruit is partly solid matter, the mixture does not require as much gelatine, eg 20 g ($\frac{3}{4}$ oz) of gelatine to $\frac{1}{2}$ l (1 pt) of water and $\frac{1}{2}$ l (1 pt) of fruit purée.

These opaque jellies should not be confused with mousses and bavarois, which, although using gelatine as a setting medium, are of a different texture and composition and require different techniques in their preparation.

Bavarois (Bavarian creams)

The basis for bavarois consists of a mixture of egg or other kinds of thickened custards, together with gelatine, whipped cream and stiffly beaten egg whites. This mixture is moulded and set, turned out and decorated in the same way as jellies. It is also used as a filling for charlottes, chartreuse and gâteaux. A lighter mixture may be produced by using less gelatine. In this case the bavarois is left in its container as it would not be strong enough to hold up.

The basic custard may be flavoured to taste by adding one of a variety of flavourings, eg vanilla, coffee, chocolate, cocoa, essences, grated zest of lemons or oranges, while the milk is being heated. Any liqueurs, spirits or wines should be added after the gelatine has been added and when the mixture has cooled. These extra liquids should be considered as part of the total liquid. Bear in mind that the juice of citrus fruits will curdle the milk and should not be added at this stage.

The pre-soaked gelatine is added and dissolved in the hot custard. Make sure that the custard is not too hot or the gelatine may curdle the milk. Use 25 g (1 oz) gelatine to $\frac{1}{2}$ l (1 pt) of milk. Strain and allow to cool to setting point (when the mixture begins to thicken). Give the mixture a good stir and quickly fold in the semi-stiff whipped cream, followed by the stiffly beaten egg whites. Mould immediately and allow to set.

A fruit bavarois is made by reducing the amount of milk and replacing the volume with the chosen fruit purée. For the purpose of measuring the gelatine, the purée should be considered as liquid. The fruit purée should be added to the custard when it is on setting point. A little colouring may have to be added to enhance the appearance.

Mousses

A mousse is made by using an all fruit purée base. Gently warm the fruit purée and then add the soaked and melted gelatine. The warming of the purée and the melting of gelatine is important, otherwise the two cannot mix together. Depending on the fruit used, the mixture may require further sweetening and colouring. When the mixture is on setting point fold in the cream followed by the beaten egg whites, mould immediately and set. The moulds may be pre-decorated with jelly cut out shapes or with dry slices of fruit, held in position on the inside of the moulds by first chilling the moulds in the refrigerator and then dipping the pieces in cold unset jelly and sticking into position.

The same method applies to savoury mousse but sugar is omitted and possibly seasoning is required, depending on the commodities used, eg fish, ham, meats, poultry, shellfish or vegetables. Savoury sauces, eg veloutés may also be used as the bases.

Cold Soufflés

Another term given to this type of mixture is 'chiffon'. Egg yolks, sugar and flavouring, eg lemon or orange juice, spirits, liqueurs or wines, are whisked to a foam over a bain-marie of hot water, or alternatively the sugar and water may be cooked to 115° C (240° F) and briskly whisked onto the yolks. While still hot, add the soaked and melted gelatine and continue whisking until cool. Quickly fold in the whipped cream and stiffly beaten egg whites. Mould immediately into a pre-prepared soufflé case. To produce an extra light soufflé, omit the cream and add double the amount of beaten egg whites. As a general guide 15 g ($\frac{1}{2}$ oz) of gelatine is sufficient to set a soufflé using four eggs.

Rice moulds

These are prepared in the same way as for milk bavarois, except that rice is used as the thickening agent instead of egg yolks: 30 g (1 oz) of rice to each $\frac{1}{2}$ l (1 pt) of milk. This preparation is also used for riz impératrice, which has the addition of chopped candied fruits and is moulded on a red jelly base, so that when it is unmoulded the top is a layer of red jelly.

■ PRECAUTIONS

When combining other ingredients with a concentrated gelatine mixture, the important points to remember are that the mixture will gel quickly when it comes into contact with other cold surfaces in the region of 15° C (60° F) and below. If care is not taken and the mixing is performed too slowly, or the gelatine base has overset, the mixture will set in lumps, have an uneven texture, or have strands of hardened gelatine within it.

If performed too fast or overmixed, most of the aeration is lost thus resulting in a dense and heavy item.

If the gelatine base is still warm, it reduces the stiffness of the whipped cream and possibly curdles, so losing aeration.

Ideally the ingredients being combined should all be at the same cool temperature, between 20° C (70° F) and 26° C (80° F) which is slightly below blood heat. Therefore the cream and the egg whites should not be used straight from the refrigerator.

If the gelatine base solution should overset, providing the cream has not yet been added, it may be warmed up to bring it back to a softer consistency and then re-cooled. Any hardened lumps of gelatine may be strained out, melted separately, and returned to the solution and mixed back in.

The quickest and easiest method when folding in the cream and the beaten egg whites is by using a whisk. This action should be done gently, not by stirring or beating, but by using the same lifting and turning motion described in the folding in method.

When using raw shell eggs, it is important that reference be made to the food poisoning precautions stated on page 105.

■ GUM ARABIC, TRAGACANTH AND AGAR-AGAR

As jellying agents these gums have a limited use in pastry work. The following descriptions and details will give some indication of their uses.

Gum arabic is extruded from the acacia tree grown mainly in Sudan and Australia. To prepare, stir warm water into the gum and place to warm until the solution is clear and liquid. It is used for brushing over petits fours, biscuits of the almond variety such as rout, parisienne and baked marzipan. It is also used on buns and fruit loaves after baking to give the surfaces a glossy finish.

Tragacanth is a substance extracted from the astragalus plant which grows in the Middle East. It is available in fine powder form. It should be stirred with sufficient cold water to give a thin creamy consistency and left to soak for at least twenty four hours, when it should be soft and pulpy without any hard lumps. It is used as a moistener and setting agent with icing sugar to make gum paste for decorative sugar mouldings.

Agar-agar is a substance produced from certain seaweeds and is obtainable in powder or strip form. It is a powerful jellying agent: 30 g (1 oz) will set 5 l (8 pt) of water to a firm gel. It is soaked in cold water for twelve hours, then boiled to dissolve. Because this gum has powerful stiffening properties, it is mainly processed by manufacturers for the sweets industry and to produce a variety of convenience jelly products such as piping jellies, semi-prepared jellies, marshmallows, jams, glazes, pie fillers and emulsifiers for artificial creams.

Many jellying products are available on the market sold under trade names. Instructions for using these are normally supplied or printed on the packet.

18 CHOCOLATES

Two main types of chocolate are available to the confectioner; each used for specific purposes and requiring different methods of preparation. Both are available as plain or milk chocolate and, for commercial use, are supplied in slab or chip form. Manufacturers and suppliers give a code to their brands of products, which indicate the blends and recommended purposes.

■ CHOCOLATE COVERING

This is known professionally as couverture. The plain variety is manufactured from cocoa mass, sugar and cocoa butter. Milk chocolate has the addition of full cream milk solids which include fat. Couverture sets very hard with a high gloss and contracts slightly. It is used for covering centres, mouldings of eggs and figures, for run outs and cutting into decorative shapes. It must be tempered before use; a necessary process, otherwise the fat content would set slowly, separate, and then rise to the surface, giving the finished product a grey patchy appearance known as fat bloom.

■ CHOCOLATE COATINGS

Sometimes referred to as bakers' or cooking chocolate, which is a ready prepared compound and only requires melting to be ready for use. The coatings contain vegetable fats and emulsifying agents with very little cocoa butter. When set they have a softer texture than chocolate covering. They are more suitable for coating items such as gâteaux and cakes as the chocolate will not break or splinter when cut or handled. It has a milder flavour; does not require tempering; is cheaper in price, but lacks the high gloss and snap of couverture.

Unsweetened chocolate is available and is mainly used as flavouring for fondants, icings, creams and recipes which are in themselves already sweetened.

The various types of chocolate should never be mixed, except when they are used for the flavouring of liquids and sauces.

■ STORING

It is essential that chocolate is well wrapped and stored in a cool, well ventilated area. A humid atmosphere will cause condensation on the chocolate which will spoil the product when the mixture is being melted. If any moisture is on the surface it should be wiped dry and scraped to remove all traces of moisture contamination. The scrapings need not be wasted; they may be used without detriment in sauces and fillings.

■ MELTING

This should always be done over gentle heat and the chocolate should be stirred slowly to prevent air bubbles forming. The ideal equipment is a chocolate melting kettle, heated by electricity, having an automatic thermostat to control the temperature. The following procedure should be adopted where equipment is limited and production is on a small scale.

Cut, grate or chop the chocolate into small pieces and place in a double jacketed container. The outer pan should contain water at 55° C (130° F). Allow the chocolate to melt and stir gently with a dry wooden spoon or spatula. Never melt over dry heat or at high temperature, this will cause the chocolate to grain. Precautions must be taken to prevent any form of moisture coming into contact with the chocolate. This would cause it to thicken during the melting process. Standing a bowl in a tray of hot water is not recommended as the steam would condense on the chocolate and in the bowl.

The degree of temperature to which the chocolate is heated is very important. With experience it can be checked by touch. Body temperature is 37° C (98° F); if the chocolate is tested with the finger and it feels warm, this indicates that it must be above body temperature; if it feels cold it is below. The use of a thermometer is advised for beginners as the difference of a few degrees can spoil the end product.

As couvertures and coatings vary in their composition and uses, procedures to adopt have been described for each type. Special reference is made to temperatures required for successful results. The temperatures must be carefully noted and strictly adhered to.

■ PREPARATION OF CHOCOLATE

Couverture

Couvertures needs to be tempered. The reason is that the cocoa butter in it is composed of two types of fat crystals. One has a low melting point of 28° C (83° F), the other a high melting point of 34° C (93° F). The method of tempering involves the melting of both. It is followed by cooling the mixture almost to setting point, when most of the fat crystals will solidify. The mixture is then reheated, but only to the point where one of the types of fat crystal melts, retaining the other in solid crystal form.

PLAIN COUVERTURE
Melt the couverture, stirring all the time, until it reaches 45° C (110° F). Remove from the heat and cool to 27° C (80° F), which is almost at setting point. Place back on the heat to raise the temperature to 32° C (90° F), stirring gently to mix. The couverture is now tempered and ready for use. If at any time the couverture is allowed to go above 32° C (90° F), the whole process of cooling and reheating must be repeated. It will not be sufficient merely to reduce the temperature.

MILK COUVERTURE
The procedure for tempering is the same. But because it contains full cream milk, the degree to which it is heated, cooled and reheated must be 1° C (2° F) lower throughout the operation.

Coatings
No special pre-preparation is required for either plain or milk coatings. Melt the chocolate to a temperature between 32° C and 40° C (90° F and 104° F). The lower the temperature the denser the chocolate. For a more fluid and easy flowing coating, use the higher temperature.

All chocolates must be gently and thoroughly stirred before use to ensure even distribution of the cocoa butter or fats and to produce an even consistency.

■ HANDLING PRECAUTIONS

It must be stressed that if successful results are to be achieved with chocolate work, the recommended procedures and temperatures must be adhered to. Work rooms are important and, as not all working areas are suitable, it may be necessary to adapt and adjust the conditions to meet the requirements.

Make use of heaters, lamps or work near ovens if the room is cold. Open windows, doors and use fans if the room is too warm. For ideal conditions, the room should be ventilated, but free of draughts, with a constant temperature in the region of 20° C (70° F).

Dipping, coating and moulding
Best results are obtained if the items to be coated with chocolate are also at room temperature. If the items are too warm, the chocolate will run off, or take too long to set, and the fat content will rise to the surface resulting in fat bloom. Care should also be taken that the items are not too cold. This

would cause the chocolate to set too quickly, lack gloss and have a streaky appearance.

Cooling and setting
Once the coated items begin to set, they should be transferred to a cool, ventilated area 12° C (55° F) to harden. If the cooling process is speeded up by exposure to extreme cold, a dull finish will result.

■ STORAGE

Finished items should be stored in a dry, airy room with a constant temperature in the region of 15° C (60° F). Varying room temperatures and humidity will cause the products to discolour and lose their gloss.

19 CHOCOLATE WORK

As well as adding flavour and colour in the preparation of foods, chocolate lends itself as a decorative medium for pastry cooks. It is used in many ways to finish off cakes, pastries, petits fours and gâteaux. It can be moulded and, when using sufficiently large blocks, can be carved into models and shapes. For successful results in chocolate work it is essential that the preparation and characteristics of chocolates are fully understood. The most important parts of the preparation are temperature control and the tempering of converture if used. These details will be found in the previous chapter.

■ POPULAR CHOCOLATE PREPARATIONS

The following are some of the popular chocolate preparations which may be used for various dishes which require chocolate, either as an integral part of the dish or as decoration.

CIGARETTES
Pour the melted chocolate onto a smooth hard surface such as marble, melamine or thick glass. With a palette knife spread it into a thin, even layer and continue spreading until the chocolate sets. Using a metal scraper or palette knife held at a thirty degree angle, press the full length of the blade firmly on the surface and scrape a layer of chocolate off the surface so that it rolls onto itself.

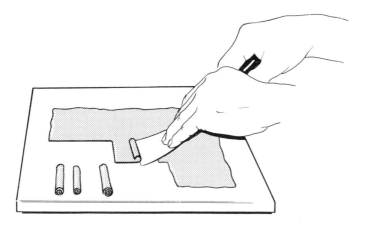

Cigarettes of equal length are best achieved by using a suitable size scraper, eg a paint scraper.

If the chocolate is not sufficiently set, it will stick to the blade and not roll. If overset it will flake instead of rolling. This may be overcome by warming the surface of the chocolate by rubbing with the palm of the hand or by leaving it in a warmer area for a short while.

PIPED DESIGNS

The following are typical of fine-line, piped designs using melted chocolate. They are suitable to use as decorations on cakes, pastries, gâteaux and petits fours and may be varied in size to fit the surface area on which they are to be used.

The design may be piped directly onto the items or prepared on greaseproof, waxed or silicone paper. To remove from the paper when hardened, slide the sheet over the edge of the table and pull the paper downwards releasing the design.

The warmth of the hands will quickly soften the chocolate so the designs must not be handled. As a piece is being released from the paper, support it with a palette knife.

Loose designs may be arranged in raised positions on a product. As well as being decorative, the designs serve the purpose of indicating the number of portions expected from the product.

The same designs may also be made using royal icing, in which case they must be piped on to either waxed or silicone paper. To facilitate their removal when hardened, use the same method for releasing from the paper as for chocolate.

CHOCOLATE CUT-OUTS

Pour the melted chocolate on to a thick sheet of greaseproof or silicone paper placed on a flat tray or board. Lift the tray and allow the chocolate to flow to a thin even layer, then allow to cool. A lightly oiled flan ring may also be used to retain the chocolate in a round shape.

When the chocolate loses its 'wet look' gloss it is on the point of setting.

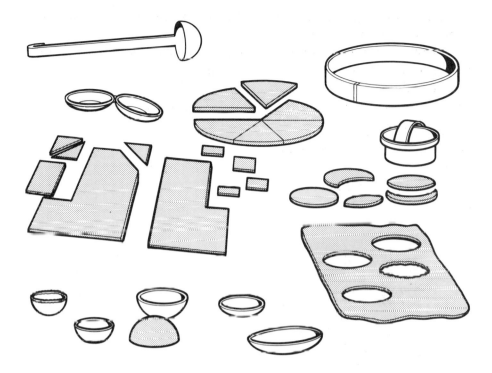

At this stage, using cutters or a knife, cut the layer into the shapes and sizes required and allow to set hard.

Take care when lifting the chocolate cut-outs off the paper. Ensure that the warmth of the fingers does not mark the pieces. If possible use a thin bladed knife or lift the set sheet of chocolate and peel the paper away from underneath, holding the cut-outs at the edges only.

Chocolate shrinks when setting; this may cause thin paper to curl. Special thick paper with a metallic foil coating is available for this kind of work and does give better and more reliable results. Shapes may be made by piping out the chocolate on to paper on which a design has been drawn. Use the same techniques as for royal icing runouts.

SPINNING CHOCOLATE
This is a quick method of decorating the tops of gâteaux, pastries and petits fours. Pour the melted chocolate into a paper piping bag fitted with either a very fine plain tube or with the tip of the bag cut to give a very small aperture. Squeeze a thread of chocolate out, moving the hand at speed over the items to be decorated. Use either a continual circular movement or pipe straight lines in different directions.

If the aperture becomes blocked it is because the chocolate has set. Hold the bag in the palm of the hand for a few moments and the warmth will soon soften it.

PIPING CHOCOLATE

If a small amount of liquid is stirred into melted chocolate (approximately $\frac{1}{4}$ teaspoon to 120 g (4 oz) of chocolate) it will thicken sufficiently for it to be piped, using either a plain or star tube.

This mixture is best prepared only in the amounts required for immediate use. It should never be added to other melted chocolates. To promote a gloss finish, the liquids used can be glycerine, glucose, sugar syrup or piping jelly. Liqueurs and spirits may also be used to add flavour but a duller finish is to be expected.

If the mixture is too soft for piping, a few drops of cold water will stiffen it. If it is too stiff it may only need warming slightly. More melted chocolate could be added if too much liquid has been used. This chocolate is mostly used for decorating Easter eggs, chocolate modellings, pastries, gâteaux and petits fours.

GANACHE

This is a mixture of melted chocolate and a liquid composed of approximately two and a half parts chocolate to one part liquid. The proportions will vary depending on the type of chocolate and the liquid used.

The type of liquid used depends on the requirements of the finished product. Sugar syrup gives a gloss finish; the higher the sugar content the glossier the finish. This mixture is mostly used for coatings on petits fours, pastries and gâteaux. Ganache is also made with cream which gives a richer but softer consistency. This mixture is mainly used as a filling or for moulding centres to use as petits fours. With the addition of a little unsalted butter, it will become firmer and have a smoother texture. Spirits and liquers are normally added for their flavour properties.

There are two popular methods for making ganache. Performed correctly, they will give the same results. The first method described is mostly used while the chocolate is still warm and at a pouring consistency. Upon cooling it sets into a firm covering. A well-known type of gâteaux using ganache made by this method is the 'Sacher torte'.

The second method may also be used as a coating but is more suitable for use as a filling and for producing the centres of petits fours such as truffles and potatoes. Both kinds will set firm upon chilling and will produce a lighter consistency if beaten before setting, making them suitable for piping.

Method I Melt the chocolate to about 40° C (105° F). With a wooden spoon stir in the liquid a little at a time. The mixture will at first begin to thicken. Continue adding the liquid until the required consistency is achieved. It should be a smooth, easy flowing mixture but not so thin that it runs off the spoon.

If, during the addition of the liquids, the mixture separates (fat content of the chocolate separates and appears curdled) stop adding the liquid but continue stirring until smooth again. The mixture may possibly require either warming or cooling slightly to achieve smoothness. The addition of extra melted chocolate will also help to bring the mix back to the required consistency. When the mixture is smooth again continue to add the liquid.

Method 2 Heat the liquid to almost boiling point, remove from the heat and then stir in the melted or finely chopped chocolate. Beat well until smooth. Continue stirring until the required temperature and consistency is achieved. If required for filling or moulding, allow to cool completely and then transfer into a container and chill.

MODELLING CHOCOLATE

Most pastry cooks refer to this as 'plastic chocolate' because of the way it can be manipulated. It can be used in very much the same way as modelling marzipan. It is used for the decoration of Easter eggs and gâteaux and for making flowers.

To prepare, warm the chocolate couverture and equal quantities of liquid glucose in separate bowls. Raise to a temperature of about 40° C (105° F). Mix thoroughly together and allow to cool. When required for use knead the required amount in the hands and use as required. When using chocolate covering compounds increase the proportion of chocolate to two parts chocolate to one part glucose.

■ CHOCOLATE MOULDINGS

If success is to be achieved when moulding chocolate, it is imperative that the following details, and those described for the preparation of chocolate, are strictly observed.

Correctly prepared and tempered couverture should be used if possible. Because of the type of fat content in chocolate compounds, they are not ideal for use, although with care they will produce a suitable and acceptable product.

There are several important points which are worth noting. The moulds used, and the temperature of the room in which the moulding is carried out, should be at an even temperature of about 21° C (70° F). This allows the chocolate to flow smoothly and evenly into the moulds being used.

The area in which they will eventually be placed to set should be in the region of 7° C (45° F) and well ventilated but free from draughts. If the temperature is too warm the cocoa butter or fats may separate, rise to the surface and appear as small speckled spots called fat bloom. Chocolate will shrink upon cooling, so if the temperature is too cold the surfaces exposed to the cold air will contract quickly and may crack or possibly set with a steaky appearance.

Because of this contraction the moulded chocolate, when fully set, will lift easily out of the mould. At most, all that may be required to free the chocolate is a light tap on a hard surface or, if a flexible mould is used, a slight bending of it to release the chocolate from the mould.

Remember that body heat will melt the chocolate, so always hold the moulds at the edges. When removing the set chocolate from the moulds, handle carefully so that finger marks are not transferred onto the shiny surfaces.

Moulds are available in a variety of shapes and sizes. They are produced using different kinds of materials suitable for varied forms of mouldings. Powders such as starches, are also used when a particular designed shape is required.

The following examples give an indication of suitable moulds required for various purposes, together with a brief description of method where necessary.

EASTER EGGS AND CHOCOLATE FIGURES

For these shapes, moulds made of copper, with a mirror silver lining, are best but expensive. Plastic moulds are mainly used and if carefully looked after, they give excellent results. They are more flexible in use, making it easy to remove the moulded chocolate. Tinned moulds are cheap but they do not last long in good condition. The tinned lining scratches and wears off quickly, leaving bare metal which spoils the surfaces of the moulded chocolate.

There are two types of moulds available. One type consists of two halves which, after the two halves have set, are removed from the moulds and joined together. In the other type, the two halves are held together with hinges and clips. The chocolate sets in the complete shape and the mould is then removed. These are mainly used for figures.

The moulded chocolate will only be as shiny and smooth as the moulds used. Any form of moisture, or any scratches or roughness on the moulding surface, will appear on the surfaces of the finished item. As well as blemishing the appearance is also makes it more difficult to remove the chocolate from the moulds without breaking or cracking it.

It is important that the moulds are clean and dry. Just before moulding they should be polished with a clean, dry, soft cloth or cotton wool, taking care that the hands or fingers do not touch the moulding surfaces. This leaves smears of moisture which show as blemishes on the finished products. All traces of cotton wool must also be removed.

A point to note is that if a thick layer of chocolate is required, it is best to build it up on two or three separate coatings rather than attempt one thick layer.

Eggs For these, half moulds are best used when preparing by hand. Half fill the moulds with the prepared chocolate, tap or shake gently to expel any air bubbles. Empty out the chocolate, turning the mould to ensure all parts have an even coating. Remove any chocolate adhering to the edges and place upside down on greaseproof paper; that is with the edges to be joined on the paper.

After about fifteen minutes, when the chocolate has started to set, check that the mould is completely and evenly covered. If using metal moulds there should not be any metal showing through the chocolate layer. Hold plastic moulds up to the light, any thin parts will show through. If necessary give a second or even a third coating.

Remove the chocolate from the edges using a plastic or a blunt instrument. Never use sharp blades as these will scrape off small particles from the moulds.

The mouldings should then be allowed to set hard in the cool area. This will take about one hour, depending on the size and thickness of the chocolate. Do not force the chocolate out of the moulds. If the work has been done correctly the chocolate should have contracted sufficiently for it to be removed easily, requiring only a slight tap or bending of the mould to release any parts that are still attached to it.

To join the parts together, all that is required is a slight warming of the edges of the moulded chocolate. This can be achieved by rubbing the edges for a few seconds on a warm plate. Hold the two parts together until set. Piping chocolate is often used on the edges to hold the parts together when some form of decoration is included.

Chocolate figures The clipped together type of moulds are used for figures. Make sure that the two halves of the mould have held firmly together. Fill the moulds with the prepared chocolate a little at a time, tapping the mould to expel any air bubbles and to ensure that the chocolate reaches all parts.

After filling, empty the chocolate out through the opening, remove any surplus and stand on greaseproof paper. Check that the mould is sufficiently and evenly coated. Clean off any chocolate at the open edges and allow to set hard. To remove the moulds, take off the clips and insert a thin blade in between the edges of the moulds. Gently ease the two halves apart, lifting them off one at a time from each side of the figure.

CHOCOLATE CASES

Chocolate moulded containers can be made using paper or foil cases, tartlet, barquette or dariole moulds, and ladles or spoons. The item used must be clean and have a smooth finish without wrinkles or folds. It should be new and, if required regularly, kept apart for this purpose only.

To prepare the chocolate cases, fill them with chocolate and allow them to stand in a cool area until a form of crust appears on the surface and at the edges. Drain off the chocolate and stand upside down on greaseproof paper in the cool area until set. Trim the edges and when set hard remove from the moulds using the same technique as for eggs. If paper or foil has been used, this may be peeled off the chocolate.

The cases may be filled as required, eg with fruits, nuts, butter cream, liqueur soaked biscuits, marshamallow, etc. If required, the fillings may be encased by covering the surface with melted chocolate and allowing to set.

CHOCOLATE COATED CENTRES

Pre-prepared centres of varying flavours, types and shapes, such as fondant creams, ganache, marzipan, praline, nougat, biscuits and nuts, may be dipped or coated with chocolate for use as petitis fours.

During the process the chocolate must be retained at the correct temperature if an even appearance is to be achieved. For dipping, a fine wire dipping fork is required. the fingers may be used. This has the advantage that the warmth of the hands helps the chocolate to retain the working temperature.

The pieces to be covered are dropped into the chocolate, lifted out and allowed to drain over the container, then placed on paper to cool and set.

For coating, the pieces are arranged on a wire grill and the chocolate poured over. Before they are completely set they should be cut off the wires and allowed to harden on paper. If they set hard while still on the wires, they may crack while being removed.

It is usual to overpipe or have some form of decoration to enable identification of the type of filling.

CAST CHOCOLATE

Small moulds made of rubber, plastic or paper of different shapes, and with an impressed design, are filled with melted chocolate and allowed to set. This produces moulded pieces for use as petits fours or decorative plaques.

For particular designs, die mouldings can also be made using plaster or a starch such as cornflour or arrowroot. Special plasters are available, or plaster of paris may be used. Any embossed design or pattern may be used.

Water is placed in a bowl and sufficient plaster is gently stirred in to produce a thick creamy consistency. The mixture is then poured into a container, levelled off and gently tapped or shaken to expel air bubbles. Lightly oil or wax the item from which the impression is to be made and then press it firmly on to the surface of the plaster while it is still soft and allow to set hard. When set remove the piece and allow the plaster to dry overnight at room temperature. For an extra smooth surface the hardened plaster may be given a thin coating of lacquer or varnish. This type of moulding may also be used for marzipan and pastillage (gum paste).

Cast mouldings may also be made using a starch. The starch box is prepared by filling a tray or container of suitable size and depth with firmly packed starch. The shape, or embossed design from which the impression is to be made, is pressed into the starch and carefully lifted out. If a handle is made with some form of paste or plasticine, the piece can then be lifted up easily without spoiling the impression in the starch.

After the chocolate has set it is lifted out and the starch removed using a soft brush.

20 SUGAR BOILING

Sugar may be used diluted and cooked in syrup form. This is achieved by boiling sugar and water together to the required degree, using a saccharometer to test the density and a sugar thermometer to check the temperature. Different degrees of density and temperature are required for specific purposes. At this point it must be stressed that sugar reaches very high temperatures during cooking. Extreme care must be taken when cooking and handling it.

■ THE TECHNIQUES OF SUGAR BOILING

The techniques are simple but unless done with care, taking the appropriate precautions, the results will not be satisfactory or may not be suitable for the purpose required.

The sugar used must be clean and pure. Loaf sugar is the best but not easily obtained. Lump or cube sugar may be used but tends to have a residue of coating deposited on the lumps during the moulding process used to manufacture it, and this could cause complications. Uncontaminated granulated sugar is recommended for use when loaf sugar is not available.

It is important that the equipment used is clean and grease free. A pastry cook will not use sugar boiling equipment for any other purpose.

Because of the high temperatures needed when boiling sugar, an untinned copper pot with a pouring lip is ideal for use. The rivets that are used to fix the handle should have a tight and smooth fit, to prevent residue forming. The sugar thermometer is usually made of brass or stainless steel.

The best way to ensure clean and grease-free equipment is to fill the pot with water, place the thermometer in and boil for several minutes. Drain away the water. Rub the pan with lemon or vinegar and salt. Then rinse both the pan and the thermometer several times in hot water. Dry them well with a clean cloth.

The main problem experienced during the boiling of sugar is that, during the cooking programme, water evaporates, so the solution will gradually develop a higher concentration of sugar. It is during this stage that sugar crystals begin to form on the side of the pan and it only requires small amounts to drop in the pot to 'grain' (crystallize) the whole mass. It is vital for success that the work be carried out cleanly and accurately. To guard against graining of sugar, cook only in small quantities: 1 kg (2 lb) is ideal. Never stir or agitate the boiling solution and when it starts to boil make sure it boils fast and continually. Remove any sugar crystals that form on the sides of the pan as directed in the notes on cooked sugar. When the solution has reached boiling point, glucose or diluted cream of tartar or lemon juice are added as 'grain cutters'. They invert the sugar to prevent it crystallizing. Care must be taken, for if too much is added the cooked sugar may be sticky and will not set for the required purpose.

When the syrup gives a reading of 31° on the saccharometer, the temperature of the boiling syrup starts to increase above boiling point, 100° C (212° F), then the solution becomes saturated. This means that the water will not dissolve any more sugar unless it is boiled to higher degrees of heat. It is when this point is reached that the grain cutter is added to invert the sugar and prevent the sugar crystallizing. It must then be boiled fast and continually until the required stage is reached.

When a sugar thermometer is used it will be noticed that as the temperature increases, the bubbles will gradually get smaller and more numerous. This gives a visual indication of the changing condition of the sugar. If the cooked sugar has 'gone past' the stage required, or it is necessary to slow the cooking speed down, sprinkle with warm water. Do not take the syrup off the boil as this will cause it to crystallize when it is returned to the heat.

■ STOCK SYRUP

Place the sugar and water in a pot. Allow to heat slowly until the sugar has dissolved. Bring to the boil and remove any scum from the surface or sides of the pot with a clean damp cloth. Continue boiling until the required density is reached. Test with a saccharometer placed in the solution. The saccharometer will float, rise or sink, depending on the sugar strength of the syrup. The Baume degree of density will be indicated on the line that is level with the surface of the syrup. If too thick, adjust the syrup with water. If not thick enough, add more sugar or continue to boil. Strain through a clean cloth. Depending on requirements, the syrup may be used hot or cold, flavoured with fruits, herbs, spices, wines, spirits, liqueurs or essences.

A good practice is to have syrup in stock; one which is heavy in sugar content. This can be diluted to the correct density, as and when required. For a true reading, when using a saccharometer, it is best if the syrups are at room temperature.

The following scale indicates the amount of sugar required in 500 ml

(1 pt) of water, to give the corresponding Baume degrees of densities and examples of practical uses.

150 g	(6 ozs)	12°:syrup for fruit salad
250 g	(10 ozs)	18°:water ice cream, stewed fruits
325 g	(13 ozs)	22°:soaking savarins, babas, trifles
500 g	($1\frac{1}{4}$ lbs)	28°:for moulded ice creams
600 g	($1\frac{1}{2}$ lbs)	33°:candied fruits.

■ COOKED SUGAR

Place the sugar and water in the pot and allow to dissolve over a gentle heat. Do not boil until the solution has cleared. To each 500 g (1 lb) of sugar, add 50 g (2 oz) glucose or half a level teaspoon of cream of tartar diluted in water. Bring to the boil. Remove any scum that appears on the surface with a wet metal spoon and remove it from the sides of the pot with a clean, wet cloth. As the solution boils faster, small specks of sugar crystals will be sprayed on to the sides. These must be removed or washed down. This can be done by either dipping the hand or a piece of cloth in cold water and then rubbing around the sides of the pot, so removing the crystals or diluting them back into the solution. Do not use a brush as it could be contaminated by grease or other substances after previous uses and nylon brushes would be affected by boiling sugar. It must be stressed again that extreme care must be exercised during this operation.

To test the condition of the sugar, use a clean sugar thermometer placed in the pot, or follow the method detailed below. When the sugar has reached the required degree, add a few drops of lemon juice and gently shake in. To stop the sugar cooking further plunge the pot in cold water until the bubbling stops.

Although a sugar thermometer is used as a guide to temperature, it is the physical condition of the cooked sugar that is being tested. Cooling some of the solution and observing the state of the sugar will indicate the stage it has reached. It will also be noticed that as the solution gets hotter, the bubbles will become smaller and more numerous. The following hand testing methods are used to check the stages of cooked sugar most frequently used in confectionery products. These are examples of some uses of each stage or termperature. These hand testing methods are used by experienced pastry chefs and a novice must use them with extreme care.

Stage	Temperature	Hand test
Short thread Candied fruits and peel Turkish delight	105° C (220° F)	Quickly skim the tip of a dry finger on the surface of the sugar; rub the mixture between thumb and finger and draw apart. A thread will form. At this stage the thread will break if stretched more than 25 mm (1").
Long thread Crystallized fruits and peel Marron glacé Cold soufflé base	110° C (230° F)	Test as above. The thread will stretch as far as the span of the fingers without breaking.

To test for higher degrees, have at hand a bowl of cold water; cool the finger in the water; pick out a little of the cooking sugar and quickly return the hand to cold water. The sugar solution will solidify. The softness or hardness of the manipulated sugar will denote the stages reached in the following sequence.

Stage	Temperature	Hand test
Soft ball Fondant Marzipan Fruit Cold soufflé base	115° C (240° F)	The sugar can be shaped into a ball, but will just hold its shape and be soft and pliable.
Medium ball Crystallized fondant Soft fudge Soft nougat	121° C (250° F)	The ball will now be much easier to shape, but can still be pressed flat.
Hard ball Hard fudge Soft toffee Soft Italian meringue Fondant creams	125° C (260° F)	The sugar can now be moulded very easily into a ball and is very firm when pressed between the fingers.
Soft crack Hard toffee Hard nougat Firm Italian meringue Rock sugar	137° C (280° F)	When placed in water, the sugar will form a film on the finger. It will snap, but has a tendency to be pliable.
Hard crack Dipped fruits Pulled sugar Spun sugar Glass-like modelling sugar	155° C (312° F)	Test as above; the sugar will be hard and brittle. A true test can be made by biting. It should snap but not stick to the teeth.

After this stage the sugar will begin to colour gradually to darker shades of brown; this is the caramel stage. If allowed to continue cooking, it will turn black and can only be used as colour, by adding more water and reboiling. This is known as 'blackjack'.

■ REVIEW OF PRECAUTIONS AND CARE WHEN COOKING SUGAR

1 Equipment should be clean and grease free.
2 Sugar should be clean and pure. If in doubt, boil the syrup, remove scum and strain through a thick clean cloth.
3 Make sure sufficient water is added to the sugar so that it will dissolve.
4 Allow the sugar to dissolve over a low heat before bringing to the boil.
5 Add the grain cutter before the solution reaches boiling point.
6 Once the solution has reached 101° C (215° F) it must be boiled fast and continuously until the required stage is reached.
7 Never stir or agitate the sugar solution.
8 Keep the sides of the pot clear of crystals and of any scum that appears on the surface of the boiling solution.
9 When the required stage has been reached, stop the cooking by cooling the pot in a bowl of cold water.
10 If the sugar has gone over the stage required, adjust by adding warm water. Should it be necessary to delay the boiling sugar reaching a higher temperature, the process can be slowed by adding water, but the sugar solution must continue to boil. If the boiling is stopped after the solution has reached 110° C (230° F) it could crystallize.
11 If colour or essences are used, ensure that they are oil-free. Aniline powders diluted with alcohol are advised.
12 The cooking of sugar requires 100 per cent attention. Do not divert from the procedure; it will not take care of itself.

21 COOKED SUGAR WORK

Before attempting any kind of cooked sugar work it is important to thoroughly understand the principles involved. The section on sugar boiling must be studied and the procedures to adopt and the precautions to take must be fully learned and consistently used.

Pulled sugar work is a skilled art form. Success can only be achieved with continual practice. Practice makes perfect. The cost involved of practising is nil because any sugar work which is not successful need not be wasted. Providing it is clean and of the colour required, it may be dissolved in liquids for sweetening purposes. Uncoloured sugar may be used for any purpose. If, for example, the sugar has been coloured red, it can be used to sweeten jellies, ice-cream, sauces, or for making into stock syrup for poaching rhubarb or pears in red wine. The sugar may also be caramelized to use as caramel or as brown colouring.

It is not advisable to cook large amounts of sugar at any one time because if it is to be kept hot for too long, or it has to be reheated, there is a danger that is may crystallize or caramelize. 1 kg (2 lb) of sugar is an ideal amount to cook for most types of work. Until experience has been acquired a beginner should attempt to cook and work with only half this amount.

It must be stressed that the sugar used must be pure; the equipment must be clean and grease free; the sugar must be cooked to the correct degree and the required amount of glucose, cream of tartar or lemon juice, which inverts the sugar, must be used. Too much additive will make the worked sugar soft and sticky, while insufficient will make it hard and difficult to manipulate.

Strong colourings should be used and are added when the cooked sugar is still hot so that any liquid, which should be minimal, is evaporated by the heat of the sugar. Aniline colours diluted with alcohol are the best to use.

The cooked sugar will quickly deteriorate if any form of moisture is present. Avoid preparing cooked sugar work if the general atmosphere of the workroom is damp. If precautions are not taken to ensure complete dryness the cooked sugar work will at first become sticky and then dissolve into a syrup. Cooked sugar work should be stored in an air-tight cupboard containing a moisture absorbing agent, such as lime or silica gel.

Fruits which are dipped in cooked sugar to use as petits fours are best made at the last possible moment.

■ PULLED SUGAR

This medium may be used to produce items of varying shapes and colours. While it is hot it has a pliable, plastic-like consistency which can be manipulated to make flowers, baskets, ribbons etc for display purposes. It may also be flavoured and coloured to use cut into pieces as a type of petit four.

A marble slab is required to work the sugar on. It must be smooth and free from any chips or cracks. To prevent the cooked sugar sticking to it, apply a light film of oil to the surface, using a soft paper tissue or cloth. A palette knife is required and when used should also be lightly oiled. The hands must be clean and dry. Do not use oil on the hands as the oil will get hot when pulling and manipulating the cooked sugar and it may cause blisters. If the hands and fingers feel sticky rub them with a little cornflour or starch. This is not detrimental to the cooked sugar but it may slightly reduce the shiny appearance of the finished pulled sugar.

The pulled sugar will have to be manipulated while hot. An open oven or an overhead heating lamp that will maintain the pulled sugar at a temperature of 70° C (160° F) may be used. The temperature must not get too hot or the sugar will crystallize.

PREPARING PULLED SUGAR

Observe the sugar boiling procedure. Take the appropriate precautions and remember to add the grain cutter (glucose, cream of tartar or lemon juice) when the sugar solution starts to boil. Cook the sugar to the hard crack stage: 155° C (312° F). Remove from the heat and gently shake in a few drops of lemon juice.

Plunge the base of the pot into cold water to stop the cooking process, then pour the sugar onto the prepared marble slab. Make sure no water drips off the pan. While the sugar is still hot add the colouring if required. When the edges of the sugar can be lifted with a knife, commence working it by lifting the outside edges and folding over toward the centre. Take care that it is only folded over. On no account should it be stirred.

Continue slowly working the sugar in this manner to ensure that the mass of cooked sugar is of equal temperature throughout. When the sugar is cool enough to handle, lift it to a cool part of the marble. Hold one end with the palm of the hand and gently pull the sugar with the other hand and fold over together. Reverse the hand holding the sugar and repeat the process by pulling the other way. After a few times the sugar will begin to take on a shine. When it is firm enough to be lifted, hold each end with the hands and gently pull to form a long strand, aiming to keep it in equal thickness throughout its length. Bring the two ends together and continue the pulling and bringing together until the sugar is firm but still pliable.

Form the pulled sugar into a ball and place on a lightly oiled tray. Keep it hot by using one of the methods suggested earlier. The sugar should be used as soon as possible. Taking only the amount required for manipulation, keep the remainder hot.

The main problem that often worries a beginner is the thought of handling hot sugar. With correct cooking methods and manipulation, it will be found that, although the sugar is hot, it will not burn providing it is held lightly in the fingers without using undue pressure.

When the pulled sugar has been formed into the shapes required it must be cooled quickly. Working by an open window or door, or using a fan at this stage, will achieve this. Any pieces that have lost their shape and have set hard may be reshaped by gently warming the piece and re-forming as necessary. Do not attempt to bend pulled sugar pieces that have gone cold and hard. It is very brittle and will easily break. Pieces, such as ribbons or rods that have been cut to size, should first be made warm to soften them and then cut, using sharp scissors or a knife, while the pieces are still hot, soft and pliable.

Remember it is important that the pulling, moulding or shaping of the sugar is performed in a hot area, but the assembly of the pieces must be done in a cool, dry atmosphere. To 'weld' the pieces together when assembling, a small spirit lamp or gas flame can be used to soften the edges to be joined. Alternatively the edges may be softened by dipping in hot cooked sugar, or by using a rod made of pulled sugar which has had the end melted over a flame. This can be used as a 'soldering iron' to fuse the edges together. The pieces are then held in position until set.

When the techniques of pulling and shaping the sugar have been mastered, it will assist in achieving a close similarity to an item if a model is available to look at. When making flowers and leaves, for example, use a real flower to copy. The petals when taken apart will serve as patterns to copy regarding their size, shape and colour. A second whole flower will assist when assembling the pieces into formation. Leaves, stems, or other suitable items, can be copied to produce realistic imitations.

SUGAR BASKET

To make a wicker-type basket using pulled sugar, it is necessary to have a basket-making frame. Wooden bases of different shapes and sizes can be used. All must have an odd number of 5 mm (about $\frac{1}{4}$") holes drilled about 25 mm (1") apart, all around the outer edge. The holes are to support metal or wooden rods in an upright position. They should, however, have a slight outward incline. The rods should be a good fit in the holes but must be sufficiently loose for easy removal. To prevent the sugar sticking the bases and the rods must be lightly oiled. The diagrams shown give four

shapes of basket that can be woven. These can be bought or are easily made.

Using a small amount of pulled sugar, pull it several times to form it into a 12 mm ($\frac{1}{2}''$) thick rope about 300 mm (12″) long. Rub a closed hand over the length of sugar to smooth it and to ensure even thickness throughout the piece. Standing over a table, carefully pull it further so that the thickness reduces to about 5 mm ($\frac{1}{4}''$). The table surface acts as a third hand to support the strand.

The strand must now be woven in and out of the rods. Aim to start and finish with the ends inside the basket so that the joins are hidden. The sugar strands must be pliable but should be just on the point of hardening so that they will be sufficiently firm to retain their position in layers. Continue the weaving up to the height required but stop to allow the top 25 mm (1″) of the rods to remain uncovered. This is so that the rods can easily be handled when removing them.

A quicker method of weaving pulled sugar, which requires much more skill and experience, is to pull the strand directly from a ball of sugar held in one hand (see diagram).

This method involves holding the ball of sugar in the hand and pulling it

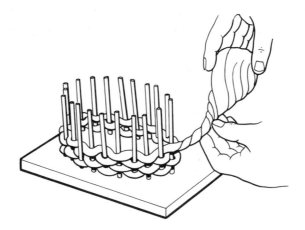

out into a strand while weaving it in and out of the rods, turning the frame with the other hand. With this method it is therefore more difficult to obtain a strand of uniform size. The pulled sugar strand does not always set firm sufficiently before the next layer is placed on top, consequently the build-up of layers can have an uneven and clumsy appearance.

When the woven section has set hard, carefully remove the rods by twisting them out of their holes. Replace with rods of the same thickness made from pulled sugar. Cut the rods level with the top of the basket using a hot knife.

If a base to the basket is required, roll out a piece of pulled sugar, using an oiled rolling pin, on an oiled surface and cut to the size and shape required. Wipe it clean using a cloth and fix to the underneath of the basket using hot sugar.

To decorate the top edge and base pull three or more thin strands of sugar and twist them together to form a rope. Bend it into shape and use it to fit the top edge of the basket, then fix it to the edges with a little hot sugar. Another rope prepared in the same way can be fixed around the base of the basket.

To make the handle, bend a suitable length of clean, stiff wire to the shape required so that the two ends meet the top edges of each side of the basket. Pull the sugar into a 5 mm ($\frac{1}{4}$") strand and wind closely around the wire so that it covers it completely, leaving about 50 mm (?") of bare wire at each end. When the sugar has set hard, heat the bare wire ends or dip them in hot sugar and insert between the gaps of the weaving on each side of the basket and hold in position until the sugar had hardened.

A more decorative and colourful effect is achieved in the weaving by using different coloured strands of pulled sugar. A width of thick, pulled sugar ribbon can also be inserted during the weaving of the basket. Different coloured strands may be used for the preparation of the rope used for decorating the top, base and handle. A taller basket of different appearance could be made by using two baskets of similar size and shape, joined together at their bases. They can be joined by using some melted sugar or by carefully heating the bases and holding them together as they set.

FLOWERS

To make petals, raise from the mass of pulled sugar a small piece and, using a twisting action, pull it off. Using the fingers, thin the edges and pull it into shape while forming the contours of the petal. This must all be done while the sugar is still hot and pliable, which may entail working near the source of heat.

Flowers such as roses and tulips require the petals to be bulging with curved edges. This is achieved by pressing the shaped petal over the thumb and curling the edges into shape. For pansies, sweet peas and carnations, the petals are laid flat. Sweet peas are slightly crinkled at the edges using the fingers. The serrated edges of the carnation petal may be made by either using a warm knife or by warming the edge of the petal and pressing it on to a lightly oiled sieve.

Daffodils require six flat, oval petals and the trumpet section. To make the trumpet use a small ball of fairly hot pulled sugar. Mould it by pressing it on top and working it down the sides of a lightly oiled cork or something of similar shape made of wood, metal or plastic. While it is still hot, trim with an oiled knife to straighten the open edges. Remove from the moulding. Warm the open end and thin edges with the fingers, giving the trumpet a slight outward curve at the same time.

A CALYX

May be made by moulding a small ball of pulled sugar and pinching or pulling out several points from the ball. If necessary trim neatly into equally pointed lengths using warm scissors.

STEMS

If they are to be presented on a flat surface, pull the sugar into a strand to the thickness required and cut into the lengths needed. If a stem has to support a flower, flatten some of the pulled sugar into a layer about 3 mm ($\frac{1}{8}''$) thick and push a length of fairly stiff wire through the layer so that it comes out the other side coated with a thin film of pulled sugar. Depending on the thickness required, it may need to go through more than once. Bend into the shape required whilst it is still warm.

LEAVES

To shape leaves, use the same techniques as for making petals. The vein marks of the leaf may be made by either using a small warm knife, or by pressing the leaf, while it is still warm, on to a lightly oiled mould which has the impressions of the vein marks.

To make the serrated marks on certain types of leaves, use the pointed end of the blade pressed around the edges of the leaf. If a leaf is to appear bent, lay it to cool on a curved surface and allow to set.

To make the long leaves required for daffodils and tulips, mould a piece of sugar to the shape and size of a cork. Press it flat and hold one end firmly on the table. Pull the other end until a long leaf shape with a point is formed. Trim the leaf to shape while it is still warm.

ASSEMBLING THE FLOWER

Join the petals together by either warming the edges of the petals over a flame or by dipping the edges into warm and fluid cooked sugar. Hold the pieces in position until the sugar has cooled and set. The completed head of a flower can be assembled into the calyx using the same technique.

To fit the wired stems, either warm the end over a flame or dip it into hot cooked sugar and immediately force it into the base of the calyx and hold until set. Stems that have been made without using wire should be warmed or dipped into sugar and held in place. This type of stem is not suitable if the flower has to be mounted in an upright position.

Leaves are positioned using the same methods of fixing, either by warming or dipping the ends into sugar.

RIBBONS AND BOWS

Prepare three or four strands of pulled sugar about 12 mm ($\frac{1}{2}$") thick and 100 mm (4") long, using a single colour or two or more colours if a multi-coloured ribbon is desired.

Press the strands together side by side to form a band about 50 mm (2") wide. Pull it out evenly to about twice its length and lay it on a lightly oiled marble slab. Using the palm of the hand, rub along the whole length to flatten and smooth it. Make sure that the thickness and width is even throughout. Pull it out evenly to about twice its length and bring the edges together, again pressing them so that they join. Rub again to smooth the surface. Do this about two or three more times. The band should now be approximately 1 metre (3 ft) long and about 50 mm (2") wide.

Use a heavy weight, or get some assistance, to hold one end of the band firmly on the table while pulling the sugar longer. Use the hand to lift it off the table and gently rub it along its wholke length while it is being pulled to achieve a thin, smooth, even ribbon. The ribbon should now be about 2 metres (6 ft) long and about 25 mm (1") wide. Remember that as the sugar band becomes thinner it will harden much quicker, so this final process must be done fairly quickly.

Using a hot knife cut the ribbon into the required lengths and warm the pieces to make them pliable for shaping or draping in position. To make bows use suitable lengths and bend or curl to shape and join together by either warming the ends over a flame or by using hot cooked sugar.

BUTTERFLIES

Shape the four wing sections using the same techniques as for making petals, using small pieces of suitably coloured pulled sugar. If additional colour markings are required, press small pieces of a second or third colour on to the already shaped wings and gently smooth together. Make the body with a small cylinder of pulled sugar and fix the wing into position by warming or dipping the edges in hot cooked sugar and holding until set.

SPIRALS

These look like stretch-out coil springs and are useful to place among the flowers or draped over the sides of the basket, or hung from the handle. Using a small amount of pulled sugar, pull it to form a strand about 6 mm ($\frac{1}{4}''$) thick. Hold one end pressed at the base of an oiled sharpening steel and wind the strand around the steel, pulling gently to make it thinner as it is being wound on. Slide it carefully off the steel and break off the thick piece of sugar where it was being held.

COMPOSING A FLOWER BASKET

It is important to remember that if sugar work needs re-adjusting to form a required shape, the sugar must be made pliable by warming before any bending is done.

If the flowers are to be arranged in the inner part of the basket, place a piece of expanded polystyrene cut to shape, or a plastic bag tightly packed with rice or cornflour, in the hollow of the basket. Push the wired stems firmly into this so that the flowers are held in an upright position. Observe in flower shop displays how flowers may be composed artistically. A few flowers, neatly arranged, will look more effective than an over-filled basket.

Flowers may also be arranged against the inner sides of the basket and on the handle, attaching them with a little hot cooked sugar to hold them in place. Warm a ribbon piece to make it pliable and form it around the top part of the handle to trail down the sides into the basket. Arrange the bows and butterflies in suitable positions, attaching them with a little hot cooked sugar. The butterflies will also look attractive if some are fixed on the flowers and to the stems. Any blemishes or joins showing in the sugar work may be camouflaged by covering with pieces such as leaves, spirals, or by laying ribbon over the parts.

Spun sugar may be used to fill the basket by arranging it in between the flower stems, together with some spirals overlapping the edges of the basket.

As well as being an embellishment for sugar baskets, the flowers, bows and butterflies may also be used as decoration for pastries, cakes and gâteaux.

To keep the sugar work in good condition it must be kept dry at all times. If it is to be placed on open display it is advisable to place some silica gel or lime inside the basket so that any atmospheric moisture is absorbed.

Unless on display, sugar work should be stored in the special cupboards described earlier.

■ BLOWN SUGAR

Prepare a batch of pulled sugar, coloured as required, and keep it at a warm temperature. Note that all the following procedures should be performed in a warm area, that is, in front of an open oven, under a heating lamp, or with a fan-operated drier blowing warm air gently on to the sugar.

Take a small amount of sugar, pull it 2 or 3 times and shape it into a ball. With a dry finger, or a suitably sized piece of dowel (the round handle of a wooden spoon may be suitable), press into the ball to form a cavity.

Connect a small tube (a clean, empty case of a ballpoint pen may be suitable) to the edge of the open cavity and pinch the sugar so that it adheres to one end of the tube. Ensure that there are no gaps and it is airtight.

Ensure that the sugar is warm and pliable and gently blow air into the cavity. This can be done by using a foot operated air pump of the same type that is often used to inflate beach beds and cushions. The small tube may have to be adapted to connect it to the pump air outlet. Because the pump can be foot operated, both hands will be left free.

The blowing can be done with the mouth, but there are two main reasons for not using this method: first, the moisture from the breath will affect the sugar and, second, it is not hygienic.

Force the air in gently; when the ball starts to expand, control its movements with the fingers and the palm of the hand. At the same time, control the pressure of the air entering the cavity and shape the expanding sugar to the form required.

When the shape is complete, cut it off at the tube end using a hot knife or scissors and neaten the cut edge while it is still warm.

Additional colouring may be brushed or sprayed on, but care should be taken when using liquid colourings, as they could dissolve the sugar if applied too liberally.

■ SPUN SUGAR

It must be remembered that spun sugar will not last long. It must be kept absolutely dry and if possible made and placed on the items at the last possible moment.

Spun sugar is used to cover sweet dishes to which the terms 'voilé', or 'oriental', are given, which mean 'with a veil'.

It can, in many ways, serve as a decorative representative medium, such as in a sugar basket. Green coloured spun sugar could be used to represent moss or grass; a model of a boat could be surrounded by blue and white to give the effect of the sea or, in a mountain scene, white spun sugar could be arranged around the peaks to appear as clouds or mist.

Arrange to have two bars of metal or wood 30 mm (12″) apart, projecting from a table by about 300 mm (12″). The bars must be held on the table by using a heavy weight such as a tray, which will also serve the purpose of being a convenient place on which to lay the spun sugar as it is being made. To avoid unnecessary cleaning, it is wise to place a large tray on the floor underneath the bars where the sugar is to be spun. Two other trays should be propped upright, one on each side, to prevent splashes of sugar dropping on the floor and the surrounding areas. Make sure that no one is standing alongside because, as the sugar is thrown off the wires, droplets of sugar tend to splash out and could cause serious burns to the face.

Cook the sugar following the usual procedure but omit the glucose and only use half a level teaspoon of cream of tartar to each 1 kg (2 lb) of sugar. When it reaches the hard crack stage, 155° C (312° F), add any colourings required and gently shake the pot to mix it. For a golden coloured sugar allow to cook longer until it starts to caramelize and is a light brown colour. Plunge the base of the pot into cold water to stop any further cooking.

If a lot of spun sugar is being made it will be necessary to keep the sugar hot. Have the pot standing over gentle heat so that it retains its fluid consistency without the need to reheat.

Using two forks with the prongs interlocked, or a sugar spinning whisk which is a bundle of wires bound together, or a thin wire whisk with the ends cut off, dip then into the cooked sugar taking care not to stir or it may crystallize. Allow the surplus to drain back into the centre of the pot. Move the whisk back and forth across the two bars allowing the mixture to form fine strands of sugar as it falls and solidifies. When sufficient has been made, lift it off the bars and lay it on a paper lined tray and keep in a dry room temperature.

■ CLEAR 'GLASS' SUGAR DESIGNS

This method of producing flat, decorative designs involves pouring cooked sugar inside shallow framed casings set out on oiled silicone paper or kitchen foil which has been laid on a flat surface, or directly on to a marble slab. Separate sections of the design are made which are eventually joined together with a dark coloured cooked sugar to simulate stained glass windows or leaded lights.

First, draw the design on the surface being used. There are several methods which can be used to prepare the frame casings which should be about 3 mm ($\frac{1}{8}$″) thick by at least 6 mm ($\frac{1}{4}$″) high. Royal icing may be piped over the design and allowed to dry for at least twelve hours, or plasticine can be rolled into strips and pressed on to the marked lines. For more permanent types of frames, pliable soft metal strips, such as aluminium or copper, may be bent to the shape required, or the section can be cut out from polystyrene tiles and lined with smooth kitchen foil. The frames and the surfaces which are to receive the sugar should be given a thick film of oil to facilitate the removal of the sugar when it has set hard.

Cook the sugar to slightly above the hard crack stage, ie 157° C (315° F). For this purpose add only a pinch of cream of tartar. When cooked, colour as required and allow the sugar to cool but ensure that it will still be sufficiently hot to spread. Pour into the prepared frames to form a layer between 3 mm ($\frac{1}{8}$″) and 6 mm ($\frac{1}{4}$″) thick, then leave to set hard. If a frosted or cracked glass effect is desired, when the sugar has formed a skin and it has cooled sufficiently to stop spreading, remove the frames and lift the sections, bend them slightly to cause the surfaces to crack and lay them back on a flat surface until they set hard.

For a clear glass effect, when the sugar has set, remove the frames and wipe the sugar with a clean non-fluffy cloth, or absorbent paper, to remove all traces of oil. It is important that there is no oil left at the edges as this will prevent the pieces from being joined together.

Arrange the sections into the pattern on a flat, oiled surface and run some darker coloured cooked sugar in between the edges to join them together and give the effect of the lead strips. To enclose the outer edges of the design, arrange a frame about 3 mm ($\frac{1}{8}$″) away from the edges and pour cooked sugar into the gap and allow to set before removing the frame casing. This hot sugar used to join the sections may be poured in by using a hot spoon or by using a metal funnel with a well fitting, tapered rod in the aperture. Pour the sugar into the funnel and control the amount allowed to drop through by lifting or lowering the tapered rod.

The sections, or the completed pattern, may be bent into a curved shape by gently warming them to make them pliable, laying them on a suitably curved surface to harden. The designs, when completed, may be mounted on a background such as a sheet of pastillage or of clear, run-out sugar by using a little hot sugar to fix and hold in place. A mottled or marbled effect may be achieved by pouring threads of different coloured sugar over the surface as soon as it have been run out. Use the funnel and rod method.

1	2	3	4

The above are examples of designs using the methods described. The lines shown would represent the framed casings required to make the sections.

Fig. 1 As well as being used flat, this design could be curved so that it could be displayed standing upright.

Fig. 2 The rose design could be mounted on to a suitable background with the stem and leaves placed on separately.

Fig. 3 Before assembling, the sail and the boat could be curved to give a three dimensional effect. The pointed ends of the sail are attached to the mast and to the boat by warming the points over a flame, or by using hot cooked sugar and holding in place until set.

Fig. 4 See below.

■ FROSTED OR CRACKED 'GLASS' SUGAR MOULDINGS

Sugar is prepared and coloured as desired as for the clear sugar designs. It must be allowed to cool to the point when it will stop spreading but is still sufficiently warm to be pliable for shaping over suitable oiled moulds. During the shaping and moulding the surface of the sugar will naturally crack, giving it the appearance of frosted or cracked glass.

The following are suggested methods for making a bowl, a basket, a vase and other models.

BOWL

Run out the cooked sugar on an oiled surface in a round frame; an oiled flan ring will serve the purpose. The round should be at least 50 mm (2″) wider than the mould that is being used. When the sugar is ready lay it over an oiled bowl or mould, such as a pudding basin or fluted jelly mould, and shape the edges. This can be done by fluting evenly all the way round and then folding and lightly pinching the edges with the fingers before allowing it to set hard. Using pulled or cooled cooked sugar, make some feet and fix to the bowl with hot sugar when it has been moulded. To remove, give the mould a sharp tap and lift off the bowl.

BASKET

Run out the sugar as for the bowl but allow a wider area so that the moulded item will have more depth. The basket will also look more effective if the sugar has been run out into an oval and afterwards shaped over the oiled underside of a pie dish.

For the handle use pulled sugar, or run out a wide strip of cooked sugar and shape over a suitably curved surface, so that the two ends will meet close to the upper edges of the basket.

When hardened, remove the basket base from its mould, wipe off the oil and attach the handle by warming the ends over a flame and holding in position until set.

VASE

Run out the sugar to the pattern shown in Fig. 4, page 149, so that it has a 75 mm (1½″) hole in the centre. While it is still warm, rub the surface with a little oil to prevent it sticking together while shaping and place the hole over the neck of a lightly oiled bottle, or on top of an upturned tall glass, and arrange the sugar draping down the sides into neat, evenly spaced folds.

Prepare a suitable size disc of sugar for the base of the vase. In this case do not run the sugar into a frame but pour the hot sugar in one spot on an oiled surface and allow it to flow freely so that it achieves a fine edge. While it is still warm mould it over the bottom of a suitably sized saucer or tartlet mould. The actual size required for this round base will depend on the size and height of the vase. It must have a sufficiently wide base to hold the vase upright.

When both the vase and the base have set hard, remove from the moulds and attach the base to the bottom of the vase by either using hot sugar, or by warming the bottom of the vase over a flame and holding in position on the base until set.

Curved handles made of pulled sugar may be fixed to the sides of the vase. A rope made of pulled sugar and formed into a ring, fixed between the bottom of the vase and the base, will add to its decorative appearance.

Many of the patterns and techniques of shaping and making models described in royal icing run-outs and pastillage, eg the cottage (see page 178), may be adopted and used to make models with cooked run-out sugar. The shapes are run out as described in prepared frames or cut with an oiled knife from an area of cooked run-out sugar while it is still warm. The pieces are then joined together by warming the edges over a flame.

The roof tiles for the cottage may be made by using the funnel and rod method described earlier, or they may be cut into squares from a layer of warm run-out sugar. As with pulled sugar work, it is important that the items are kept dry, preferably in a sugar cupboard.

■ GRAINED SUGAR MOULDING

This method of making table ornaments is a simple procedure but one that is not widely used. It is only suitable for the heavier and bulky type of ornaments such as bowls. The items are of a thick construction and have a coarse appearance which does not lend itself to the preparation of the finer, and more decorative types of displays, possible by other mediums.

There are two basic methods of preparing the sugar for this kind of modelling: firstly by using cooked sugar, causing it to grain and then moulding it in either clay, plaster or metal moulds. Secondly, it can be prepared by moistening castor or granulated sugar. Flexible types of moulds, such as plastic, may be found more suitable for this method. In either case the moulds should be lightly oiled or waxes and given a fine coating of cornflour.

COOKED SUGAR METHOD
Without adding any form of grain cutter, cook the sugar to between the soft and hard crack stages: 150° C (300° F). Take off the heat, colour if desired and to each 1 kg (2 lb) of cooked sugar add a tablespoon of fondant or ordinary sugar crystals and allow to cool slightly. Stir the sugar slowly until it crystallizes and while it is still fluid, pour it into the prepared moulds. As the mixture becomes firmer, press it down using the back of a metal spoon. On curved mouldings press it in so that the mixture will achieve and retain the shape of the mould. Once cold, it may be removed from the mould and the surplus cornflour brushed off.

RAW SUGAR METHOD
To each 1 kg (2 lb) of sugar mix in 50 g (2 oz) of cornflour. Moisten the sugar with either royal icing or egg white. Take care that only sufficient is added to moisten; if too much liquid is used it will melt the sugar crystals. If the mouldings are required coloured, add the colouring and rub it into the sugar thoroughly before it is moistened.

Press the mixture into the prepared moulds and allow to dry out in a warm ventilated area for at least twenty four hours. Remove with care as this method produces mouldings that are more fragile and are therefore easily broken.

Pieces may be assembled and joined together with royal icing, allowed harden and then decorated with royal icing.

■ CARAMEL NOUGAT

The confectionery term for this cooked sugar product is referred to as nougat croquant. Basically it is sugar cooked to the caramel stage and combined with nuts such as almonds or hazlenuts which may be used whole, split, stripped, flaked or nibbed, depending for which purpose the nougat is required. If the nougat is to be rolled out into thin layers do not use whole or split nuts.

Nougat croquant is a preparation that can be used for modelling. It may be cut into shapes for use on pastries, gâteaux and for petits fours, or it can be crushed and powdered into praline for use in masking the sides of gâteaux. It can also be used as a flavouring for creams and ice-creams. Lastly it can be made into a paste for petits fours.

One method of making the nougat is to cook the sugar (using one level teaspoon of cream of tartar to each 1 kg (2 lb) of sugar) with about 250 g ($\frac{1}{2}$ lb) of nuts in a sugar boiling pot over a slow heat, stirring continuously to prevent the sugar burning before it has melted. The cooking is then continued at a higher temperature until the sugar has caramelized. It is them poured onto an oiled marble slab to cool and is worked as required.

This second method will be found to be a more practical approach, giving equally good results.

Colour the nuts in the oven or under the grill to a light brown. Cook the sugar (using only half the amount of cream of tartar) to the caramel stage and plunge the base of the pot in cold water to stop any further cooking and darkening of the sugar.

Pour the caramel sugar onto an oiled marble slab and immediately sprinkle on the nuts. Allow the mixture to cool until the edges can be lifted with an oiled knife. Mix in the nuts by lifting the edges and folding over several times. When the sugar has cooled sufficiently to be handled, fold and press the nougat until the nuts are evenly mixed in.

Using an oiled rolling pin, roll out the nougat as thin as possible. Finally, before it hardens, turn the sheet over and rub across the surface with the pin instead of rolling to achieve a smooth even finish. If the nougat is to be cut, it should be done while it is still warm and pliable.

MODELLING

Most of the designs used in pastillage and in cooked run-out sugar may be used for nougat, following almost the same procedures with regard to shaping and moulding. Instead of forming the shapes by running the sugar into frames, cut them out while the nougat is still warm, using an oiled knife or shaped cutter, and lay or press into or over the moulds to set into shape.

Nougat is especially suitable for making into woven baskets. Cut the nougat strips and weave them in the same way as pulled sugar strands. Cooked sugar nougat may also be coloured; in which case, the sugar is cooked to just above the hard crack stage 157° C (315° F). The colouring is added then the mixture is processed in the same way as for nougat, using the second method described.

DECORATIVE CUT OUTS

While the nougat is still warm, cut it into the shapes required for decorating pastries and gâteaux.

CRUSHED AND POWDERED PRALINE

Using a sheet of rolled out nougat, place it between two clean and dry cloths and using a heavy rolling pin crush the nougat. First, sieve through a coarse breadcrumb sieve to remove any large pieces, then through a fine sieve to obtain even-sized granules, allowing the finer powder to go through. The granules are used for masking the top and sides of gâteaux and the powder is added to mixtures, such as butter cream, as flavouring.

A praline paste can be made with the finer powder by packing it firmly in a tray or bowl. Cover with a dry cloth and leave in the refrigerator for a few days. The moisture in the refrigerator and the oils contained in the nuts will make it sufficiently soft to be manipulated into a paste. It can be used as centres for petits fours.

■ PETITS FOURS USING COOKED SUGAR

The following are some example of petits fours made using cooked sugar. Reference should be made to the appropriate sections dealing with the methods of preparing the sugars.

PULLED SUGAR
For petits fours the cooked sugar should be suitably flavoured and coloured. Remember that the flavouring and colouring are added when the sugar is poured onto the marble slab. The pulled sugar petits fours should be light and crunchy to eat. To achieve this, incorporate as much air as possible during the pulling and folding of the strands, working with only small amounts at any one time.

Pull the sugar into 6 mm ($\frac{1}{4}$″) wide strands. Bring the two ends together so that the strands are attached alongside each other, forming a wide but short band. Continue in this manner until a 100 mm (4″) wide band is formed. Fold the band so that the two edges join to form a tube. With the tube enclosed in the palm of the hand, rub along its entire length to make it of equal thickness.

Pull out the tube so that it is about 12 mm ($\frac{1}{2}$″) thick. Bring the two ends together and pull out again. Repeat this process four times altogether so that it forms a band composed of sixteen small tubes attached alongside each other.

Re-form the band into a tube, which is now made up from a circle of sixteen smaller tubes as shown in the diagram. Pull out gently to achieve a

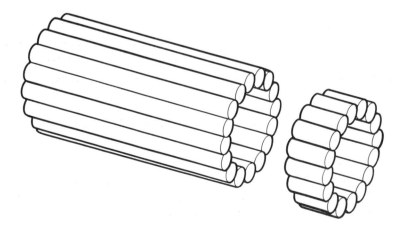

tube about 25 mm (1″) diameter. With the hand closed over the tube, rub along its length to smooth it and ensure that it is of equal thickness and joined at the edges.

PEPPERMINT CUSHIONS
Using plain or green coloured, peppermint-flavoured cooked sugar, prepare the pulled sugar as previously described. Lay it on the table and while still warm cut into 25 mm (1″) lengths with a cold oiled knife. The action of pressing the knife will squeeze the ends being cut and the pieces will appear as puffed up cushions.

RHUBARB SUGAR
Use raspberry or strawberry red-coloured, pulled sugar prepared as described. When forming the tube in the final stage, do it in a very cold area so that the sugar sets quickly. Hold it, or fix it suspended, until cold and completely set hard. Lay it on a flat surface and, using a hot knife, cut through the tube of pulled sugar into 25 mm (1″) long pieces.

The temperature of the knife is important and should be tested on a separate piece of sugar tube easily without any undue pressure. If the knife is too hot it will burn and discolour the sugar; if it is too cold and pressure is applied the sugar will crack. As the knife cools, clean the blade to remove any stuck sugar and reheat.

STRAW SUGAR
To achieve a golden colour cook the sugar until the caramel stage. Pull as described for rhubarb sugar but at the final stage pull the tube so that it is about 6 mm ($\frac{1}{4}$″) thick. Allow it to harden and cut with a cold knife into 75 mm (3″) lengths. As it is cut it will splinter slightly to give the appearance of cut straw.

The above are suggested colourings and flavourings, other flavours and colours may be used if desired.

NOUGAT CROQUANT
Prepare the nougat rolled out to about 3 mm ($\frac{1}{8}$″) thick. While it is still warm cut it into strips, then into 25 mm (1″) squares or diamonds, using an oiled knife. If an oiled cake-cooling-wire is pressed hard on the surface it will mark lines to use as a guide for cutting into even sizes and shapes.

PRALINE CENTRES
Using praline paste made as described, shape by moulding with the hands into rounds or ovals, or by pressing and rolling out into a 12 mm ($\frac{1}{2}$″) layer and cut into the required shape.

Lay the pieces on a wire grill and coat with fondant or melted chocolate. Decorate the tops with nuts, or by piping a design, or by sprinkling with praline granules or with crystallized violet or rose petals.

Centres may also be made by adding a little melted chocolate to praline granules to form a paste. Finish as above.

TOFFEE AND FUDGE

These sweets may be produced in varying degrees of hardness and richness and in different flavours and colours, depending on the temperature to which the sugar has been cooked, and on the amount of butter and cream added, or on the type of sugar and flavourings used.

The following temperatures and amounts will produce a semi-hard toffee which may be used as a basic guide and adjusted according to requirements. Cook the sugar and glucose to the soft crack stage: 137° C (280° F), using 250 g (8 oz) of glucose to 1 kg (2 lb) of sugar. Remove from the heat and stir in a few drops of lemon juice, vanilla essence, 150 g (6 oz) of unsalted butter and 50 g (2 oz) of fresh cream. Mix together thoroughly and pour a 12 mm ($\frac{1}{2}$″) thick layer into a tray lined with oiled greaseproof paper, and allow to cool.

Using an oiled knife, mark the toffee slab deeply to the size and shape required. When set, remove from the tray and cut the pieces through completely. As petits fours they may be served as they are or coated with melted chocolate and then decorated.

A variation of flavours may be achieved by using white or brown sugars, adding grated or melted chocolate at the same time as the butter and cream, or by using flavouring essences and spirits or liqueurs, or by using treacle instead of glucose.

If a darker coloured toffee is required, cook the sugar to the caramel stage. Slowly add hot water to reduce the density and re-cook the sugar solution to return it to the degree of temperature required.

To achieve different degrees of hardness, the range at which the sugar is cooked may vary between the soft ball stage, 115° C (240° F), for a soft fudge type consistency, to the crack stage, 148° C (300° F), for a hard toffee. By increasing the amount of butter and cream used, a softer and richer toffee will result. To produce a harder and more chewy toffee the butter and cream used should be reduced in quantity.

CLEAR MINT DROPS

Cook the sugar as for 'glass' sugar run-outs. Flavour with peppermint essence and allow it to cool in the pot until it achieves a fairly thick but still runny consistency.

Using the funnel and rod method, drop rounds of the sugar onto an oiled surface. When removing, wipe off any surplus oil. Different coloured and flavoured sugars may be used if desired.

PASTILLES

Cook sugar to the soft ball stage, 115° C (240° F), using 100 g (4 oz) of glucose to 1 kg (2 lb) of sugar. Take off the heat and flavour with spirits or liqueurs; colour as desired and stir in 250 g (8 oz) of icing sugar. With a spoon, or using the funnel and rod method, place or drop 25 mm (1″) rounds onto lightly oiled greaseproof paper, or into shapes pressed out in a starch tray as described in the chocolate section, and allow to cool and set. When removing, wipe or brush off the oil or starch.

An alternative method for making pastilles is to allow the prepared sugar mixture to cool slightly, then knead it until smooth and pliable. It may then be rolled out to a 6 mm ($\frac{1}{4}$″) layer, using icing sugar for dusting. Cut out into shapes with a lightly oiled knife or cutters. The mixture may also be moulded into a 25 mm (1″) thick roll and cut into 6 mm ($\frac{1}{4}$″) thick rounds and laid flat to dry.

GLAZED FRUIT AND MARZIPANS

Prepare the fruits and the marzipan shapes as described in Mise en place (Chapter 7) and Marzipan (Chapter 23). Make sure that the fruit is dry and that the marzipan shapes are prepared the day before to ensure that they form a dry skin. Following the sugar boiling procedure, cook the sugar to the hard crack stage, 155° C (312° F), and plunge the sugar pot in cold water for a few seconds to stop any further cooking.

With fruits such as grapes that have stalks, hold the stalk, either with the fingers or with a pair of tweezers, and dip into the sugar to completely coat the fruit. Allow the surplus to drain off and place on a lightly oiled tray to set. When dipping fruits and marzipans which cannot be held with the fingers or tweezers, drop them into the cooked sugar and lift them out, using a fine wire dipping fork or loop. Allow to drain then place on a tray.

Marzipan shapes may also be dipped by piercing them with a wire rod or dipping fork in order to dip them into the cooked sugar. They are removed from the wire by pushing them with an oiled knife and sliding them off the wire onto the tray.

Orange segments may be dipped half at a time and placed on the tray. When cool and set, dip the other half. Because of the moisture content, dipped fruits will not last long in good condition and soft fruits, such as strawberries, are best dipped at the latest possible moment.

To prevent the cooked sugar from graining, the following precautions should be noted.

1 Take care when dipping that the sugar is not stirred.
2 The items to be dipped should be clean and dry, with unbroken skins.
3 The sugar should be kept sufficiently hot and fluid to allow the dipped items to be coated quickly and evenly.
4 When lifting the items out of the cooked sugar make sure that the surplus sugar draining off falls into the centre of the pot. Any cooked sugar settling and hardening on the sides may drop in the cause the bulk of the sugar in the pot to grain and crystallize.

CANDIED AND CRYSTALLIZED FRUITS

Except for the very soft fruits with a high moisture content, most fruits are suitable for candied and crystallized petits fours. The basic process is to cook the fruits in stages, over a long period of time, in heavy syrups. The fruits used should be in good condition and not over ripe. The fruit is peeled and unless of the very large type, may be prepared whole, in slices or in chunks.

Dried fruits, such as prunes and figs, should first be soaked in water for several hours and drained. Dried chestnuts should be soaked for at least twenty fours hours, partially cooked, and skinned whilst hot. Prepare sufficient vanilla flavoured stock-syrup registering a density of 16° B (Baume) when tested with a saccharometer. Place the prepared fruit in a pot and cover well with the syrup. Bring it slowly to the boil and continue cooking until the syrup registers 20° B. Cover the fruit and syrup with greaseproof paper and leave until the following day. Repeat the boiling on successive days, increasing the density by 4° B each day until it reaches 34° B. Of necessary replenish the pot with syrup to ensure that at all times the fruit is covered.

Store in an airtight jar or tin and keep in a dark cool area. To serve as petits fours drain the fruit and place in small paper cases.

To prepare crystallized fruits Drain the candied fruits and place on a wire grill, over a tray, in a hot cupboard which maintains a temperature in the region of 80° C (175° F) until they are dried out. As they dry the syrup will form a layer of dry crystals over the surfaces of the fruit.

This dry kind of fruit may be coated with either fondant or chocolate, or may be decorated by dipping the ends of the pieces, or by over piping with chocolate.

22 FONDANT

It is generally accepted these days that fondant is purchased ready made as it is less expensive and more convenient than making your own. The proprietory products give consistent, excellent results, provided the necessary care is taken in preparation. Making one's own fondant should, however, be attempted. It is an interesting operation, the cost involved is very small and the knowledge gained may be useful when stocks are not available. If the fondant was not a success, the sugar would not be wasted. It can be used as a sweetening agent in stock sugar, syrups and sauces.

■ MAKING FONDANT

Using 1 kg (2 lb) of sugar, 100 g (4 oz) of glucose, or 5 g ($\frac{1}{4}$oz) of cream of tartar, cook the sugar to 115° C (240° F) following the sugar boiling procedure. Arrange four steel or brass bars to form a square on a wet marble slab. Pour in the cooked sugar and sprinkle the surface with cold water. When it has cooled to 40° C (100° F), stir backwards and forwards with a wet spatula. It will gradually thicken and eventually turn into a white mass. Knead with the hands to form a smooth pliable consistency. Cover with a damp cloth and allow to cool completely. Store in an airtight container, covering the surface of the fondant with a damp cloth.

If only a small amount of fondant is being made, a flan ring may be used to contain the cooked sugar. Alternatively, a wooden frame wrapped in aluminium foil would be suitable. If metal bars, a frame or a marble slab were not available, fondant could be made in a large, stainless steel bowl. It takes longer to cool, but is easier to stir.

Preparing fondant for use

Re-warming the fondant is important and has to be exact in temperature and consistency to achieve a smooth finish with a high gloss.

Break the fondant into small pieces and place in a bowl or pot. Moisten with sufficient water to barely wet the fondant then stand the container in a tray of hot water. Allow contents to reach a temperature of 43° C (110° F); they should just feel warm to the touch. Stir to break down any lumps and produce a smooth consistency. Flavour and colour as necessary and adjust the consistency by adding sugar syrup. Remove from the hot water and use at once.

While using the fondant to cover goods, the above temperature must be maintained. Replace the pot back into hot water to keep warm and stir to distribute the heat evenly throughout the mixture. It may be necessary, because of evaporation, to adjust the consistency with sugar syrup.

CONSISTENCY
Some form of liquid will have to be added to fondant if it is to flow easily and cover evenly. The amount and type of liquid used will vary, depending on the purpose for which it is to be used. Sugar syrup, which has a high density of sugar, will give a good, hard and lasting gloss. A creamier consistency will be achieved if egg whites are used. This addition produces a softer texture, but does not set with a very high gloss.

Using only water is not advisable as the coatings will shrink, crack and become unsightly. Block chocolate may be melted with fondant but it must be realized that adding chocolate will thicken it and extra liquid may be required to make it flow easily for coating.

Coffee, cocoa, and chocolate powders are suitable as colouring and flavouring but should first be diluted with boiling water. Liquid colours, flavours, liqueurs, spirits and fruit juices may be used. Bear in mind that these liquids will tend to thin fondant. Care must be taken, and allowances must be made, to retain the required consistency.

COLOUR AND FLAVOUR
Colouring and flavouring must be practised with care and moderation. The coatings should be soft-hued but not look dull. Avoid using strong and vivid colours. Make sure that goods will look edible and appetizing. Blues and deep greens are best avoided. Use pastel shades which are more pleasing to the eye. Whenever possible add the colouring by daylight. Colour shades are deceptive under artificial lighting. The use of a drop dispenser bottle is ideal as a means of adding small amounts gradually.

Points for special attention
Prepare only the estimated amount of fondant required for the work in hand. Fondant that is re-warmed several times will start to crystalize and lose its shine.

When the work is finished, transfer any left overs to a clean container and sprinkle the surface with water or cover with a damp cloth to prevent a crust forming. Make sure that the surface is kept damp. Do not use syrup as the water content would evaporate and crystals would form. If the fondant is left in the used pan, the fondant on the sides dries very hard and when re-used this would not dissolve into the bulk and so would spoil the appearance of goods. A few moments spent transferring the mixture and cleaning the extra pan will save fondant and produce subsequent better finishes.

Make sure the fondant is warmed to the right temperature and the consistency adjusted to requirements. If at the correct temperature the fondant is too thin, it will run off the items and not set hard; if it is too thick it will not flow evenly and lumpy surfaces will result. When used too hot the coating will, within a short time, lose its gloss or crystallize, giving the product a grainy appearance.

The surfaces to be coated with fondant must be dry, smooth and free from any loose crumbs. Better results will be achieved if the items with a porous surface, such as sponges and biscuits, are first coated with a thin layer of marzipan or boiling apricot jam. The fondant is then protected from the absorbent tendencies of the goods being covered, this gives a smoother surface for the fondant to flow over and the gloss is retained for a longer period of time.

Small items, such as petits fours and fancies, are best covered if placed on a wire grill standing over a wet tray. The prepared fondant is poured over. To achieve a smooth even finish, the fondant should cover completely with a single pouring. the surplus fondant will drain through the wires onto the tray. Providing it is free of crumbs, it may be scraped off and returned to the pan for re-use. Better and faster results are obtained if the pieces are arranged on the wire in straight lines. This makes is easier to control the pouring motion and in this position they are more easily decorated by overpiping with straight lines.

When centres to be coated contain butter cream, they should first be chilled and allowed to become firm. Otherwise, the effect of the warm fondant poured over them would soften the filling and possibly slip off the surface. Any fruit used should be dry or the moisture would cause the fondant to dissolve and slip off.

23 MARZIPAN WORK

Marzipan is a paste composed of ground almonds and sugar mixed in varying proportions according to the quality and purpose for which it is required. The usual proportions being one part ground almonds to two parts sugar, moistened with either eggs, glucose or warm fondant to form a smooth paste.

For modelling purposes, icing sugar should be used in the proportion of three parts sugar to one part ground almonds. After mixing, press the mixture through a fine sieve to give a smoother texture. To each 1 kg (2 lbs) of dry mix add 25 g (1 oz) of gelatine or 12 g ($\frac{1}{2}$ oz) of gum tragacanth dissolved in water as part of the moistening agent. This will improve the hardening qualities of the modelling paste and consequently it may be used in the same manner as pastillage.

A modelling marzipan should be smooth, pliable and sufficiently firm to retain its shape. If the made-up paste is wrapped in a cloth and placed in a warm place for a short while, the oils and the moisture in the paste will blend while being kneaded and improve the texture.

Another method for producing marzipan, which has a longer lasting quality, is by adding the ground almonds to cooked sugar. Use 100 g (4 oz) of glucose to 1 kg (2 lb) of sugar and cook to the hard ball stage, 120° C (250° F). Mix the ingredients well and thoroughly knead on a marble slab.

■ USING MARZIPAN

In confectionery, marzipan serves many purposes. It can be used for cake coverings, modelling and petits fours. The following are some examples.

COVERING A CAKE
Marzipan is used to cover celebration cakes prior to icing. The reasons are to enable flavour and moisture to be retained within the cake, to prevent the moisture and fat content in the cake from staining and spoiling the icing and to provide a smooth surface to take the icing.

The cake to be covered should be brushed clean of any loose crumbs. A thin coating of boiling apricot jam should be brushed onto the surfaces to act as an adhesive for the marzipan.

The following is suggested as an easy and efficient method to adopt for covering the cake with marzipan.

Roll out the marzipan to a size a little wider in diameter than the top surface of the cake, using caster or icing sugar as a dusting medium. The thickness required depends on personal preference. The normal thickness used being between 6 mm ($\frac{1}{4}$") and 12 mm ($\frac{1}{2}$"). Brush the top of the cake with the boiling apricot jam. Invert the cake and press its surface firmly down on the marzipan. Push the marzipan in at the edges to ensure that any small gaps around the circumference are filled. Trim the surplus marzipan off level with the sides of the cake. To cover the sides, mould the marzipan into a roll of sufficient length to surround the cake. The roll must be wide enough to produce a band of marzipan of the required thickness when pinned out to cover and slightly overlap the sides of the cake. Trim the edges straight then roll the strip up.

Brush the edges of the cake with boiling jam. Lay one end of the band of marzipan against the side and unroll it onto the inverted cake, pressing it flat against the sides all the way round. Using a suitably sized tin, as illustrated, will help roll on the paste more evenly and a good join at the base (which eventually will be the top surface) is more likely to be achieved.

The surplus marzipan on the top of the band is folded towards the centre of the cake to ensure a good seal when the cake is turned over onto the cake board.

MARZIPAN BASKET

Colour the modelling marzipan to choice. The same type of frames and techniques apply when weaving marzipan strands as for pulled sugar.

The strands are prepared by either moulding into 6 mm ($\frac{1}{4}$") thick lengths, or by rolling out a layer of marzipan and cutting into suitable widths. They should be used immediately, before the paste forms a skin.

When the surfaces of the completed basket are dry, they may be given a shiny finish by brushing with edible oil. A solution made by dissolving gelatine or gum arabic in hot syrup may be applied in a thin coat while the solution is still warm. Alternatively the basket may be brushed with egg white and covered with granulated sugar to achieve a crystallized effect. Piped white or coloured royal icing may be used to decorate the basket.

WOOD EFFECT MODELLING PASTE

Prepare the modelling paste incorporating sufficient melted chocolate to colour it to a light brown. Press the paste out into a thick layer on the table and pipe thin lines of chocolate over the surface. Before it hardens, mix the line in slightly to achieve the effect of wood grain.

This paste may be rolled and shaped in the same manner as pastillage. Before the pieces are cut out, rub the surface of the layer with the back of a lightly oiled spoon to give it a 'french polish' shine. Before assembling the pieces, clean off any oil from the edges and join together using a thin application of brown royal icing.

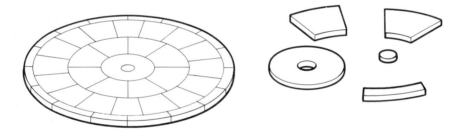

To make a 'wooden' marzipan bowl, roll out the paste to about 10 mm ($\frac{1}{3}''$) thick and cut into suitably sized shapes as illustrated above. Brush the edges to be joined with egg white and arrange the pieces to fit tightly, coverind the inside of an oiled bowl. Rub the inner surfaces with the back of a lightly oiled spoon to smooth it and give a shine. Allow to harden for a few days. Remove from the bowl and, using the palm of the hand, gently rub the outer surface with a little oil.

The bowl will look more effective if the marzipan pieces are of slightly different shades and have the grain effect going in opposite ways to the piece next to it.

FLOWERS

When preparing marzipan paste for flowers only, use gum solution if the items are to be used for display purposes. If they are for consumption, and form part of the decoration on products such as gâteaux, pastries, cakes and petits fours, do not use the gum as it makes the items too hard and unpleasant to eat.

The petals and leaves are made by rolling out the paste thinly to 1.5 mm or $\frac{1}{16}$") on a smooth surface, using icing sugar or cornflour as the dusting medium. Cut the paste into the shapes and sizes required and thin the edges by pressing and rubbing between the fingers. The vein marks on the leaves and any serrated edges are made with a small knife. The pieces are then formed or moulded into the required shape.

To join the pieces together, moisten the edges with a thin film of egg white and press into place. When preparing larger types of flowers it may be necessary to place the made-up sections in suitable moulds so that they retain their shape.

The marzipan may be coloured before moulding, or the colourings can be either painted on with a soft brush or sprayed using a fine aerograph pressure spray.

The finished flowers may also be glazed by dipping into sugar cooked to the hard crack stage, 155° C (312° F); in which case it is best if they are made slightly thicker and allowed to dry out for at least twenty four hours to form a skin before dipping. To dip, hold the flower with either a wire rod or a fork pressed into the base, dip into the sugar, allow to drain then place on an oiled tray to set.

The following illustration and details describe quick methods for making three popular kinds of flower: the carnation, the rose and the

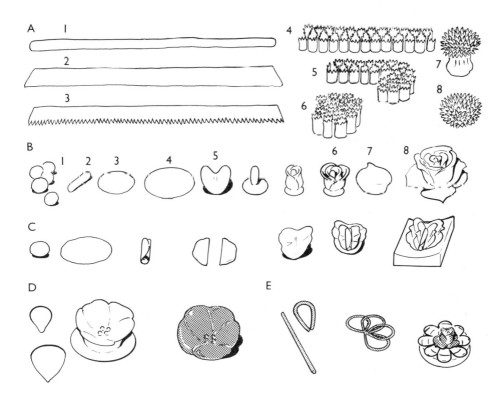

sweet pea. Also shown are a thick petal rose and a small woven basket which have been shaped and moulded over a tartlet mould. The rose (D) has been dipped in cooked sugar and the basket (E) glazed with a solution of gum arabic.

Many other flowers can be made as described in the pulled sugar section. Using a real flower as a model will assist in shaping and assembling the petals. It must be remembered that unlike cooked sugar, marzipan will take a long time to harden.

Carnation (A) Mould the paste into a 12 mm ($\frac{1}{2}''$) wide roll about 300 mm (12") long (1). The thickness and length of the roll may be varied according to the size of the finished flower required. For a two-tone carnation, use two strips of different coloured marzipan placed alongside each other and mould into a roll. Place the roll on a smooth board and with the rounded end of a palette knife press down on half of the width of the roll along its length, flattening it onto the board to form a thin edge (2). Using the points of a fork, press at the thin edge to make serrated marks (3).

With the palette knife, scrape the length from the board. Stand the strip upright with the thin edge uppermost. Fold the strip into pleats like a concertina (4).

Starting at one end roll it into a round (5 and 6). Using the thumbs and forefingers press gently, a little at a time, the centre of the sides all the way around. At first the thin edges of the flower will close and then they will open out (7). When fully open cut off the surplus paste from underneath the flower (8).

Rose (B) The rose may be made with as many or as few petals as needed, depending on the shape, type and size required. The following describes the method used for making a rose using ten pieces.

Colour the marzipan to choice. Divide it into ten equal sized pieces and form into balls about 12 mm ($\frac{1}{2}''$) in diameter (1). Form one of the balls into an elongated shape (2). Flatten the remainder onto a smooth board (3).

Using the back of a spoon or small ladle, rub the surfaces of the flattened rounds with a circular movement to smooth the surface and thin the edges, leaving the centre parts of the rounds slightly thicker (4). Scrape the rounds off the table and keep covered to prevent a skin forming.

To hold the sections upright as the petals are being assembled, place them on a large plain piping tube or pierce them onto a spike.

The first two inner petals are curved by pressing the rounds over the thumb (5) and attaching them close together around the elongated piece (6). The following seven petals are shaped with a bulge in the centre part, with the top edges curved slightly outwards (7). These are attached one at a time around the central piece already made. Overlap each petal as it is fixed into place (8).

Sweet pea (C) Prepare three round shaped petals. Cut one of them in half and roll one up tightly. Place the whole one on the table and crinkle the edges. Fix the cut edges of the two halves with the cut edges near the centre and curve them slightly upwards to the centre. Attach the rolled piece in the centre of these two and lay in a barquette mould so that the whole assembly sets in a curved shape.

Calyxes are made using green marzipan and attached to the under parts of the flowers.

The rose and sweet pea can also be made using 'plastic' chocolate, which is ideal for decorating chocolate pastries and gâteaux.

CAST MOULDINGS

Modelling marzipan can be made into various shapes by using casting moulds. Plaster of paris moulds can be made to a required design as described in the chocolate section, or by using plastic moulds. Children's plasticine modelling kits are ideal for this kind of work.

The plaster moulds should be dusted lightly with starch or cornflour. The plastic moulds should be given a thin coating of oil.

Press the marzipan firmly into the moulds and cut away surplus marzipan level with the surface edges of the moulds. To remove, use a piece of marzipan or a piece of fine wire mesh pressed on the surface and lift the shape out of the mould. A sharp tap on the mould may be necessary to loosen the filling and sometimes it is sufficient to allow the shape to drop out on its own. Use colouring to emphasize any special details on the pattern.

When the models are dry they may be glazed with gum arabic diluted in sugar syrup or, providing the pieces are of a manageable size, dipped in cooked sugar.

PETITS FOURS

Marzipan lends itself to the production of petits fours and can be used in many ways to produce a wide variety of shapes, finishes and flavours.

As a guide to amounts and yield, 500 g (1 lb) of made up marzipan paste will produce approximately fifty pieces of petits fours. It may be cut or moulded into shapes and finished, if required, by coating or dipping into chocolate or flavoured and coloured fondant. Marzipan may also be shaped to represent fruits and vegetables which may then be dipped in cooked sugar for glazing, or rolled in sugar as if crystallized.

Marzipan dipped centres Although the term 'dipped' is given, these are best made by coating.

Roll out the marzipan to about 6 mm ($\frac{1}{4}$") thick and cut into fancy shapes using a knife or cutters. Shapes may also be moulded by hand. It is important for presentation and portion control to produce pieces of equal size, even though the shapes may differ. Place the pieces on a wire grill standing over a tray and coat by pouring either chocolate or flavoured and coloured fondant over them so that they are completely covered. The variety of the marzipan dips may be increased by using different flavoured marzipans or by the addition of different toppings, such as butter cream, ganache, praline paste or glacé cherries before coating.

In addition, the dips may be decorated by overpiping with different coloured icing or by using neatly cut pieces of angelica or glacé cherry, or nuts such as almonds and walnuts.

Toasted marzipan Roll out the marzipan to about 12 mm ($\frac{1}{2}''$) thick. Use either an embossed decorative rolling pin or alternatively a knife, fork, spoon or cutters to mark a pattern on the surface. Brush with egg-wash and allow to dry. Cut into shapes and dust heavily with icing sugar. Place under a hot grill to caramelize the surface. For another variety of toasted marzipan, shape the pieces as fancy bread roll shapes, brush with egg-wash and colour under the grill.

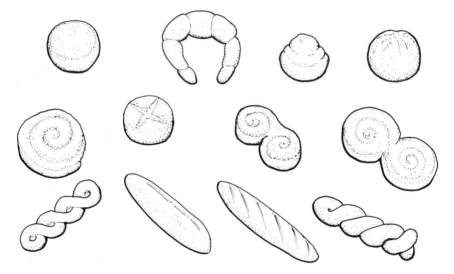

Shaped marzipans There is no limit to the shapes that can be made with marzipans. They may be finished by either dipping in cooked sugar, in which case they must be allowed to dry overnight before dipping, or they may be rolled in caster sugar. For this latter method keep the hands slightly moist with either water or egg white while moulding and shaping so that the marzipan is tacky and when rolled in sugar will coat more readily.

When preparing the marzipan for fruit and vegetable shapes, the marzipan should be coloured and flavoured with liqueurs corresponding to the item it is meant to represent. For items such as vegetables, flavouring is not possible and it is best if the marzipan is coloured and left a neutral flavour. For fruits that have more than one colour, such as bananas or peaches, the secondary colour is best applied after shaping. Use a fine brush or the finger. In all cases avoid using straong and vivid colourings.

The following descriptions give examples of shapes and textures acquired when using different methods of finishing to achieve a specific effect.

Strawberries Mould the marzipan into balls and roll firmly over a cheese grater to give the effect of the seedy surface of a strawberry. Hold the piece with three fingers and press in lightly on the sides, at the same time press the top. This will form a point to the ball with impressions at the sides and top. Attach a piece of angelica on top for the stalk.

Oranges and lemons Mould into balls and roll over a coarse sieve to give the pitted surface. Keep the orange round and press a currant on top. Form the lemon into an egg shape, slightly pointed at one end.

Apples and pears Use three colours of marzipan such as red, green and yellow lightly mixed together. Shape the apple round and indent with a current pressed in at one end and a piece of angelica for the stalk at the other end. Roll the pear to a point and attach a piece of angelica for the stalk.

Peaches Mould into a ball and colour lightly with red and green. Do not roll the peach in sugar but give a light dusting with cornflour to give the effect of bloom. Press a diamond of angelica in the top for the leaf.

Bananas Mix some streaks of green colouring into yellow marzipan. Mould into a ball, then into an elongated shape pointed at each end. Place the pieces on the board and with a knife flatten the top and the sides and curve slightly. Dip the two ends in melted chocolate and brush marks along the edges. If they are to be dipped in cooked sugar use brown colourings instead of chocolate.

Cherries Mould the marzipan into a ball-shape and position between halves of glacé cherries, then roll in the hands to reshape into a ball.

Walnuts Sandwich a ball of marzipan between two halves of a walnut. It may be necessary to moisten the walnut with a little egg white to make it stick.

Dates and prunes Split the fruit about halfway, using a knife to remove the stone. Fill the cavity with marzipan and mark a pattern on the surface of the marzipan with either a knife or a fork.

Carrots Mould into rounds then into a pointed, elongated shape. Roughen the surface with marked lines around the shape, using the back of a small knife.

Peas in the pod Mould and press the marzipan flat on the board to achieve an oval about 30 mm ($1\frac{1}{4}''$) long by 12 mm ($\frac{1}{2}''$) wide. Thin the edges with the back of a spoon and lay small pea shapes along the centre of the oval. Fold the sides upwards and over to almost enclose the peas. Join the ends of the pod completely.

Cauliflower Press three balls of green marzipan flat onto a board to make 25 mm (1") round pieces.

Press a ball of white marzipan through a coarse sieve, turn the sieve over and scrape up the marzipan with a palette knife, pressing the segments lightly together. Arrange the three green round pieces around the sides, curving the top edges slightly inwards to form leaves.

Potatoes Roll the marzipan into suitable shapes. Using a little melted chocolate in the palm of the hand, roll the pieces to give them a light coating of chocolate then roll immediately in chocolate powder. With the point of a skewer mark the eyes in the potatoes. These petits fours may also be made using praline or ganache pastes.

Acorns Mould coffee flavoured marzipans into egg shapes. Dip about one third of the base in melted chocolate, allow the surplus to drain and dip into chocolate vermicelli. If they are to be dipped in cooked sugar, dip and allow to set before proceeding with the chocolate and vermicelli.

24 ICING SUGAR WORK

■ ROYAL ICING

This type of icing is traditionally used as a decorative coating and piping medium for celebration cakes. It is also used for preparing ornamental designs known as 'run-outs' which are used as separate pieces to embellish iced cakes. Another use of royal icing is for making artistic plaques, pictures and models for display and show purposes.

Royal icing is composed of icing sugar and egg whites. The approximate proportions in weight being one part egg white to six parts sugar, or two egg whites to 450 g (1 lb) sugar. For larger quantities use 500 ml (1 pt) of egg whites to 3 kg (7 lb) of sugar. Because the size and quality of eggs vary, more or less sugar may be required to achieve the correct consistency. A few drops of lemon juice or acetic acid may be added to develop the proteins in the egg whites, although this is not essential. For convenience and to avoid waste, reconstituted dried albumen or substitute egg whites can be used.

When preparing royal icing make sure that the egg whites and all equipment used is clean and grease-free. It is best if the whites are separated from the yolks a few hours before use to allow for evaporation of moisture. The icing sugar should be passed through a fine sieve to ensure that it is free of any lumps.

If a mixing machine is used it should operate at low speed only. A certain amount of aeration is required but if the mixture is overbeaten it will be difficult, if not impossible, to achieve a smooth surface when coating the cake because of the excessive quantity of air bubbles in the mixture.

To prepare the icing place the egg whites in a bowl. Add approximately a quarter of the icing sugar and beat for about five minutes, using a wooden spoon if mixing by hand, or the cake beater at slow speed if using a mixing machine. Gradually add the remaining sugar, beating all the time with a circular movement so that the aeration is even throughout the mixture. Continue beating for about ten minutes. A soft consistency is required for coating; one that can easily be spread smoothly over the top and sides of the cake. The icing must be stiff enough to stay in place on the cake. This quality is achieved when the icing is light in texture but will not quite hold in a peak when lifted with the spoon. A point to note is that it is not necessarily the amount of sugar which determines the coating and piping consistencies of the mixture but the prolonged beating.

Icing required for piping must be beaten until it retains its peak shape when lifted. It should not require any excessive pressure to pipe out and will be suitable for fine line and fancy piping, using either small or large, plain or decorative nozzles.

A mixture which is hard to pipe is due either to insufficient beating or it has had too much icing sugar added, making it stiff and hard to work. When set this mixture would be hard and brittle, with a dull colour and appearance. If too much icing sugar has been added the mixture may be corrected by adding more egg white and beating until it is light in texture and holds itself in stiff peaks when lifted with the spoon.

If the royal icing is to be used white, a few drops of blue colouring will promote brilliant whiteness. Do not however use blue if the icing is to be coloured. The use of a dispenser bottle or drop dispenser is recommended for adding colours, so that the amounts used are easily controlled.

Another method of preventing royal icing becoming hard and brittle is to add 10 ml (2 level tsp) of glycerine to each 1 kg (2 lb) of sugar used. Glycerine should not be used in icings which are required to dry and set hard, such as run-out designs or for top coatings on a tiered cake. For these purposes hardness is necessary so that the icing is firm enough to support the weight of the tiers, or in the case of run-outs, to support itself.

Royal icing will improve in texture if made in advance and kept in an air-tight container in the refrigerator for a few hours, or even overnight. This allows for the aeration to settle. It requires only a little further beating to smooth it out ready for use. It is at this stage that the glycerine and colours are added if they are to be used.

Royal icing will very quickly form a crust and while using it, it must at all times be kept covered with either a tight fitting lid or a damp cloth. The same applies to piping bags filled with royal icing. When they are not actually being used, keep them covered with a damp cloth.

If a damp cloth is the method adopted, make sure that it is not in contact with the icing, as the moisture will dilute and soften the mixture.

RUN-OUT DESIGNS

These are specially designed, pre-prepared pieces made with royal icing which are used to decorate cakes or to display artistic plaques, pictures, ornaments and models. Items may be prepared in advance and stored between sheets of tissue paper in trays or in boxes until required.

A pastry cook does not have to be an artist for this kind of work. With an inventive imagination and an appreciation of colour, texture, size and proportion, attractive pieces of work can be produced. A beginner should at first attempt simple designs. Children's colouring and painting books, which have pictures outlined and easy to trace, are ideal to start with. Very little cost is involved in this work, but time and patience is essential.

To ensure that finished items are easily removed when dry, they are prepared on waxed or silicone paper and placed on a flat surface such as glass, firm plastic or a wooden board. The paper for use must be flat and smooth without creases or scratches of any kind. The design which has been drawn in outline is placed underneath the waxes or silicone paper. Both sheets of paper must be held firmly in position by using some form of fixing method such as weights, sticking tape, drawing pins if the surface is wood, or by using a little royal icing.

The procedure is first to outline the sections of the design with thinly piped lines of royal icing. The sections of the drawing are then filled in up to the outlines, with icing that has been adjusted with egg white so that the consistency is just soft enough to allow it to flow smoothly. The section should be filled with icing. Sufficient should be used to enable a slightly convex surface to be retained.

The correct consistency of the icing is most important; if the icing is too runny, the finished appearance will be flat and have an uneven surface, and the mixture could possibly overrun the outlines. If it is too thick, it will not smooth out and may have streaks and joins apparent. When using liquid colourings, add them to the mixture before adjusting the consistency with egg whites. There is a danger that the icing will be too thin if the colouring is added after the egg white. It is advisable to test a little of the prepared icing on a separate paper to assess its flowing tendencies before running it into the sections.

The running-in of the icing is best done with a paper piping bag with a small hole cut in the tip for the mixture to be pressed through. To achieve a smoother finish and avoid streaks keep the end of the bag in contact with the icing that has already been run out.

The bag being used should be large enough to hold sufficient icing to fill the section being worked. If only part of the area is filled in and the work stops for the bag to be refilled, the area will start to dry out and when the piping is restarted a joining line will show.

It is also important that air bubbles do not rise and remain on the surface. If they do the run-out will appear pitted with small holes as the bubbles burst. To prevent this, prepare the icing about an hour before required, cover with a moist piece of greaseproof paper and keep it in the refrigerator. Just before using, remove the paper and give the mixture a gentle stir so that some of the air will come out. It is useful to have a pin handy when preparing run-outs, as any bubbles that do appear on the surface can be pricked immediately, allowing the icing to remain smooth. Care must be taken to ensure the pin is not lost during the process.

When one section is filled in, do not start running in on the adjacent section until the surface of the first one forms a dry skin, because the icings will run into each other. An electric table lamp with the light beamed at the design will radiate sufficient heat to accelerate the drying process. On some designs, however, the colours are meant to run into each other to achieve the desired effect. For fine details, colours may be painted on. To avoid the iced surface melting during painting, use a fine small brush and ensure that it is not overloaded with liquid. It is advisable to slightly thicken the colourings with a little icing sugar before use.

Removal of the run-out designs from the paper must be done slowly and with care. The icings are thin and brittle and can easily crack. Slide the whole sheet to the edge of the board, pull the paper gently, slowly and evenly away from the underneath of the run-out while it is on the edge of the board, holding the run-out level at the same time as the paper is pulled away. With very large pieces this process should be performed a little at a time all the way round the edges of the run-out, while gradually working towards the centre.

STENCIL DESIGNS
Stencils may be used with royal icing to produce silhouettes. This method is especially useful if a stock of items is required for future use, eg initials and numbers to decorate celebration cakes. The stencils may be purchased or can be made by cutting out the pattern required from $1\frac{1}{2}$ mm ($\frac{1}{16}''$) thick plastic, metal or cardboard. The stencil must be placed flat on waxed or silicone paper. Using a stiff royal icing, spread the mixture evenly inside the aperture. Lift the stencil off carefully and allow the icing to dry. The piece may then be overpiped to decorate, or may be coated with a thin icing or fondant, or a design may be painted on with colourings.

Run-out designs and modelling with royal icing

RUN-OUTS
The following diagrams have been selected as typical examples of this type of work. Methods of approach to adopt, and suitable colours to use, are suggested. Variations of technique required to achieve the desired effect or pattern are described. Larger or smaller designs may be used, depending on the purpose for which they are required.

It is important to remember that if distinct colours are required when running-in the icing must be allowed to set with a dry skin before proceeding to fill in any adjacent areas. As the icing for this kind of work has to set hard, do not use glycerine.

Bear in mind that liquid colourings will dilute the icings and if allowances are not made for this, the icing may be too soft and runny. When using the paint brush to emphasize colour and details of the design,

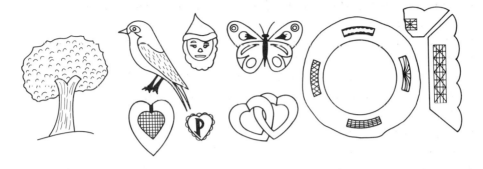

make sure that it is not too wet and that the run-out is hard and dry. Any excessive liquid will melt the icing.

Tree Pipe out the outlines of the trunk and overhead leaf area. Fill in the trunk part with a brown icing and allow to partly set and form a skin. To achieve the bark effect, press lightly with the fingers to make the surface crack and allow to dry hard. Fill in the leaf area with a green icing and, while it is still soft and wet, sprinkle with green coloured coconut or granulated sugar. For a winter effect, keep the icing and the coconut or sugar white. Any surplus loose coconut or sugar is brushed off when removing the run-out from the paper.

An alternative method for producing this kind of design is to pipe the trunk with a firm brown icing using a star nozzle. For the top area, fill a paper bag with firm green icing. Cut the tip of the bag into a triangular point and pipe the leaves, completely covering the top section. Because of the extra thickness of the icing used in this method, it will take longer to dry out and set hard.

Bird Pipe out the outlines, including the separate sections of the bird. First fill in the front breast part with a pale coloured icing, then the head section, using a slightly deeper tone. Deepen the colour more and fill in the wings, using a very dark tone for the tail and the beak. The legs are added by piping them on using a stiff, dark coloured icing. When set and dried hard, pipe on a white circle with soft icing, with the centre filled with a darker dot for the eye. Use a fine line brush to paint the eyebrow and the feather lines with dark brown colouring.

Different colours may be used. Look at birds in books or on greeting cards to promote variations of this idea.

Father Christmas Pipe out the outlines, fill in the face with a peach coloured icing and leave to dry hard. Using a stiff, white icing, pipe the edge of the hat, the beard and the eyebrows. While the icing is still soft, dab the beard with a soft brush to roughen and raise the surface slightly. When dry, run in deep red icing for the hat. With a stiff, pink icing, pipe on the lips, an oval for the nose and a thick line on each side of the face for the ears. Lightly brush in the cheeks with pink and the eyes with dark brown colouring.

Butterfly This design is best if made in three separate parts and assembled when the wings are set hard.

First outline the left and right hand sides of the wings separately. Fill in the lower parts of the wings with a chosen colour of icing. The secondary colourings should be piped on while the icing is still soft so that the two icings will blend together; this gives a smoother effect. The patterns may have more than one colour piped on top of each other, or a pattern may be made while the icing is still soft, using the same technique as for the feather design on gâteaux (see the section on chocolate work).

When the lower parts of the wings have set, repeat the process for the upper parts.

When the wings have dried hard, remove from the paper. Any additional colourings may then be painted on if desired.

Pipe the body of the butterfly on waxed or silicone paper using stiff, dark coloured icing. Immediately press the inner parts of the wings into position and allow to set.

To achieve the impression that the butterfly is in flight, raise the wings slightly at the edges and prop them up in this position before the icing of the body has set. The antennae can be piped on when the butterfly is placed in its final position on the cake or wherever it is to be used.

To change the effect of the surface of the butterfly and give a different finish, brush very lightly with egg white and sprinkle with castor sugar. Different colours and different types of finishes make the butterflies look very attractive, especially when several are used to decorate an item or to build up a picture.

Plaques and pictures With imagination, many attractive plaques and pictures can be made using royal icing run-outs. The diagram (on page 175) shows a heart-shaped background with a pronounced initial in the centre.

First, pipe out the outlines of the letter and fill in with the chosen colour. When dry, pipe the outline of the heart around the letter and fill in, using a different coloured icing.

Another method is to prepare the heart and the letter separately. When they have both dried hard remove from the paper, place a little royal icing on the back of the letter and affix to the top of the heart. This gives a three dimensional effect.

Other plaques or pictures may be made by adopting these methods of run-out work and using different shapes and colours and background designs.

The bird, for example, could be set in a large oval with a branch piped at the feet. The butterfly or the tree could be set in a rectangular plaque, with further decoration of flowers in the surrounding areas. The face of the Father Christmas may be set in a round, with the border of the plaque piped with green leaves.

When the run-outs are set hard the edges may be piped in stiff royal icing, using a decorative type of nozzle to form a frame around the picture. Suitable colourings, designs and pictures may be observed in books and on greetings cards.

Hearts First, pipe out the inner and outer outlines. Run in the icing using the desired colour. When making the double interlocking hearts, remember to allow the first one to set dry before filling in the adjoining one, so that the overlapping effect shows.

The shape of the hearts are emphasized if the V shape at the top is over-piped with thicker icing.

If the design is to be finished with a trellis, as shown in the diagram, allow the run-outs to set hard, remove from the paper and turn them upside down. Pipe the trellis with a fine line, using stiff icing, and then allow to dry hard.

Using the same techniques, other shapes, such as ovals, rounds, squares etc may be made according to the shape of the cake of ornament on which they are to be used.

Cake borders These are used on top of iced cakes instead of piped, decorated borders.

They are prepared in the same way as the hearts. The diagram (page 175) shows spaces left in the run-outs, with infilled variations of fine, line piping which may be used to add additional interest.

When preparing the designs on paper, measure the cake carefully. Plan the size and design to overlap the top of the cake by 10 to 15 mm (about $\frac{1}{2}''$). Run-outs for a square cake are best made in four separate sections with carefully measured mitred corners (see page 175).

The outer and inner lines are piped first and, if spaces are to be left for fine line piping, these should also be outlined. When running-in the icing on a large round design, do not start at one point and continue all the way round. The first part will dry out and a join line will show where the final icing meets. The running-in should be done by alternating the piping a little on one side then the other, so that there is always an edge of soft icing available to blend smoothly together with the icings being run in.

The edges may be left plain or a decorative border may be piped on, using stiff icing with a plain or decorative nozzle, when the icing has set hard.

MODELLING

The following model of a cottage is a simple example which may be using the run-out or stencil techniques. With a little thought and careful planning many variations of models can be made.

Plan and draw the sections on paper to the size required. Place the drawing under the waxed or silicone paper and pipe out the outlines, remembering to leave the space for the doors and windows. Run in the icing. The roof tiles do not have to be outlined; they are piped out to a suitable size as round discs.

When the pieces are set hard, fill in the door in a different colour. Alternatively the door may be prepared separately and put in position, using some stiff icing to hold it in place. With some stiff icing, pipe the ledge below the window space.

To achieve the effect of leaded lights on the window, turn the piece over and pipe fine lines over the space. Alternatively, some suitable coloured paper may be used to cover the window area; a little icing should be used to hold it in position.

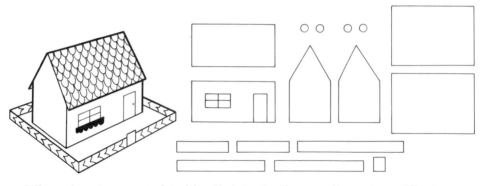

When the pieces are dried hard, join the four walls, using stiff icing on the edges to 'cement' them together. The tiles are placed in position with a little icing so that they completely cover the two roof sections. Start at the base of the roof and work upwards.

Make sure that the icing has dried hard and that the sections are firmly fixed before placing the roof in position. To fix the roof, pipe a few dots of stiff icing along the top edges of the walls and place the two roof sections in position. Do not pipe complete lines of icing along the edges of the wall as excessive icing will cause the roof to slip off.

When set, the apex of the roof may be piped with small shells of still icing, using a plain nozzle.

 Alternative wall finishes The walls may be left plain as described, or, before they are assembled, different surface effects on the walls may be achieved by using one of the following methods.

 Tudor When the icing has set, pipe the timber effect by using either melted chocolate or a brown icing.

Pebble dash While the icing is still soft, sprinkle with some brown sugar, or with crushed praline or rock sugar.

Log cabin Do not run in the icing as described. Colour the icing brown and keep it slightly stiffer than for running in. Pipe thick lines across the walls, leaving a gap of equal thickness between each line. When it is dry fill the gaps with another line of icing.

Stone work Use a stiff icing and pipe dots of different sizes close together to completely cover the wall area. With a small soft brush dab the icing to flatten it slightly and to give it a roughened surface, but still show the separate piping. An alternative method for stone effect is to spread some stiff icing over the area then press pieces of rock sugar of suitable size into the icing.

The fencing surrounding the cottage is made by piping the design in a stiff royal icing of suitable colour. This is held in position with stiff icing at the base and at the joins.

25 CAKE DECORATING

The art of decorating a cake is in creating an attractive item which is edible and appealing to the eyes of the consumer. The decorating may be in the form of designs piped directly on the cake or onto its prepared surfaces. The decoration can take the form of arranged set pieces denoting the feature of the cake, eg numbers on a twenty first birthday cake or denoting the composition of a specific cake, eg fruit on the surface or a fruit flavoured gâteaux.

Depending on the produce and presentation required, the right decorating medium should be used. Royal icing is needed for celebration cake because it has lasting qualities and properties which allow for finer and sharper definiton of design. Creams, soft icings and chocolate are used on gâteaux, sponges and the lighter varieties of cakes. They may also be used as flavoured fillings for a particular type of cake.

A mistake often made, which spoils the final appearance of a cake, is in overdecorating. Simple designs, evenly piped and neatly executed, will look much more attractive than a cake which is overloaded with piping and trimmings, or one which has too many combinations of pattern and design.

A beginner should practise and experiment with piped designs and patterns before attempting to decorate the cake itself. The basic principles of piping are the same whichever medium is used. With softer icings and creams, however, the finished details will not be so pronounced. An economical mixture for practising may be made by beating together equal quantities of white fat and soft flour until light and creamy. A little egg white may also be added, but this tends to aerate the mixture and, although easier to pipe, it will be more difficult to achieve a smooth base layer. The practice may be performed on a board or on an upturned cake tin. The mixture can be scraped up and re-used repeatedly.

■ COATING THE CAKE

So that any decoration projects itself as a definite design, it is important that the base coating on the cake has an even and smooth finish. This can only be achieved if the surface of the cake is level and free of crumbs and the mixture used for decoration is of the right consistency. When

required, it is advisable to seal the surfaces by brushing with boiling jam to prevent crumbs from becoming loose and spoiling the icing. It is necessary to cover cakes with a layer of marzipan when coating with royal icing.

The procedure to adopt for spreading and smoothing a coating is the same for cream and royal icings, but it must be remembered that royal icing will dry out fast and it is not always possible to remove or correct a mistake which has been made, unless it is done quickly.

To coat a round cake place it on a turntable or, if one is not available, use an inverted plate placed on a saucer. Put sufficient icing on top of the cake with a palette knife; spread the mixture evenly over the surface using a paddle action to force out the air bubbles. To smooth the surface of the icing clean the knife and hold it at a slight angle, pressing it lightly onto the surface a little more than half-way across the surface of the cake. Revolve the turntable, keeping the knife still and in the same level position to enable it to remove the surplus coating, and smooth the top

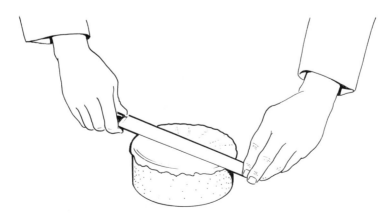

surface. It may be necessary to repeat the process more than once to achieve a smooth finish and each time the knife must be cleaned.

An alternative method for smoothing the top is to use a rigid strip, such as the back of a carving knife or a ruler. Using both hands, hold the strip at a slight angle on the surface; start at the opposite edge and draw evenly across the surface towards the nearside edge.

When the top is level and smooth remove any surplus icing overhanging the edges.

To coat the sides, spread the icing all around the sides of the cake, using the same paddling action to level and distribute it evenly. Clean the knife and with gentle pressure hold it upright at a slight angle to the sides. Revolve the turntable, keeping the knife still and in the same position. This should give a smooth surface on the sides. Remove any surplus icing at the base and top edges. A plastic baker's scraper may be used as an alternative tool when coating the sides.

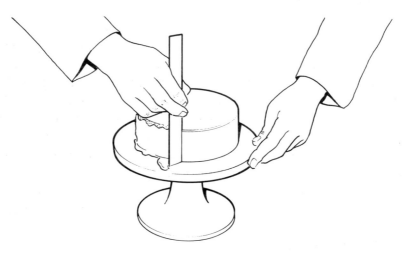

For a square cake the turntable is not required. Place the cake flat on the table or on a board and spread the icing as previously described. To smooth the top, draw a long rigid blade across and afterwards remove the surplus icing from the edges. To smooth the sides, hold a rigid metal or plastic scraper at a slight angle and in one clean action draw it from one corner of the cake to the other. Remove the surplus from the base and top edges.

When coating with royal icing it is best if the covering is allowed to harden before decorating. This allows for corrections to be made to the piped decorations as they can be removed easily without spoiling the base coating. If covering with creams, the decoration may be continued immediately. If masking of the sides is required, this should be done before the top surface is decorated.

A form of icing which is becoming increasingly popular is a roll-on icing sugar paste. This can be handmade by mixing together 1 kg (2 lbs) of icing sugar, 75 g (3 ozs) of egg whites or substitutes and 25 g (1 oz) of glucose to a smooth, pliable paste. This type of icing is sold commercially in bulk, or from retail outlets in small packaging. It has to be kept in airtight wrappings or containers to prevent the paste hardening before use.

To ice a cake, roll out the paste to the required thickness and to a size suitable for the cake's surface area. Brush the marzipaned cake with egg whites or substitute and lay the paste on top. Use a rolling pin to press and smooth the paste on to the cake, and then trim the edges. The same procedure is adopted for the sides. It should be noted that this paste does not harden to the extent that royal icing would, but it can be piped on and decorated immediately, which is an obvious advantage. It can be coloured and used for, modelling flowers and for small cut-outs for use as decorations.

■ PIPED DECORATIONS

The following details describe some of the basic methods of piping a design which are ideal for a beginner to follow when performing a piping exercise. Once the techniques of handling and controlling the flow of piping mixtures have been mastered, variation on designs and patterns may be achieved by using these examples as a basis for work. Remember that varying the pressure applied when forcing out the mixture will vary the size of the piping; the type of nozzle used determines the form of the piped medium; and the movement of the bag and position of the nozzle during the forcing of the mixture give it its shape.

Always apply the pressure from the top of the bag with one hand, and guide the nozzle with the fingers of the other. Make sure that the guiding hand is kept below the bag so that the point of the nozzle and the surface being piped are not obstructed from view.

To retain the mixture when using a large piping bag, close the top by holding it between the thumb and forefinger. Force out the mixture by applying pressure with the fingers and the palm of the hand. When using small or paper piping bags fold the top over to seal in the mixture. Hold the bag with fingers, almost as if holding a pen, to force out the mixture and control the flow of icing. Apply pressure on the top with the thumb still using the fingers of the other hand to guide and steady the bag.

The following photograph illustrates a tilting turntable which will make the piping of decorations on the sides of a cake much easier. It is fitted with adjustable grips which will hold most sizes and shapes of cake boards firmly in position on the turntable. It can be tilted to varying degrees, and the pivot is held at an angle with a pin, which slots through a series of holes.

FINE PIPING

The following illustration shows some line and dot pipings, which can be made using chocolate, fondant, cream and royal icings. These are best piped using a paper bag either fitted with a small plain nozzle (No. 2), or by cutting a hole at the tip of the bag.

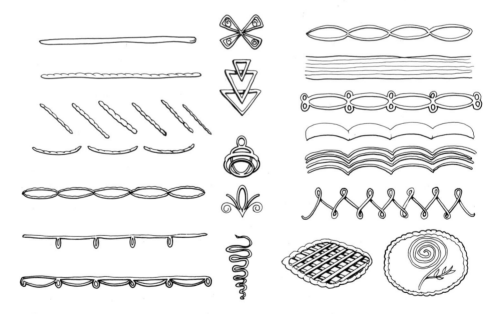

LINES

To pipe straight or curved lines start with the point of the bag touching the surface, apply an even pressure, and as the icing begins to flow, lift it off the surface so that a thread is formed. Continue the pressure and guide the thread into a straight or curved line as required. Do not attempt to 'write' with the bag but allow the thread to fall into position.

To ensure that a continual, even thread is drawn from the bag the pressure applied must correspond with the speed of movement. If there is insufficient pressure and the movement is fast, the thread will break. If too much pressure is applied and insufficient speed of movement, the thread will drip in uneven thicknesses and in wavy lines.

When the required length is reached, stop the pressure and lower the point of the bag into the position required on the surface, then lift off the bag. A good design to use to practise curves it to write one's own name. When the ability to pipe the curved and straight lines has been mastered, progress to the other designs. The same basic designs may be extended by filling in suitable patterns with run-out icings or by piping lines of different thicknesses on top of each other to produce a raised effect.

DOTS

Prepare the piping bag as for line piping and fit it with either a small plain or star nozzle. Hold the bag slightly above the surface and apply pressure, holding the bag still. Continue the pressure until the required size is achieved; stop the pressure and sharply lift up the bag.

A dot design looks most effective if the dots are graduated in size by increasing or decreasing the pressure when piping.

BORDERS AND BOLD CENTRE DECORATIONS

These are best piped using a piping bag fitted either with a large nozzle or with an adaptor, when using smaller nozzles, depending on the design and the type and size of item being decorated.

When piping always hold the point of the nozzle just above the surface and press or lay the mixture in position so that the pattern is more definite. As with all piping, the size is controlled by the amount of pressure applied when forcing out the mixture.

The illustration shows an example of piping shapes when using an eight point star and a plain nozzle. It shows how they can be joined to form a pattern suitable for borders and base designs and for general use.

> Rope (1) Hold the bag in a slanting position and, maintaining an even pressure, pipe out the mixture with a spiral movement of the nozzle, overlapping each section as the mixture is forced out of the bag.
>
> Shells (2) Hold the bag on the slant and keep the point of the nozzle in the same position, press until the size required is formed, then gently move the nozzle forward, easing off the pressure at the same time. Stop the pressure and draw the nozzle away. Repeat the movement, overlapping the previous shell. If watching an expert piping this pattern, it appears that the joining is one continual movement. But if seen in slow motion it would be apparent that each shape is piped individually.
>
> Double shell pattern (3) Pipe as for shells but pipe alternatively one shell

positioned to the right and the other to the left, overlapping them each time.

Scrolls (4) Hold the bag slightly slanted and pipe out question mark

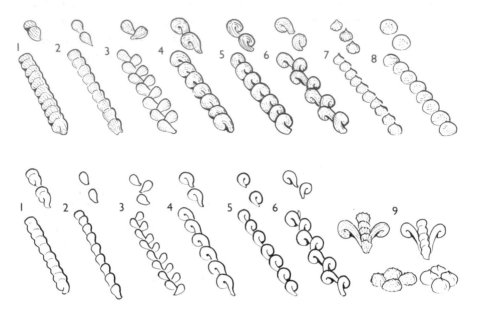

shapes, gradually easing off the pressure towards the end. Overlap each section when used for a border. The curve of the mark may be piped left to right or vice versa, as shown (5).

Double scroll (6) Pipe as above alternating the curve of the mark to the left and right as they overlap.

Star (7) Hold the piping bag upright and press until the size required has been formed. Stop the pressure and lift up sharply.

Rosette (8) Holding the bag upright, force out the mixture and, at the same time, give one circular movement at the point of the nozzle. Any combination of these designs may be combined to form patterns as shown in (9).

This illustration shows a complete design using most of the lines and bold types of piping. It shows a mixture of patterns on the border. It is stressed that this has been done only to show the effects and is not recommended for use as an example of suitable design. Any one pattern would be suitable for use as a border on a cake.

PIPING RAISED DESIGNS

To pipe royal icing to set in a raised or suspended position it is necessary to use some form of support, such as a rolling pin, spoon, ladle, plate, tartlet or barquette mould, so that the icing remains in that position until set hard. A lattice design is normally used.

The mould requires some form of non-stick surface so that the icing is removable when set. Depending on the design of the mould, it may be possible to fix waxed paper over the shape.

If using items which do not allow the paper to attain the contour of the mould, one of the following methods may be adopted. The mould may be waxed or lightly oiled and given a fine dusting of cornflour. The shape may be obtained by filling the mould with firmly packed starch, such as cornflour or arrowroot, then turning it out on to a flat surface.

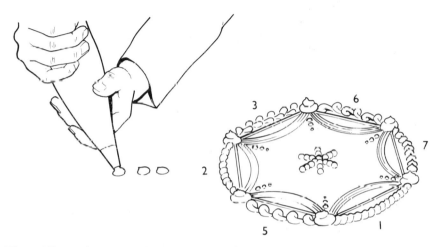

The stiff royal icing is then piped, in the desired pattern, over or into the prepared moulds or over the shaped starch and allowed to set hard. When set, remove by lifting the designs carefully from the moulds, or by gently peeling away the paper, or by brushing off the starch using a soft brush, depending which method was used to retain the shape of the icing.

Any additional decorative piping is best done when the design has been removed from the mould.

MODELS
Run-outs, stencils and piped designs can be used to build models. These require a pre-planned, ready made set of pieces which, when set and dry, are joined together with royal icing.

It may be necessary to build the models in separate stages to allow the icing 'cementing' the pieces together to set hard before the other pieces are added to complete the model.

■ ROCK SUGAR

This is a combination of cooked sugar and royal icing. It produces a crunchy, honeycomb like texture and is used to make snow scene effects on cakes and models. For coloured rock sugar incorporate the desired colour into the royal icing.

It is recommended that only 1 kg (2 lb) of sugar is cooked at any one time and that a deep pot is used which allows plenty of room for eventual stirring of the mixture. Cook the sugar to 150° C (300° F), following the sugar boiling precautions.

Take off the heat and when the sugar has stopped bubbling, use a spatula to briskly stir in two tablespoons, about 50 g (2 oz), of well beaten royal icing. Mix thoroughly. The mixture will immediately begin to froth and expand. Pour quickly into a lightly oiled bowl or a bowl lined with oiled greaseproof paper. Cover immediately with a thick cloth or tray, or turn the bowl upside down on flat surface. Allow to stand covered for about fifteen minutes. Tap the bowl sharply on the table for the rock sugar to drop down. It is now ready for use and may be broken up into pieces or cut into the required shapes and sizes using a saw knife or balde.

■ FEATHER OR MARBLE DESIGN

This method of decorating is often used for covering the tops of gâteaux, pastries and slices. It is recognised as the accepted design for vanilla and cream slices and gâteau milles feuilles.

The top of the item to be coated should be flat and smooth; better results are achieved if the surfaces are first brushed with a very thin coating of boiling apricot jam. This seals the surface and the moisture helps to retain a longer lasting gloss. It also produces a smoother base for the icing to flow on.

The process involves a layer of fondant or water icing, over-piped with fine lines of chocolate which are drawn along with the point of a knife to form the pattern. Icings of different colours may be used, alternating the colours of the lines.

To be effective, the work must be done quickly before either of the icings set. The pattern will not be achieved if there is delay between the stages. It is therefore important that the icing or chocolate for piping the lines is ready prepared in paper piping bags, and that the required tools are at hand, before the icing is poured onto the cake.

LARGE ROUND SHAPES
Pour the prepared fondant or icing onto the centre of the cake; spread it out to the edges. Immediately pipe fine lines in a spiral about 25 mm (1") apart (1).

Before the icing sets, draw the point of a knife from the centre towards the outer edges (2).

Immediately draw lines with the knife between the previous lines, but start from the outer edges and draw towards the centre (3).

1	2	3

LARGE SQUARE AND RECTANGULAR SHAPES

Pour the icing along the centre of the cake and spread it to the edges. The same procedure is used except that straight lines are piped about 25 mm (1″) apart (1). The knife should be drawn from one edge to the other at about 50 mm (2″) intervals (2) and then drawn in between in the opposite direction (3).

For covering smaller items the procedure is the same but the distance between the piped lines and the drawing is reduced accordingly.

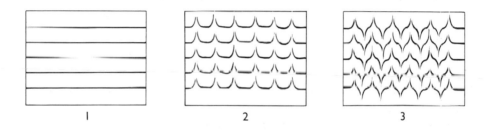

1	2	3

26 GUM PASTE (PASTILLAGE)

This modelling paste is a mixture of icing sugar and cornflour bound together with a diluted edible gum such as gelatine or tragacanth. It may be coloured as required.

To each 1 kg (2 lb) of icing sugar add 100 g (4 oz) of cornflour, a few drops of lemon juice and, as with royal icing, a few drops of blue colouring to promote whiteness. Mix into a paste with either 15 g ($\frac{1}{2}$ oz) of soaked and dissolved gelatine in 150 ml ($\frac{1}{4}$ pt) of cold water and allow to soak for twenty four hours.

Once the gum has been added it must be quickly mixed and thoroughly kneaded until smooth. The consistency should be firm but pliable (like plasticine) so that it can easily be rolled out or manipulated into shape.

If it is too hard, add a little hot water or if too soft, mix in more icing sugar. Kept in an airtight container pastillage will keep for several days. With storage it tends to harden and requires a lot of kneading to smooth it. Mixing a new batch is just as quick; it is therefore advisable to make only the amount required for immediate use.

Once made, it forms a skin very quickly and must be kept covered with a damp cloth. Take only the amount required for the piece being made and knead again before using. Keep the trimmings to a minimum and as they are cut away, place immediately under the damp cloth.

Pastillage does not achieve such a smooth surface as royal icing run-outs but it has the advantage that it can be moulded over curved surfaces and can be made into almost any shape desired. It is used mostly for the preparation of ornaments, caskets, flowers and models for show pieces.

Although it is entirely composed of edible materials, because of its hardness when set, it is not ideally suitable for use as an edible decorative medium for cakes.

The following describes a method of using pastillage for modelling. To try out the procedure, the pattern for making the cottage (see page 178) in royal icing run-out could be used.

The surface on which the paste is rolled must be hard and smooth. Only a very light dusting of the table and the surface of the paste with cornflour is necessary. This dusting is best achieved if the cornflour is enclosed in a double layer of muslin and shaken or gently rubbed over the surfaces. The surfaces on which the pastillage is placed to set should also be dusted with cornflour and the excess shaken or tapped off so that only a thin film of cornflour adheres to the surfaces.

Roll out the pastillage to about 3 mm ($\frac{1}{8}''$) thick and cut out the shapes with a thin sharp blade without distorting the paste by dragging the knife.

It will be easier to cut out shapes from the rolled out paste if it is first marked in the shapes required. This marking may be achieved by using prepared templates made from thin metal, stiff plastic or cardboard. When the pastillage has been rolled out press the template on the surface. It will leave an outline which is easy to follow with the knife.

The cut pieces should be laid on a flat smooth surface, such as glass or laminated plastic, and lightly dusted with cornflour. Cover them with a sheet of greaseproof or silicone paper and place a flat board on top. This is done to prevent the paste drying out too fast and also to retain a smoother surface.

Allow to dry for about twenty four hours, occasionally turning the pieces over carefully so that both sides dry out evenly. If only one side dries out completely, the shape tends to become distorted. Brush off the cornflour before assembling.

If desired, different types of surfaces may be achieved by marking a pattern on the pastillage, while it is still soft, after being rolled out. Alternatively when hardened, the surfaces may be brushed with a soft royal icing and coated with white or coloured sugars. The pieces may then be assembled, using the same techniques as with set royal icing run-outs.

For shaping pastillage on curved surfaces or in hollow-ware moulds, the surfaces are prepared in the same way with a thin coating of cornflour. The pastillage must be moulded as soon as it is rolled out. Lay it over or into the moulds. Gently, but firmly, press the layer of paste on to the surfaces so that any trapped air is expelled and it takes on the contours of the shape. Do not press too hard or it may stick to the surfaces and when set it may be difficult to remove without breaking.

To prevent the pastillage drying out too fast, cover with a thick layer of cornflour or with plastic sheeting. Allow to dry out for about twelve hours. Gently remove from the moulds and leave to dry out completely then brush off the loose cornflour. Assembly of the pieces and any further decoration is done with stiff royal icing. Using suitable plans and moulds, a variety of containers, such as caskets, boxes, bowls, plates, vases, etc may be made for petits fours.

The following illustration shows some models made of pastillage, together with the equipment used for moulding. The box and cottage are made from cut out sections. A possible pattern idea is on page 178.

A flat sheet of set pastillage may serve as a background for pictures and plaques, using run-out icing, fondant, melted chocolate, or the background may be painted with colourings.

Freshly made pastillage, used while it is still soft, may be manipulated in the same way as marzipan for making flowers, or it can be shaped by pressing it into cast moulds.

27 MAINTAINING STANDARDS

When products are not of the quality and standard expected, the reasons should be investigated and corrected.

In pastry work there are a multitude of small, fundamental details which a skilled pastry cook has learned, and practised. These have become second nature in the approach to work and in the methods adopted. Only by experience can one learn sufficient of the techniques to be skilled at the craft.

There are reasons for doing things a certain way and it must be remembered that if variations are made to the recipes or methods of production, or if there has been a change in the working environment, special care and attention is necessary. Often the weather or temperature can affect the results of recipes and methods which are usually successful. Faults can occur through lack of understanding regarding commodities used, or in the manner of handling, or perhaps both. Faults often develop through lack of knowledge or skills. In these cases instructions are required.

If there are not sufficient staff, or working time is limited, or the wrong type of equipment is used, it could mean adopting different methods and using short cuts. This would make it very difficult to perform the work correctly, be ready by service time and achieve good results.

Experience alone will not produce good results if the commodities are of poor quality, or if the ovens and other necessary equipment do not function properly or are unsuitable for the work to be done.

In all sections of industry there are operatives who have no incentive to acquire knowledge or who have no sense of loyalty to their employer. Their only concern is to do a job of work to earn money and they have no interest in extending their ability or in promoting the reputation of the firm employing them. Good operatives will know their own value and will expect to be paid accordingly. To this end they should always give of their best to maintain and improve standards while continuing to develop and improve their own knowledge and skills.

■ ASSESSING WORK AND PRODUCTS

It is the responsibility of the pastry cook to judge products and to assess whether or not they have reached the required standards.

There are three main points that the pastry cook should consider when assessing work.

1 Customer appeal and appreciation of the food to be consumed and paid for.

Sweets, cakes, pastries, or any product, should be neat, look attractive and appetizing and be correctly garnished and decorated. The flavour, texture, colour and quality must all be appealing. The type, quantity and final appearance should be of the kind expected. If a sweet is meant to be hot or cold, chilled or iced, this is how it should reach the customer.

A well-known saying is, 'the proof of the pudding is in the eating'. A test of customer approval is whether or not the item has been eaten, for if many customers request the same dish, or hope to have it at some other time, it suggests that the dish is popular and appreciated and therefore worth producing again.

2 The business point of view: the economics of the whole process. The costs of producing the sweets must be controlled. This must include the cost of commodities, energy used for cooking, preparation time taken and staff used for the production of the items. The aim should be to adopt methods which save time, labour, and energy while keeping waste of foods to a minimum.

Employers and administrators do expect and require a profit. Has an adequate profit margin been achieved? Would it have been possible to reduce the costs by more conscientious and effective working methods, or by using bulk- or multi-production systems and making better use of food, labour and energy? All these aspects of the work must be considered.

3 The challenge of the work and the self satisfaction that the results have achieved the required standard.

All self-respecting pastry cooks take pride in their craft and aim to maintain their standards. They will always look for ways and means to improve every aspect of their work. It is said that 'one should never cease to learn'; this is true. An ambitious pastry cook will find that there is always room for improvement when trying to achieve perfection. Constructive self criticism of the product and working method should be continuous when aiming at the highest possible standards of quality and professionalism.

■ BASIC FAULTS

Success in food production is more than using a good recipe. It is the combination of correctly balanced ingredients, the use of correct methods of preparation, handling and cooking, together with a good working knowledge of the commodities being used.

It is not possible to describe every detail of all the difficulties encountered or give reasons for all failures. Indeed, not all problems can be solved.

Where results have not been altogether satisfactory and difficulty is experienced in comprehending the reason for the sub-standard product, the following examples of faults and the possible reasons for their occurrence will be of use. These examples will be especially helpful to the novice who, although diligently following a recipe, is unaware of the reason for imperfection in the product.

To understand the reasons for such faults occurring, the relevant sections in the book dealing with the area of work must be studied, together with any recipe being used. Before detailing individual products a few general rules must be noted.

1 Measure ingredients correctly.
2 Make sure that the right kind of commodities are being used for the purpose required and that they are of good quality.
3 Ensure that the equipment is clean, in good condition, properly prepared and of the correct type for the work being done.
4 When baking, make sure that the ovens are on and will be at the right temperature when required. Remember that ovens do vary with regard to temperatures and controls.
5 Ensure that oven shelves are correctly positioned. Bear in mind that the temperature of the oven is hotter at the top.

Pastes

Except for choux and hot water pastes, keep all the ingredients that are being used for mixing as cool as possible and work as quickly as possible.

If baking powder is used, sieve together with the flour to ensure even distribution in the paste or mixture. It is best if liquids are added all at once to avoid the paste being lumpy or not well mixed. Remember that overmixing develops the gluten in the paste and produces a tough dough. Any pastes that are meant to be short should never be over kneaded.

To prevent the paste from shrinking, or going out of shape during baking, allow to rest before rolling. Do not stretch the pastes when rolling or moulding and allow to rest again before baking.

Pastes may be prepared, rolled and cut the day before. They should be placed on clean sheets of paper and covered to prevent a crust forming. Transfer to the baking tray just before baking. If allowed to stand overnight on metal trays or in moulds, the metal will stain the paste and spoil the appearance.

Keep the pastes cool and always work on cool surfaces when mixing, rolling or moulding, except when using hot water paste for raised pies which requires the paste to be moulded while it is still hot. Avoid excessive use of flour when dusting during rolling; use only sufficient to prevent the paste sticking to the table. Too much flour will toughen the paste.

Fault identification	Possible reason for fault
Short paste	
Hard and tough	Insufficient fat. Too much liquid. Over-mixed. Over-handled. Cooked too slowly or too much. Too much flour used for dusting.
Crumbly and too short Blistered when cooked	Too much fat. Insufficient liquid to bind the mixture. Fat not well rubbed in. Insufficient liquid. Insufficient mixing. Crust formed when paste left uncovered.
Shrinkage during cooking	Insufficient rest time. Over-handling or over-mixing. Paste stretched when being rolled or moulded.
Puff pastes	
Lack of lift	Oven too cold. Soft flour used. Fat too soft. Rolled out too thin when giving turns. Too many turns causing fat layers and dough to mix. Blunt cutter used. Sides of cut edge sealed by excessive eggwash.
Hard when baked	Oven too cold. Under cooked. Over-handling. Excessive use of dusting flour between rollings. Too much water in dough. Too many turns.
Uneven rising	Dough too stiff. Insufficient mixing of dough. Uneven lamination of fat. Fat too soft so leaked out of paste. Not kept square when given turns. Insufficient rest time between turns and prior to baking. Fat too hard so broken through surface of paste. Uneven temperature throughout the oven.
Excessive shrinking during cooking	Not enough rest times. Stretched when rolled and shaped. Baking tray over greased.
Sugar paste	
Pitted appearance of baked paste	Sugar not dissolved or granulated sugar used
Difficult to handle or mould	Too much fat. Insufficient liquids to bind. Not mixed sufficiently. Too much sugar. Too much egg. Insufficient fat. Paste not cool enough. Working surfaces too warm.
Hard after baking	Too much sugar. Insufficient fat. Too much egg.

Fault identification	Possible reason for fault
Choux paste	
Cooked items close and heavy	Too much fat. Water allowed to evaporate when preparing the base mixture, resulting in high proportion of fat. Soft flour used. Insufficient eggs. Not enough beating. Eggs added when mixture was too hot. Oven too cool.
Items collapsed after being removed from oven	Oven too hot. Insufficiently cooked. Too much water. Not enough egg. Weak or stale eggs used.
Hot water paste	
A dry paste that breaks when being moulded	Insufficient fat. Not enough water. Fat and water too cold when flour was added. Dough cold when kneaded. Too cold for moulding.
Moulded pastes collapses when removing moulding block	Paste still warm. Paste moulded too thin. Uneven moulding. Careless handling when removing moulding block. Excessive dusting flour used.
Suet paste	
Tough after steaming	Not enough baking powder. Cooked too fast. Suet not chopped small enough to dissolve. Too much flour.
Heavy and soggy after steaming	Too much liquid. Undercooked. Not enough steam pressure. Cover not sealing so water allowed to penetrate into paste.

Yeast mixtures

A well-kneaded and elasticated dough or mixture is required for all doughs using yeast as a raising agent. To prevent drying out and a crust forming, the doughs should always be kept covered and proved in warm, moist temperatures.

The process of mixing and mouldings should be carried out away from draughty and cold areas and moulding should be done as quickly as possible so that the items being made will all be proved and ready for baking at the same time. When producing large amounts, batches of dough being prepared should be staggered to enable the ovens to cope with the baking.

Fault identification	Possible reason for fault
Doughs	
Not proving	Yeast killed by contact with salt or by the use of water which was too hot (50° C/127° F maximum).
Slow proving	Used stale yeast. Not enough yeast. Liquid too cold. Proved in cold place. Too much salt.
Soft dough	Too much liquid. Used soft flour. Too much fat.
Sour dough (smell of fermentation)	Too much yeast. Overproved. Liquid too hot. Not 'knocked back'. Used stale yeast. Not enough salt. Too much sugar.
Dough has rough texture	Not kept covered. Proved in dry heat. Insufficient kneading. Overproving.
Baked goods	
Close of course texture	Insufficient proving. Not well kneaded. Insufficient yeast. Soft flour used. Too much salt. Dough too hard (not enough liquid or fat).
Cracked crust or rough appearance	Under proving of items. Roughly moulded or shaped. Oven too cold or too hot (outer crust sets while centre part of item is still expanding).
Flat items	Overproved. Soft flour used. Too much liquid. Knocked when transferred from prover to oven.
Poor colour	Overproved. Oven too cold. Not enough cooking time.

Cakes

Creaming and rubbing in of fats are the two main methods of preparation used in cake mixing.

As a general guide the creaming method uses between two thirds and equal parts of fat to flour and because of the aeration produced by the beating of the fats and sugar, the mixture requires less baking powder. The rubbing in method uses between a quarter and a half part of fat to flour and, as very little air is introduced to the mixture, more baking powder is required.

A point to remember when baking cakes is that large or heavy fruit cakes require longer cooking times at lower temperatures, while smaller or plain cakes make sure that the fruit is clean, dry and is not heavy with sugar or syrup.

A good quality cake should be evenly baked all round and inside, with only thin, coloured surfaces. It should rise evenly, have a flat top or be slightly domed towards the centre. It should not be peaked or cracked on top. Arranging the raw mixture in the baking tins with a slight concave will assist in achieving this.

Make sure that the mixture is not curdled before cutting in the flour. This can be prevented in two ways. First, by ensuring that the ingredients and equipment used are all at the same temperature. The best way to achieve this is to bring everything together well beforehand and to allow them to reach the same room temperature. Second, by adding the beaten eggs gradually and beating them in well between each addition.

When the baked cake shrinks from the sides of the tin, this indicates that it is cooked. Further checks may be made as follows. After the estimated cooking time it is possible to test to see if the cake is cooked. For small cakes and sponges, press lightly on the surface; the impression should spring back immediately. For large, heavy fruit cakes, insert a thin, clean and warm bladed knife or a skewer. On withdrawal it should not have any moist mixture clinging to it. If cakes are not cooked do not delay in returning them to the oven.

After removal from the oven, allow the cakes to stand in tins or moulds for a few minutes before removal. Do not allow them to cool completely in the containers as this would make removal difficult and possibly break them.

Fault identification	Possible reason for fault
Creamed mixtures	
Cakes lack volume	Insufficient creaming. Oven too hot. Insufficient baking powder. Overmixing of flour.
Uneven rising	Baked too fast. Temperature of oven uneven. Baking powder not well mixed with flour. Uneven greasing of tins.
Sinking in the centre	Too much raising agent. Not cooked enough. Too much sugar. Too much liquid. Cake moved when not set.
Speckled surface	Too much sugar. Coarse sugar used or not dissolved. Baking powder not well mixed with flour.
Hard texture	Overmixing of flour. Too much liquid. Insufficient creaming. Insufficient baking powder. Oven too slow. Too much flour.

Fault identification	Possible reason for fault
Dry and crumbly	Too much baking powder. Not enough fat. Not enough liquid. Cooked too slowly and too long. Flour poorly incorporated (cut in) to the creamed fat.
Texture close and heavy	Too much fat. Insufficient creaming. Insufficient liquid. Oven too slow.
Uneven texture	Air pocket when mixture placed in tins. Flour not well mixed with creamed fats. Baking powder not well mixed with flour.
Sticky and sugary crust	Cooked too slowly. Too much sugar. Excessive steam in oven.
Poor colour	Oven too hot or cake too near the top. Too much sugar. (For a long cooking time, when the cake begins to colour, cover with paper of foil.)
Outer crust too brown or thick	Insufficient lining of tins. Tins too thin. Overcooked. Tins over floured.
Peaked or cracked top	Oven too hot (the outside has cooked before the centre and raw mixture has broken out).
Fruit sinking to bottom of cake	Mixture too light. Too much liquid. Too much fat. Too much baking powder. Overcreamed. Fruit wet or heavy. (In all cases the structure is not of sufficient strength to carry the fruit.)
Rubbed in mixture and scones Poor shapes	Rough handling. Careless dividing of pieces.
Dry and hard	Oven too cold. Overcooked. Overmixed. Too much sugar. Insufficient fat. Too much egg.
Crumbly texture	Too much baking powder. Too much fat. Undercooked.
Spread during baking	Oven too cold. Too much fat. Trays overgreased. Too much liquid. Insufficient eggs.
Scones not risen	Rolled too thinly. Insufficient baking powder. Oven too cold. Overmixed. Pieces cut out with blunt cutter. Eggwash on the cut sides. (The sides have been sealed, preventing rise.)
Open texture	Too much raising agent. Too much sugar.
Too pale	Insufficient egg or milk wash. Oven too cold. Baked in lower part of the oven.
Rough surface	Insufficient mixing.

A short rest period (ten minutes) before placing in the oven allows the baking powder to activate and gives better results with the smaller cakes and scones.

Whisked egg sponges and biscuits

The aeration in these kinds of sponges is achieved by the whisking together of eggs and sugar. Further addition of raising agents is not required. If the whisking takes place over gentle heat, the air cells produced will expand quickly and easily and the slight coagulation of the eggs stabilizes the multi-cell structure into a stronger foam.

The flour is added by folding in slowly and carefully to retain the aeration. Extra care is required for Genoese sponges when melted butter is also added. Sponge fingers and drops are drier products. Here the foam is achieved by whisking the yolks and the egg whites separately and then blending together. The size of eggs is important for these sponges. The guide to follow for a balanced recipe is equal weights of egg, sugar and flour.

Fault identification	Possible reason for fault
Sponges	
Close and heavy texture	Insufficient eggs or too much flour. Eggs and sugar not sufficiently aerated. Eggs and sugar overheated Overmixed when flour added. Flour added too fast and stirred in (Genoese sponge). Too much butter. Butter too hot and sunk through foam.
Sunken top	Undercooked. Knocked while cooking. Oven too hot. Too much sugar. Insufficient flour.
Uneven rising in tin	Flour not well blended in. Uneven greasing of sides of tin. Temperature uneven in oven.
Tunnelling in cooked sponge	Strong flour used. Overmixed. Melted butter not evenly folded in (gaps caused by streaks of butter).
Low and heavy sponges	Strong flour used. Overmixing of flour. Too much butter. Insufficient aeration of eggs and sugar. Oven too cold.
Swiss roll	
Cracks while being rolled	Most faults as for sponge. Strong flour used. Too much sugar. lack of aeration. Too much flour. Overcooked. Not evenly spread in tray. Allowed to get too cold before rolling. (For cream filled swiss roll, first roll with paper or cloth inside and allow to cool).

Fault identification	Possible reason for fault
Sponge fingers Soft and runny mixture and hard and flat when cooked:	Amount of egg and flour not balanced. Insufficient beating of whites. Overmixing of whites to yolks. Overmixing when adding flour. Too large a batch made (mixture softens when allowed to stand). Taking too long to pipe out. Continual dipping of spoon into mixture.
Biscuits spreading during baking	Trays overgreased. Trays not floured. Grease in mixture. Oven too cold.
Biscuits too hard	Too much sugar. Overbaked. Too slow oven. Overmixed.
Soft and sticky	Not enough flour. Icing sugar used in mixture. Steam in oven.

Meringue

Meringue is simply a mixture of stiffly beaten egg whites, combined with fine grain sugar for ordinary meringue, or with cooked sugar for Italian meringue.

The ratio of sugar to whites is one part albumen to between $1\frac{1}{2}$ and $2\frac{1}{2}$ parts sugar depending on what the meringue is to be used for. For a crisp, dry meringue use a high proportion of sugar. A softer meringue, which is suitable for toppings, requires less sugar.

Although meringue may be baked in a slow oven, a lighter and crisper product is obtained if it is 'dried out' for at least three hours at a temperature of 90° C (200° F), with the oven door slightly open to allow steam to escape.

Details on methods and precautions for using egg whites will be found in the egg section.

Fault identification	Possible reason for fault
Ordinary meringue Whipped whites appear curdled	Stale eggs used. Egg whites contaminated with grease. Thick wire whisk used. Egg yolk in whites. Bowl too large for amount of whites used (part of the whites remain untouched by the whisk and when mixed with the remainder the whole quantity becomes soft). Whisking in a plastic bowl.
Take a long time to produce a stiff foam	Stale eggs. Whites contaminated with grease. Too much sugar added. Not lifting the mixture sufficiently to introduce air. Bowl too large.

Fault identification	Possible reason for fault
Too soft for piping	Left too long a time before using. Overmixed when adding sugar. Insufficient whisking before sugar added.
Hard solid appearance of cooked meringue	Too much sugar. Too much sugar when commencing to mix. Using too fine a sugar. Continued whisking after sugar was added.
Meringue shells etc cracked and discoloured	Oven too hot. Not enough sugar. Too long in the oven.
Syrup runs out of meringue	Moisture on the tray or in oven. Granulated sugar used. Left to stand too long before being placed in oven.
Syrups runs out when covering flans etc	Not cooked enough in oven. Sugar dissolves when the oven is too cold to cook the meringue quickly and when meringue is piped on to a cold filling and is left to stand
Italian meringue Finished meringue too soft	Not enough sugar. Sugar not cooked to high enough temperature. Stale whites used. Mixture curdled when sugar was added.
Pearls or strands of cooked sugar in mixture	Sugar overcooked. Sugar poured in too fast. Mixture not whisked fast enough. Sugar too cold when added.
Poached meringue Breaking up while cooking	Cooking liquid boiling too fast. Meringue mixture not strong enough. Too much sugar. Cooked too long. Cooking liquid not hot enough (soaking the meringue and causing collapsing).

Miscellaneous Items

Fault identification	Possible reason for fault
Whipped cream Fresh cream that does not whip up stiffly	Single cream could have been used. The cream or equipment used should be chilled. If possible whip the cream in a bowl standing over ice or in very cold water.
Combining fresh and synthetic creams	Better results will be obtained if the synthetic cream is first whipped very stiff on its own, then the fresh cream added and beaten until the required stiffness is reached.

Fault identification	Possible reason for fault
Fresh cream that has curdled and is watery	Has been overbeaten or cream was warm and it is at the stage of the fats and liquids separating (further beating would produce butter in the liquid).
Bavarois and derivatives A heavy rubbery layer on top when the bavarois is turned out	If the folding in of the cream is done while the gelatine base is still hot, the heat melts the whipped cream, causing the gelatine part of the mixture to sink to the bottom of the mould with little if any cream in it.
A bavarois with white specks in the texture	This has been caused by the whipped cream being folded in while the gelatine base was still warm, consequently it has slightly curdled the cream.
A rough or lumpy texture	The whipped cream has been folded in when the gelatine base was past setting point; it was already too hard for the cream to blend in smoothly. (If the base mixture does overset, it may be brought back by gentle warming and re-cooling to setting point).
A heavy and dense texture with little volume	Whipped cream and egg whites overmixed when being added to the base mixture expelling the air.
Cream charlottes that have sunk in the centre	Indicates that either the bavarois was not set or it was not filled sufficiently. (Think of it as the filling holding up the biscuits, not the biscuits holding up the filling.)
Cream charlottes that have split their sides	Either the bavarois was not set, or it was overfilled and the surplus filling has pushed the sides apart.
Charlottes which when turned out have cream on the outside of the biscuits	Either the bavarois was runny or insufficient gelatine was used. The biscuits lining the moulds were not close enough to ensure a tight fit.
Chartreuse of fruits which when turned out has a split jelly	Most of the faults applicable to charlottes apply to chartreuse. The jelly was not of sufficient strength to hold the fruit. The fruit used was wet or syrupy.
Apple charlottes Collapses after it has been turned out of the mould:	Bread slices too thin, insufficiently cooked or not overlapping properly. Apple mixture overcooked or too wet. Insufficient filling or too much filling. Apple filling not packed tightly. Cooked too slowly.
Mixture leaked to the outside of the bread lining	Too much sugar in the filling. Filling too wet or overcooked. Bread slices insufficiently overlapped. Cooked too long.
Bread crust very pale colour	Not cooked enough. Oven too cold. Other fats used instead of butter. (Apple charlottes should never be turned out immediately after removal from the oven. They should be allowed to stand for a few moments to allow the

Fault identification	Possible reason for fault
	steam to escape; the filling should then be pressed down into the mould and the bread trimmed to the same level as the apple filling.)
Fruit flans The flan breaks when being cut for service	Paste lining too thin at sides. Paste undercooked. Apple purée too wet (the purée should be allowed to cook out so that most of the moisture is evaporated). Any base filling should be dry and fairly firm. Rhubarb flans should have a layer of cake crumbs under the fruit to absorb the surplus moisture.
Baked egg custards Texture appears pitted and watery	Overcooked or allowed to boil. Insufficient sugar. Cooked too fast. Water splashed into custard while being place in the oven.
Custard collapsing after unmoulding	Turned out while still too hot. Not cooked for sufficient length of time. Insufficient egg.
Custard seeped under the paste of tarts or flans	Pastry shrunk due to incorrectly made paste or insufficient resting time. Moulds over greased (causing paste to slip in the mould).
Fried goods 1 *Doughnuts* Raw in centre, badly shaped and cracked	Fat too hot (outside cooked too fast). Insufficient proving of dough. Cooked too slowly (outside cooked but inside still expanding).
Badly shaped and flat	Careless handling when transferring into fat. Overproving of item
Heavy and greasy	Underproved and cooked too slow. Fat too cold. Not well drained.
Pale colour	No sugar in dough. Fat too cold. Water in fat.
2 *Choux fritters* Do not expand while cooking	Most faults as for doughnuts. Insufficient egg mixture. Weak flour used. Fat too cold. Choux paste not made as per specification.
3 *Pancakes* Hard and breaking	Too much flour used. Overcooked. Cooked without sufficient greasing of pan. Allowed to dry out after being made. Too much egg in proportion to milk. Made too thick.
Greasy and stodgy	Overgreasing of pan. Too much fat in mixture. Made too thick. Piled together while very hot.

Fault identification	Possible reason for fault
Savarins etc	
Mixing and proving	The same rules apply as for any other product using yeast as the raising agent.
Too light and dry texture	Soft flour used. Too much sugar. Overcooked or oven too hot. Dough and item overproved. Insufficient fat.
Heavy and solid texture	Insufficient yeast or proving. Soft flour used. Too much fat. Too much egg. Insufficient mixing.
Item does not soak up the syrup.	Heavy and solid texture. Syrup not hot enough.
Item does not soak up the syrup Soaks the liquid but items break up:	Heavy and solid texture. Syrup not hot enough. Texture. Too light and dry. Oversoaked. Careless handling.
Soufflés and pudding soufflés	
Heavy and greasy	Too much fat in base mixture. Insufficient flour. Insufficient whites. Panada base not cooked out. Overmixed. Oven too cold.
Streaks of egg white in the cooked product	Whipped whites not completely folded in. Air gaps allowed to form when filling moulds.
Texture too light and dry	Too much sugar. Too many whites. Insufficient flour.
Uneven rising	Moulds not evenly greased. Oven temperature uneven.
Will not rise	Left too long before cooking. Too much flour. Too much fat. Overmixed. Insufficient whites.
Top cracked or peaked	Insufficient greasing of mould. Overmixing of whipped whites. Oven too hot. Too much sugar. Too much flour.
Collapses immediately when taken out of the oven:	Oven too hot (undercooked). Rough handling when taking out of the oven or turning out of the moulds. Insufficient yolks. Insufficient flour.

28 MENU PLANNING

Listing dishes on a menu serves two main purposes. From the customer's point of view it shows the food available and states at what price it is being sold. From the cook's point of view it serves many purposes. The following points give a guide to its usefulness and discuss the points to consider when planning menus.

The prime consideration when selecting dishes to be included on the menu is to attract the customer. Therefore a study of the type of customers and their requirements is needed. Although it is not possible to please all the customers all the time, a good varied selection should be available to suit the majority.

The menus assist the organizer and the operators when requisitioning the necessary ingredients and when planning the work of the section, therefore menus should be clear, comprehensible and detailed. Planners should have adequate knowledge of the composition of dishes, the methods required for producing them, the facilities available for production and the types of dishes suitable for particular meals.

The commodities required for dishes may have to be ordered so consideration as to whether the ingredients are to be purchased fresh, or will come from dry stores, will affect the choice of dishes. The availability of produce which is in season, its price and quality will also be a determining factor.

The control of expenditure and the percentage of profit required must be taken into account. The planner and the organizer must ensure that staff and equipment are put to full use. Staff concerned with the preparation and service of food must be sufficient in number and have the necessary skills and the appropriate equipment to cope efficiently, and to a satisfactory standard, thus avoiding waste of food and time.

Preparation areas and service facilities, whether they are to keep the foods hot or cold, should be adequate. Transfer of prepared dishes from the production areas to the customer must be efficient to ensure service of the dish in prime condition.

When planning a programme of work which begins with compiling a menu, the pastry cook must consider other departments. It is essential that liaison exists between the head chef, larder, kitchen and food service areas. The dishes should not clash with others listed on the menu as a whole, ie if savoury pies, puddings, mousses, flans, rice dishes were to appear on the savoury part of a menu, it would not be correct to have fruit pies or puddings, bavarois, fruit flans, and rice puddings as the selection of sweet dishes. When allocating work, the pastry cook must also consider the savoury items required by the kitchen and larder, eg tartlets, vol-au-vents, pastes, etc.

■ TYPES OF MENU

Table d'hôte is the term for a meal of a fixed number of courses at a fixed price. The sweet course will normally offer four to six choices. Some establishments keep the same menu for a period of six to eight days and will insert a 'carte du jour' which lists the dishes of the day. It is more usual in hotels to change the menu daily and have a separate menu for the evening service.

Sweets listed on this type of menu should be of the popular type, costed in relation to the whole menu and to the customer. They should be ready on commencement of service as the customer will expect fast service.

A la carte menus consist of a wide range of dishes which are individually priced. Most dishes are prepared to order so the sweets listed should be of the type that can be prepared to order from available commodities or from partially or pre-prepared ingredients, eg coupes, vacherin, meringues and moulded ice-creams. Some sweets the customer will pre-order and will expect to wait for them to be prepared, eg soufflés, pancakes and fruit fritters, which can take up to thirty minutes to prepare for service.

A la carte menus change periodically, mainly with the seaons; this allows the pastry chef to include freshly available produce.

■ SWEETS SUITABLE FOR VARIOUS MEALS AND TYPES OF SERVICE

BREAKFAST
Apart from preparing stewed fruits, no other dishes are expected from the pastry section.

LUNCH
All sweets are suitable to eat at lunch time but some are deliberately left off the menu because of the length of time required to prepare them and because they can only be made at the last moment, eg soufflés. It is usual to select the heavier type of sweets, eg puddings, pies, flans, apple charlottes, fruit fools and trifles. These can be served easily during the busier, shorter period of service time.

AFTERNOON TEAS
These require a selection of pastries, gâteaux, flans, plain and fruit cakes.

The selection should vary in shape, colour, flavour and texture, and have a variety of fillings.

DINNER AND SUPPER

The customer generally has more time to enjoy the food and atmosphere of a restaurant. The dishes offered should be more exotic; be made with extra finesse and use flavours, ingredients and methods of cooking which give pleasure to the palette. The choice should offer a variety of light hot and cold sweets, such as soufflés, liqueur flavoured pancakes, fruit flambées, cream filled profiteroles, sabayons, fruit salad, coupes, bombes and biscuits glacés and other icecream dishes. Petits fours can be served with the coffee. A full evening menu may feature sorbet; a light fruit, wine or liqueur flavoured water ice which is served between the fish and main courses, or between the entrée and relevée or roast.

Banquets and special parties require special planning. The dishes have to reach the customer in prime condition. Such meals are difficult to plan and prepare, especially for large numbers of customers. The pastry chef submits a list of sweets for the customer to pre-select the dish required.

When compiling this list the numbers being catered for should be borne in mind. Dishes submitted should be of a suitable kind for large scale production. Remember they will have to be pre-prepared and stored until required for service. Certain dishes may deteriorate during storage, others may be very difficult to serve as speedily as is required.

As a general rule the dishes for banquets are made up in services of ten portions. For a banquet of 500 this would mean fifty dishes. It would not be possible to prepare and serve fifty soufflés surprises unless the cold storage and oven facilities were sufficient.

During banquets the sweets are served to all the customers at the same time. The aim is to have sweets which may be prepared in advance and, at the most, require only final decoration before service and sauce, if applicable.

For cold buffets and sweet trolleys the dishes offered are presented and arranged to give as much variety as possible. Items should be prepared to give contrast in shape, colour, flavour, texture and size of dish. The presentation and decoration of the sweets should be such that it indicates the portions to be expected from each dish. If the customers are to help themselves, it is best if the sweets are pre-portioned or pre-cut.

It must be remembered that the dishes may be on display for a period of time, in which case hot sweets and ice-cream dishes are not entirely suitable. The sweets should be of the type that will withstand time without deteriorating in appearance or being affected from the hygiene point of view. If they are to be on display for a long period, some form of refrigeration must be used. Ideally some form of protection against air contamination should be provided.

A limited display should be arranged initially which can be replenished from a stock held in hygenic conditions.

■ COMPILING THE MENU

It will be much appreciated by the customers if the sweets on the menu are selected for quality, nicely prepared, well presented and suitably balanced to follow the main meal. To have a long pretentious list of dishes requiring an unlimited stock of ingredients and extensive basic preparations could place a strain on the staff and equipment and may result in lower standards of achievement.

All dishes featured on the menus should be different and distinctive. No two items should be the same with regard to ingredients, composition or method of cookery. Ice-creams are a possible exception; these can be the main ingredient presented in many ways, either on their own, in a choice of flavours, or as moulded ice-creams such as bombes and biscuit glacés. They can be combined with fruits and sauces for coupes and composite dishes, or sandwiched with meringue shells and as fillings for vacherins and omelettes soufflées.

The balance of the menu is the factor that should be foremost in the mind of the compiler. Other points to consider for the sweet menu should be to provide a selection of hot and cold sweets using a variety of ingredients of differing flavours and colours. They should be produced by variety of methods of preparation and cookery to give contrasting textures and finishes.

Organizational points which need consideration are: costs, business promotion, type of customer and their requirements, seasons of the year, local popular dishes, festive occasions, special requests, type of meals that require different methods of presentation and service, eg banquets, buffets, self service and out-door catering. Also, as already mentioned, the skill and availability of cooking and service staff and the cooking and service environments and facilities are important. Lastly, from the economy point of view, the utilisation of suitable left overs.

■ MENU TERMINOLOGY AND LAYOUT

A well laid out menu will be more attractive and helpful to the customer. A cluttered list of dishes, with a mixture of very long and short names written down one after the other, is difficult to follow; it requires extra concentration by the customers to select suitable dishes of their choice.

It is usual to have the hot and heavy sweets listed first, followed by the lighter and colder dishes, ending with ice-cream compositions. Avoid the repetition of names and terms, such as baked apples, apple pie, or cream caramel, creamed rice, or pudding soufflé, soufflé milanaise.

In a classical menu the English and French terminology should not be mixed, eg pancakes au citron, rice à l'impératrice, or apple chausson. If a dish cannot be translated into the same language as the rest of the menu, it is usual to put the term between inverted commas, eg 'Trifle', if the menu is written in French, or 'Gâteaux Pithiviers' if the menu is written in English.

Many dishes are classical. Their composition and manner of presentation are standard throughout the world and should not be changed. Knowledgeable customers will expect to be served with the dish they understand it to be. It is quite in order for a pastry chef to compose a dish and give it a name; this is often done when a dish is developed for a special person or an occasion, or to gain recognition for the establishment as renowned or progressive caterers. In the past this has happened many times. It is one of the main reasons why certain names are given to dishes.

Dishes have been named after a personality, a patron of the restaurant, or a famous gourmet. Others have been used to honour an artist, or a character played by an actor or actress in a play or an opera. Sometimes the play and opera itself is featured in the name of a dish. In some cases these dishes were the creation of the chef; in others the dish was commissioned by the customer when requesting certain compositions in flavour, shape, or presentation, eg Melba, Savarin, Aida, Alexandra, Romanoff. Some are named after the originator or the establishment, eg Sacher torte, Gâteau Suchard.

A name was often given because the main flavour or ingredients used were from a particular area, or because it was prepared in an obvious and typical style or in the distinctive manner of a district, eg Maltaise (oranges), Montmorency (cherries), Normandie (apples), Mont Blanc (chestnuts topped with cream), bavarois (bavarian style cream), Créole (rice), bonne-femme (housewife).

When the finished product has a certain colour, it may be reflected in the name, eg neige (white as snow), cardinal (red, symbolic of the red worn by Cardinals), demi-deuil (half-white, half dark as half mourning), Africaine (chocolate or coffee).

Using the method of production or cooking in the name of the dish will help to describe the type of sweet, eg Baked egg custard, Steamed syrup sponge, Poached pears with red wine, Omelette soufflée, Pudding soufflé, Whipped jelly, Bombe glacé.

The main flavouring ingredient can determine the name, eg Cream caramel, Apple pie, Baked jam roll, Raspberry bavarois, Sabayon au marsala, Steamed currant roll, Meringue Chantilly. This helps describe it to the customer.

The shape or cut is also used when naming a sweet, eg biscuit glacé, vanilla slice, jam tartlet, banana flan, rocher de glace panachée, apple turnover, cream horns.

It must be remembered that the name or term given must be descriptive. It is not enough to say pudding soufflé, the flavour must be given, eg chocolate pudding soufflé, biscuit glacé prâline, baked apricot jam roll or strawberry bavarois.

■ TYPES OF SWEETS SUITABLE FOR DIFFERENT KINDS OF CATERING ESTABLISHMENTS

Hotels and restaurants are more concerned with the gastronomic appeal and presentation of dishes than with nutritional value, although high priority should be given to retaining the natural nutritive properties of the food used. The pastry chef is relied upon to end the meal with a delicate sweet presented in an artistic manner and is sometimes expected to create a selection of imaginative petits fours for service with coffee.

Quick meal restaurants, cafés and non-subsidized cafeterias generally have the same type of clientel, ie customers with limited time and spending power. The sweets provided by these establishments need to look attractive to encourage impulse buying. In cafeterias and cafés the sweeets need to be of the kind that can easily be portioned for service and once cut will display well, eg gâteaux, fruit flans, fruit tart and meringue flan. Individual creams, jellies, trifles and cream pastries are also ideal sweets for inclusion on the menu. Quick meal restaurants will feature dishes from the above selection with the addition of a variety of ice-cream coupes and sundaes.

With few exceptions the customers in industrial catering require more substantial meals. Because of the work commitments of the customers a speedier service is required, so the sweet selection must be a type that is ready and can withstand the length of service time without deterioration, or can be quickly made up. Pies and puddings are much more in demand than the gourmet type of sweet.

Welfare, hospital and school meals are much more conscious of food values, but will still present the sweets in an attractive manner. When planning these menus consideration should be given to the delay in service, for in these cases the meals have to be transported from one area to another and certain sweets may not withstand the passage of time. The times of service are very important as most meals have to slot in to the day's timetable of other activities. In hospitals especially, the diets are important because many foods may not be suitable. The menus are usually planned in conjunction with the doctors and dietetic kitchens.

Outdoor catering menus require social consideration. The foods are semi-prepared and transported to the venue. With regard to menu planning, the site and the amenities have to be considered. There should be provision for keeping foods hot or for reheating and finishing or, in the case of cold sweets, suitable refrigeration. Because of the difficulties with transport, storage and service, the selection should be limited but of quality.

To assist in the selection of suitable variations of sweets for menu compilation, the following dishes, together with an indication of their suitability for different meals, have been listed.

The names of all the sweets in a particular category, for example, gâteaux, flans, bavarois, pies, puddings, fruit fritters, coupes, soufflés, ice-creams and pastries, have not been given. They are listed only with a main heading, each type followed by (* * *), indicating that they may be prepared and served in various flavours and with different fillings.

For the menu an appropriate name must be given that will specify the product, eg chocolate gâteau, banana flan, vanilla bavarois, apple pie, steamed jam roll, pineapple fritters, coupe Jacques, soufflé Grand Marnier, bombe glacée Aida, etc. In the case of pastries for afternoon teas, it is expected that an assorted selection would be served.

Many dishes are classical and definite in name, composition, method of preparation and presentation. For these the name should never be changed and each must be served with the appropriate garnish and accompaniment and, in many cases must be made in a particular shape.

A pastry cook will often develop a variation of a sweet dish, in which case the dish should not be given a name that is already a recognised term. A new name must be found for the dish created, preferably indicating its nature and content.

The following list is by no means comprehensive. The suggested meals do not have to be strictly adhered to. Planning the menu should be flexible. The selection of dishes and the consideration given to the balance of the commodities used, flavours selected and types of dishes, will vary with the consumers' preference.

	Lunches	Afternoon teas	Suppers Dinners	Sweet trolley Buffet table	Banquets Parties	Dishes prepared to order	Pre-prepared dishes
Genoeses gâteaux * * *		√		√			√
Gâteau St Honoré	√		√	√			√
Gâteau Polka	√			√			√
Gâteau Religieuse	√			√			√
Gâteau Paris Brest	√			√			√

	1	2	3	4	5	6	7
Gâteau Mille-feuilles	✓	✓		✓			✓
Gâteau Pithiviers	✓	✓		✓			✓
Gâteau McMahon	✓	✓		✓			✓
Gâteau Tom Pouce	✓			✓			✓
Sacher torte		✓		✓			✓
Dobos torte		✓		✓			✓
Linzer torte		✓		✓			✓
Kirch torte		✓		✓			✓
Vacherin glacé * * *	✓		✓		✓	✓	
Vacherin aux fruits * * *	✓		✓	✓	✓	✓	✓
Vacherin Chantilly	✓		✓	✓	✓	✓	✓
Meringue glacé * * *	✓		✓		✓	✓	
Meringue Chantilly	✓	✓	✓	✓	✓	✓	✓
Oeufs á la neige	✓		✓	✓		✓	✓
Oeufs á la neige jour et nuit	✓		✓	✓	✓	✓	✓
Soufflé surprise * * *			✓		✓	✓	
Lemon meringue flan	✓	✓		✓			✓
Apple meringue flan	✓	✓		✓			✓
Fruit savarines * * *	✓			✓			✓
Savarin Chantilly	✓			✓			✓
Rum babas	✓	✓		✓			✓
Marignans	✓	✓		✓			✓
Pomponettes	✓	✓		✓			✓
Croûtes aux fruits * * *	✓					✓	✓
Danish pastries * * *		✓					✓
Brioche buns * * *		✓					✓
Yeast buns * * *		✓					✓
Bun dough fruit loaves * * *		✓					✓

	Lunches	Afternoon teas	Dinners	Suppers	Buffet table	Sweet trolley	Parties	Banquets	Dishes prepared to order	Pre-prepared dishes
Fruit flans * * *	✓	✓				✓				✓
Bakewell tart		✓								✓
Baked egg custard flan	✓	✓								✓
Flan aux fruits bordelaise * * *	✓	✓				✓				✓
Bande aux fruits * * *	✓	✓				✓				✓
Mincemeat tarts and pies	✓	✓								✓
Jalousie * * *	✓	✓								✓
Jam puffs		✓								✓
Cream horns		✓								✓
Palmiers		✓								✓
Eccles cakes		✓								✓
Conversations		✓								✓
Galettes/Allumettes		✓								✓
Pancakes * * *	✓								✓	✓
Crêpe Suzettes				✓					✓	
Crêpes flambée * * *				✓					✓	
Crêpes soufflées * * *	✓			✓					✓	
Fruit fritters * * *	✓								✓	✓
Soufflé fritters	✓								✓	✓
Crême fritters	✓								✓	✓
Fruits flambés * * *				✓					✓	
Pouding soufflés * * *	✓								✓	
Omelettes souffleés * * *	✓								✓	
Soufflé surprise * * *	✓			✓			✓		✓	

	Lunches	Afternoon teas	Suppers Dinners	Sweet trolley Buffet table	Banquets Parties	Dishes prepared to order	Pre-prepared dishes
Zabaglione/Sabayon	√		√		√	√	
Fruit mousses * * *	√		√	√	√		√
Bavarois * * *	√		√	√	√		√
Bavarois maltaise	√		√	√	√		√
Charlottes * * *	√		√	√	√		√
Chartreuse * * *	√		√	√	√		√
Soufflé milanaise	√		√	√	√		√
Riz Impératrice	√			√	√		√
Blancmanges * * *	√			√			√
Junket * * *	√						√
Rice and semolina moulds	√						√
Mont Blanc Chantilly			√	√		√	
Cereal milk puddings * * *	√						√
Baked rice pudding	√						√
Baked egg custards * * *	√						√
Bread and butter pudding	√						√
Diplomat pudding	√			√			√
Cabinet pudding	√						√
Cream caramels	√		√	√			√
Crème beau rivage	√		√	√			√
Crème brullée	√		√	√			√
Petits pots à la crème * * *	√		√	√			√
Crème viennoise	√		√	√			√
Queen of puddings	√						√

	Lunches	Afternoon teas	Suppers / Dinners	Buffet table	Sweet trolley	Parties	Banquets	Dishes prepared to order	Pre-prepared dishes
Fruit Condé * * *	√				√				√
Fruit créole * * *	√				√				√
Fruit salad	√		√		√		√	√	√
Trifles * * *	√				√				√
Jellies * * *	√				√				√
Jelly Moscovite	√				√				√
Cream profiteroles * * *	√				√				√
Croque en bouche	√		√		√				√
Timbale d'Arenberg	√								√
Floating island	√		√		√			√	√
Poached fruits * * *	√								√
Fruit fools * * *	√								√
Apple strudel (hot)	√								√
Apple strudel (cold)	√	√			√				√
Dutch apple tart	√	√							√
Baked apple dumplings	√								√
Baked apples	√								√
Flan Normande	√	√			√				√
Pommes paillard	√								√
Eve's pudding	√								√
Apple turn-overs		√							√
Apple flan	√	√			√				√
Apple tartlets		√							√
Apple crumble	√								√

	Lunches	Afternoon teas	Dinners	Suppers	Buffet table	Sweet trolley	Parties	Banquets	Dishes prepared to order	Pre-prepared dishes
Fruit pies * * *	✓									✓
Fruit tarts * * *	✓									✓
Jam/treacle tarts	✓									✓
Jam/treacle tartlets		✓								✓
Baked jam roll	✓									✓
Fruit tartlets * * *		✓								✓
Steamed sponges * * *	✓									✓
Steamed suet puddings * * *	✓									✓
Steamed rolls * * *	✓									✓
Steamed fresh fruit puddings * * *	✓									✓
Steamed dried fruit puddings * * *	✓									✓
Steamed apple dumplings	✓									✓
French pastries * * *		✓				✓				✓
Soft type pastries * * *		✓				✓				✓
Dry type pastries * * *		✓								✓
Small cakes * * *		✓								✓
Sliced cake * * *		✓								✓
Victoria sponge		✓								✓
Swiss roll * * *		✓								✓
Tartlets * * *		✓				✓				✓
Barquettes * * *		✓				✓				✓
Scones * * *		✓								✓
Short-bread		✓								✓

	Lunches	Afternoon teas	Suppers	Dinners	Buffet table	Sweet trolley	Parties	Banquets	Dishes prepared to order	Pre-prepared dishes
Choux buns		√			√					√
Eclairs * * *		√			√					√
Swans		√			√					√
Doughnuts * * *		√								√
Petit fours and biscuits * * *					√		√			√
Ice-creams * * *	√				√		√	√		
Coupes * * *	√				√			√		
Fruit and ice cream dishes * * *	√				√		√	√		
Water ices * * *	√				√		√	√		
Sorbets * * *					√		√	√		
Bombes glacées * * *	√				√		√	√		
Biscuits glacés * * *	√				√		√	√		
Cassata	√				√		√	√		
Parfaits * * *	√				√		√	√		

29 HINTS AND TIPS

1 Check the recipe and use the correct ingredients and equipment and work according to instructions.
2 Putting a set of small intricate cutters back into their containers often presents a problem as they will only fit one way. If a thick piece of paper is fitted into the base of the container, and the cutters arranged inside and pressed down hard, they will leave an impression of their position on the paper which can be made clearer by over-marking with a pen or pencil.
3 To straighten out the points of a star nozzle, use a cream horn mould. Push it inside and gently turn around.
4 Always keep any whisks that have broken and have no further use as tools. The wires may be cut off to use as flower basket handles and flower stems.
5 To speed up the drying of fruits for dipping into cooked sugar, use a hot air drier such as a hair drier.
6 To assist in rolling out paste to an even thickness, place two clean wooden or metal bars of the thickness required on the surface, either side of the paste. The bars will prevent the pin being pressed too heavily and the paste can then only be rolled out to the thickness of the bars. Ensure adequate dusting to prevent the paste sticking to the table.
7 Save the stones from cherries. These may be used in place of baking beans when preparing flans and tartlets baked blind.
8 To achieve a smooth surface when rolling out pastes such as shortbread, sweet paste, marzipan and pastillage, roll out almost to the thickness required then lay a piece of smooth greaseproof paper on top. Rub the surface, holding the pin in a slightly raised position with the tips of the fingers underneath.

The following suggestions will help overcome the problems of paste becoming soft when working in hot rooms.

9 Chill the ingredients before and after mixing. Keep the rolling pin and if possible the working surface, such as a board or small marble slab, in the refrigerator to cool. If using a large work table or fixed surface, place a tray of ice on the surface for a short while before using. When

rolling out small quantities of paste, use a straight sided, firmly corked bottle filled with iced water. Take care not to chip the glass while using it. Grease and chill the flan rings, tartlets or any other item which the paste has to be moulded onto. The cold fat acts as an adhesive. Use only the estimated amount of paste required for one rolling, keeping the remainder in the refrigerator. Work as quickly as possible.

10 To shape a piece of paste into a round to use for a flan, first shape the paste into a ball and place it in the centre of the flan ring and flatten the top slightly. Using the flan ring, spin the ball of paste inside the ring to form an even round.

11 To avoid puncturing pastry when fitting it into a flan ring, break a piece of unwanted pastry off, flour it, then use it to push the pastry into the angles.

12 If a thin layer of fat is required, for example when making puff paste, place the firm fat between two sheets of greaseproof paper and roll out to the thickness required.

13 To distribute and level off soft mixtures in round baking moulds or tins, such as sponges or savarins, spin the mould around on the table.

14 To prevent milk sticking and possibly burning on the bottom of a pan, sprinkle sugar into the milk so that it forms a layer on the bottom. The principle here is that the sugar will form a barrier between the milk and the heat. The milk comes to the boil before the sugar is dispersed in the liquid.

15 There is less chance of baked egg custards overcooking and becoming pitted if the liquids used in the mixture and the water in the bain-marie are at the same cool temperature.

16 Once made, cooked egg custard sauces should be transferred immediately to a cold container to stop further cooking. If the mixture has curdled slightly, it is sometimes possible to smooth it by gently whisking in a little cold cream or butter.

17 When dry ingredients are to be added gradually to a mixture, it is easier to control the flow if they are rained off a sheet of greaseproof paper held in such a way as to form a shute.

18 To soften hard fats when creaming, warm the sugar slightly. Do not overheat as this may melt the fats into an oily consistency.

19 When whisking eggs and sugar into a foam, the process may be speeded up by warming the sugar beforehand in the oven as well as using the bain-marie whilst actually whisking the mixture.

20 To prevent jams dehydrating when cooking in jam tarts, stir in a little water, approximately one part water to ten parts jam, before use.

21 It will be found that small items such as cakes, sponges and vol-au-vents will rise and cook more evenly if the tray is full. Keep items close together and allow equal spaces between them. Whenever possible fill

the oven as empty spaces result in hotter areas which are the main cause of uneven rising during the cooking process.

22 Soufflés such as 'soufflé Grand Marnier' will rise more evenly in their case if a shallow layer of water is in the baking tray surrounding the case. This will even-out the heat surrounding the case.

23 Choux pastries that have to be glazed with a hot coating and filled with cream, eg profiterole for Gâteau St Honoré, should be coated first and filled with cream after cooling. This will prevent the cream inside softening.

24 When whipping fresh cream, better results are obtained if the cream is first chilled and the whipping performed in a bowl situated over a tray of ice.

25 To remove items such as sponge fingers, macaroons or meringue shells which have stuck to greaseproof paper, place a wet cloth on the hot tray and lay the sheet of items on top. The steam produced will loosen the goods, allowing them to be removed easily. The goods will be slightly dampened and it will therefore be necessary to air them to dry them out.

26 To remove set items from moulds, eg cream caramel, bavarois and jellies, loosen the sides of the mixture, turn upside down onto the dish and move the mixture slightly to allow air to enter between the mould and the mixture. Do not shake up and down but jerk the container on the dish forwards and backwards for the moulded item to drop.

27 When preparing scooped or cut ice-cream pieces that are to be placed on top of each other in a bowl, they will be easier to separate for service if they are first placed on a sheet of greaseproof paper and kept in the freezer for a short while.

28 To prepare fat in small particles to use in rubbed in mixtures, melt the fats and allow to cool to almost setting point, then pour through a coarse sieve placed over a bowl of iced water. As the fat enters the water it will immediately set in the small particles.

29 When preparing a 'mise en place' of cooked pancakes, allow them to cool by laying them on a cool surface before stacking them with greaseproof paper between each one.

30 To save oven space when drying out meringues, stack the trays on top of each other, using sufficient dariole moulds to separate the trays and allow the heat and air to circulate in between.

31 Different coloured water may be frozen in savarin moulds which, when unmoulded, may be used to support a bowl of ice-cream or fruit for presentation purposes. A battery fitted with a light bulb placed in the cavity gives it an effective appearance.

32 To remove the rind from oranges without breaking the segments of the fruit that are to be used for dipping into cooked sugar, use the tip of a

small knife and score the surface from the top to the base of the orange, making about eight incisions. Take care not to cut too deeply. Place in boiling water for about three minutes. Cool in cold water. The rind should come off easily without breaking the skin of the segments.

33 A small quantity of oil or melted butter added to a pancake batter will help prevent sticking and make greasing during cooking almost unnecessary.

34 The following illustration shows useful improvised items of equipment, which can be obtained or made, to use for various purposes.

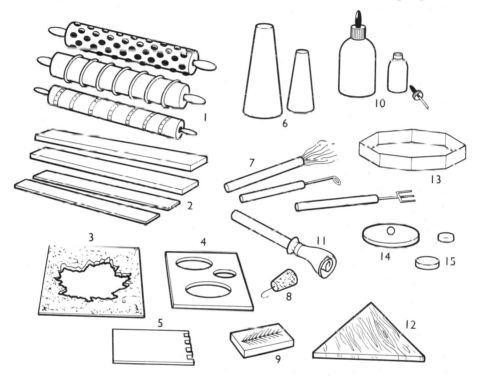

1 The three rolling pins illustrated are easily made and used for marking patterns on rolled out pastes, marzipans and pastillage. The top rolling pin is made by using a length of cylindrical wood, 50 mm (2") in diameter, into which round-headed upholstery studs are hammered to form a symmetrical pattern. The middle rolling pin is made by winding thick string around the pin at distances approximately 12 mm ($\frac{1}{2}$") apart all along its length. The string is held at each end with a tack or screw, so that it can be removed easily for cleaning after use. The third pin is made in the same way, but using a 6 mm ($\frac{1}{4}$") wide strip of patterned flexible beading.

2 Two thicknesses of wooden bars are shown. These are used to control the thicknesses of paste when rolling out. The thickness of the wood depends on the required thickness of paste. The strips should be

placed either side of the paste to be rolled out.

3 A stencil cut from a piece of flexible rubber, plastic or lino sheeting may be used as a template for spreading chocolate, icings or baking mixtures to a specific shape, size and thickness.

4 Circles of different sizes cut out from a sheet of rigid perspex. These apertures are used for spreading mixtures to standardise the thickness and size of the finished products when making goods such as brandy snaps and cornets or cigarettes from a langue de chat mixture.

5 A plastic scraper with serrated edges used to create patterns, for example on the sides of iced cakes, can be made by cutting the edges of a piece of semi-rigid plastic to the required design.

6 Plastic cones obtainable from hosiery factories are ideal to use as moulds when assembling profiteroles for *croque en bouche*, or for building up a cone of marzipan, pastillage or pulled sugar flowers to use as a form of decoration.

7 The whisk for spinning cooked sugar can easily be made by forcing a bundle of wire lengths into a piece of metal tubing with a 12 mm ($\frac{1}{2}''$) diameter, then spacing and bending the projecting wires to splay out evenly. The dipping fork and loop are shaped with wire and the ends twisted together and pushed into a wooden rod drilled with a small deep hole.

8 A cherry stoner made with a paper clip with one end cut off and pressed firmly into a cork. The stone is removed by inserting the curved end into the stalk end of the cherry and hooking out the stone. It is a quick method and does not break up the fruit.

9 To mark the impressions of leaf veins on marzipan, pastillage or pulled sugar work, engrave or file the markings on a piece of rigid plastic. Press the moulded leaves firmly on to the engraved plastic for them to take the impression.

10 Liquid droppers are available from chemists and will be found useful for adding small, controlled quantities of colouring or flavouring into mixtures.

11 To prevent contamination by grease or hair on brushes which are used for egg and milk wash or syrup and jam glazes, use an inexpensive disposable alternative. Roll a strip of clean cloth around a piece of dowelling and tie securely. This is especially recommended when used for greasing hot pans, moulds and trays.

12 A board at least 12 mm ($\frac{1}{2}''$) thick can be drilled to take the number of rods required to use as a frame for modelling baskets. The outline of the holes will determine the shape and size of the basket. The drilled holes should allow the rods to slant slightly outwards.

13 Boxes or lids of different shapes can be used as cutters, templates or moulds for marzipan and pastillage.

14 Unusual shapes can be cut by using the tops of talcum powder containers. It is possible to use them several times before they lose their sharpness. Take care to ensure that prior to use they are thoroughly washed to remove any odours from the original contents.

15 Pierced, screw on bottle tops are useful as small cutters when required for cutting out small rounds such as petits fours or decorative goods.

30 QUESTIONS AND QUIZZES

The following questions and quizzes are intended to promote research and stimulate interest. It will be necessary to read other books for the answers and it is suggested that this is done before checking the answers given at the end of this section.

Group A are in cryptic form which will suit those interested in crossword puzzles. The subsequent sections are of a more direct or selective answer type questions.

Group A

1 It's a mouthful, so say the French.
2 What is eaten as a flight in the wind?
3 The hand-made cigarette without tobacco.
4 It's hot, cold and unexpected.
5 The woman of Troy has beauty and a hot chocolate coat.
6 The sauce of an opera singer.
7 The gâteau of a thousand leaves.
8 Rhubarb and cream are mixed for the idiot.
9 A musical instrument that's filled with cream.
10 The gâteau that cracks in the mouth.
11 Sounds like a requirement, to develop a dough.
12 It's too cold to explode.
13 The lady of the explosive opera.
14 It may sound like it, but you can't wash with this bun.
15 What has become of the crushed nougat croquant?
16 These tarts are definitely not raw.
17 The egg dish full of hot air.
18 This rich egg custard is browned off.
19 The petit four that makes a person from the Middle East happy.
20 It's taken 25 years and a few cherries to name this dish.
21 The gâteau that lets us know when winter is over.
22 The cake from the dark woods of Germany.
23 Ali, the leader of forty, needs rum for the cake.
24 An explosive sweet; cold state of the USA.
25 Surrounding cream or apples, gives us the girl.
26 Piped finger biscuits, but the French say they are spooned.

27 The decoration for a queen.

28 It sounds as if the fruit is upside down, yet it's served upright.

29 You will get the French area if you whip it.

30 It's a fruit in France but termed a colour in England.

Group B

What are the French terms for the following?

1 Almond cream

2 Butter cream

3 Confectioners custard

4 Egg custard sauce

5 Frying batter

6 Gum paste

7 Hot water paste

8 Noodle paste

9 Puff paste

10 Short paste

11 Sugar or sweet paste

12 Whipped sweet cream

Group C

What are the French names for the following fruits?

1 Apple

2 Blackcurrants

3 Cherries

4 Grapes

5 Lemon

6 Peach

7 Pear

8 Pineapple

9 Plum

10 Prune

11 Raspberries

12 Strawberries

Group D

Define the meanings of the following terms.

1 Beignets

2 Chemiser

3 Compôte

4 Confiture

5 Creme renversée

6 Croûtes

7 Flambé

8 Glacé

9 Pailles

10 Panaché

11 Sabayon

12 Soufflé.

Group E

The following named dishes suggest that they are composed of certain items. Name the items.

1 Ananas créole

2 Bavarois Maltaise

3 Charlotte Russe

4 Chartreuse Montreuil

5 Coupe Jacques

6 Crêpe Normande

7 Friandises

8 Gâteau moka

9 Macédoine de fruits

10 Gâteau Cyrano

11 Soufflé Arlequin

12 Vacherin Montmorency

Group F

Match the names or terms listed in the left hand list to correspond with items in the right hand list.

(i)   1 Pineapple   a Coupe malmaison
      2 Cherries   b Omelette Soufflé Surprise Milord
      3 Fruit salad   c Ananas créole
      4 Grapes   d Coupe Edna May
      5 Pears   e Coupe Alexandra

(ii) 1 Napolitaine   a Nesselrode
      2 Praliné   b Lemon flavour
      3 Milanaise   c Raspberries
      4 Melba sauce   d Pistachio, chocolate and strawberry
      5 Chestnuts   e Caramel

(iii) 1 Short paste   a Bande aux fruits
      2 Sugar paste   b Apple pie
      3 Puff paste   c Savoury pork pies
      4 Hot water paste   d Profiteroles
      5 Choux paste   e Banana flan

(iv) 1 Bavarois   a Riz Impératrice
      2 Butter cream   b Vanilla slice
      3 Pastry cream   c Charlotte Royal
      4 Frangipane   d Gâteau Pompadour
      5 Creamed rice   e Gâteau Pithiviers

(v)   1 Marsala   a Sorbets
      2 Champagne   b Trifles
      3 White wine   c Zabaglione
      4 Sherry   d Black forest gâteau
      5 Kirch   e Syllabub

Group G

1 Express the following in grams (g) and kilograms (kg)
   $\frac{1}{4}$ kg . . . g . . . kg $1\frac{1}{2}$ kg . . . g . . . kg
2 Add together the following weights.
   308 g, 28 g, 3.55 kg, $\frac{3}{4}$ kg, 1 kg, 5 g, 0.234 kg.
3 Convert the following and show your answers in grams and kilograms.
   6 oz . . . g . . . kg $3\frac{1}{4}$ lb . . . g . . . kg
4 Convert the following and express your answers in millilitres (ml) and litres (l).
   $\frac{1}{2}$ pt . . . ml . . . 1 $1\frac{1}{4}$ pts . . . ml . . . 1
   3 pts . . . ml . . . 1
5 Convert the following temperatures and show method of conversion.
   410° F . . . ° C
   185° C . . . ° F

Group H

Select the correct answer from the three possible alternatives given.

1 When yeast is active within a dough it produces
  a) oxygen and alcohol.
  b) carbon dioxide and alcohol.
  c) hydrogen and oxygen.

2 Yeast is used as a raising agent for
  a) scones.
  b) Yorkshire pudding.
  c) Chelsea buns.

3 Strong or hard flour would be used to make
  a) choux paste.
  b) Victoria sponge.
  c) short paste.

4 A weak or soft flour is the best to select when making
  a) puff paste.
  b) Genoese sponge.
  c) hot water paste.

5 The rubbing in method is used for which one of the following?
  a) cabinet pudding
  b) steamed jam sponge
  c) rock cakes

6 The creaming method is used for
  a) Swiss roll.
  b) suet paste.
  c) butter cream.

7 Baking powder is used as a raising agent for
  a) Swiss buns.
  b) raspberry buns.
  c) choux pastries.

8 Which one of the following is used to thicken sauce anglaise?
  a) custard powder
  b) yolks of eggs
  c) cornflour

9 One of the main ingredients in diplomat pudding is:
  a) diced sponge,
  b) sliced bread,
  c) bread-crumbs.

10 A strong flour contains a higher percentage of
  a) gluten.
  b) starch.
  c) moisture.

11 What will cause puff paste to shrink on baking?

a) too many turns
b) insufficient fat
c) insufficient rest time

12 In which of the following is gelatine used?
a) bavarois
b) Blancmange
c) junket

13 At which of the following temperatures does bacteria multiply most rapidly?
a) 7° C (45° F)
b) 32° C (90° F)
c) 65° C (150° F)

14 The ideal working temperature of a refrigerator is
a) 0° C (32° F)
b) 7° C (45° F)
c) 15° C (60° F)

15 Which of the following is a water ice-cream?
a) glace vanille
b) sorbet au citron
c) parfait glacé

16 Fresh fruit salad with lemon and strawberry ice-cream served in a coupe is called
a) coupe Edna May.
b) coupe tutti-frutti.
c) coupe Jacques.

17 Poire Hélène is served with
a) coffee sauce.
b) hot chocolate sauce.
c) cream sauce.

18 Biscuit glacé is a type of
a) short-bread biscuit.
b) glazed petit four.
c) moulded ice-cream.

19 The filling for gâteau St Honoré should be
a) crème chantilly.
b) crème chiboust.
c) crème anglaise.

20 Langue de chat is a type of
a) petit four.
b) pastry.
c) hot sweet.

21 Crème Mont Blanc indicates the use of
a) meringue.

b) egg custard.

c) chestnuts.

22 Quicke Lorraine is a

a) fruit flan.

b) egg custard.

c) croûte.

23 How much flour is required when making a three egg Swiss roll?

a) 75 g

b) 100 g

c) 50 g

24 Cabinet pudding is served

a) hot.

b) cold.

c) hot or cold.

25 Jalousie is made with

a) puff paste.

b) short paste.

c) sweet paste.

26 Which of the following is the cause of puff paste rising?

a) carbon dioxide

b) steam

c) flour

27 Jelly is used to line the mould for

a) charlotte Royale.

b) chartreuse aux fruit.

c) bavarois rubané.

28 Sabayon is made with

a) whole eggs, vanilla and sugar.

b) yolks of eggs, wine and sugar.

c) eggs, cream, vanilla and sugar.

29 Meringue is used for making

a) vacherin.

b) sponge fingers.

c) othellos.

30 Beignets soufflées are made with

a) choux paste.

b) creme pâtissièr.

c) frying batter.

Group I

1 Which temperature of cooked sugar applies to each of the following terms?

a) soft ball

b) soft crack

c) hard crack

2 What are the required working temperatures for each of the following?

a) melted chocolate for moulding

b) cooked sugar for dipped fruits

c) fondant for coating

3 What type of fillings are required for making the following sweets?

a) Gâteau Pithiviers

b) Charlotte Royale

c) Black forest gâteau

4 Which commodity do the following dishes have in common?

a) Créole

b) Impèratrice

c) Condé

5 Which kind of paste is used for all three of the following sweets?

a) apple turnovers

b) jalousie damandes

c) cream slice

6 Which colours do the following names suggest?

a) cardinal

b) pistachio

c) praline

7 Which same basic mixture is used for all three of the following sweets?

a) Gâteau St Honoré

b) Gâteau Paris Brest

c) Gâteau polka

8 What do the following sweets have in common?

a) Crème beau rivage

b) Croque en bouche

c) Crème brulée

9 Which is the 'odd one' out?

a) Gâteau Religeuse

b) Gâteau Printanière

c) Gâteau Pompadour

10 Which one of the following is cooked in a shallow pan?

a) Omelette soufflé surprise

b) Omelette soufflé

c) Soufflé saxon

Group J

Answer 'true' or 'false' to the following statements.

1 Baking powder is the raising agent in puff paste?

2 Royal icing improves if left to stand overnight before using?

3 Items made with choux paste should be under baked?
4 Meringue shells are dried at approximately 90° C (200° F)?
5 Fresh egg custard sauce must come to the boil?
6 Fresh cream will give more volume if overbeaten?
7 The more turns given to puff paste the higher it will rise when being baked?
8 To produce a tender, short paste, ensure that it is well kneaded?
9 Sugar will give colour to a product during baking?
10 A yeast dough will improve if allowed to prove in a hot, dry place?

Group K

Add the missing word or words.

1 The sweetmeats served with coffee are called . . . .
2 Fécule is a . . . . . . flour.
3 The raising agent for a pouding soufflé is . . . .
4 When using couverture it must be . . . . . . before use.
5 A mixture of chocolate and cream is known as . . . . . .
6 A ring of enriched yeast mixture, cooked and soaked and served cold with fruit salad is called . . . . . . aux fruits.
7 The outside layer of a Charlotte Royale are slices of . . . .
8 Thin shallow fried 'cakes' filled with hot jam are called . . . . or . . . . (in French).
9 The protein which is developed in flour mixtures is called . . . . . .
10 A selection of sweets displayed and served from a large table in a restaurant is called a . . . . . .

■ ANSWERS TO QUESTIONS AND QUIZZES

Group A

1 Bouchées 2 Vol-au-vent 3 Chocolate cigarettes 4 Omelette soufflé 5 Belle Hélène 6 Melba sauce 7 Gateau mille-feuilles 8 Rhubard fool 9 Cream horns 10 Croque en bouche 11 Knead 12 Bombe glacée 13 Bombe glacée Aida 14 Bath bun 15 Praliné 16 Bakewell tarts 17 Omelette soufflé 18 crème bruleé 19 Turkish delight 20 Cherries jubilee 21 Gâteau printanier 22 Black forest gâteau 23 Rum baba 24 Bombe Alaska 25 Charlotte 26 Biscuit à la cuiller, 27 Royal Icing 28 Apple turnover 29 Chantilly (cream) 30 Cerise

Group B

1 Frangipane
2 Crème au beurre
3 Crème patissier
4 Sauce anglaise

7 Pâte à pâté
8 Pâte à nouilles
9 Pâte feuilletage
10 Pâte brisée or foncer

5 Pâte à frire
6 Pastillage

11 Pâte à sucré ou doux
12 Crème chantilly

Group C

1 Pomme
2 Cassis
3 Cerises
4 Raisins
5 Citron
6 Pêche

7 Poire
8 Ananas
9 Prune
10 Pruneau
11 Framboise
12 Fraises

Group D

1 Deep fried fritters.
2 To line or coat.
3 Stewed fruit.
4 Jam or served with jam.
5 Unmoulded baked egg custard.
6 Slices of brioche, toasted.

7 To set ablaze with spirits.
8 Iced (ice-cream or coating)
9 Straws (cheese or sugar).
10 A mixture (fruits or ices).
11 Whipped egg yolks and wines.
12 Aerated pudding

Group E

1 Pineapple and creamed rice.
2 Orange flavoured bavarois.
3 Bavarian cream surrounded with sponge fingers.
4 Bavarois covered with peaches and coated with jelly.
5 Fruit salad with lemon and strawberry ice-cream.
6 Apple pancake.
7 Another name given to petits fours (titbits).
8 Coffee flavoured, decorated sponge cake.
9 Fruit salad.
10 Sponge gâteau covered with meringue and flaked almonds.
11 Cooked soufflé of at least two flavours (chocolate and vanilla).
12 Meringue nest filled with cherries.

Group F

i) a–4 b–5 c–1 d–2 e–3
ii) a–5 b–3 c–4 d–1 e–2
iii) a–3 b–1 c–4 d–5 e–2
iv) a–5 b–3 c–1 d–2 e–4
v) a–2 b–4 c–1 d–5 e–3

Group G

1 $\frac{1}{4}$ kg = 250 g   0.250 kg
   $1\frac{1}{2}$ kg = 1 500 g   1.500 kg

2 308 g +
   28 g +
   3.550 kg +
   750 g +
   1.000 kg +
   5 g +
   0.234 kg =
   5.875 kg or 5 875 g
3 6 ozs × 28.35 g = 170 g   0.170 kg
   3.25 lbs × 454 g = 1 475 g   1.475 kg
4 $\frac{1}{2}$ pt = 284 ml   0.284 l $1\frac{1}{4}$ pts = 710 ml   0.710 l
   3 pts = 1 704 ml   1.704 l
5 410° F − 32 ÷ 9 × 5 = 210° C
   185° C ÷ 5 × 9 + 32 = 365° C

Group H

1 b) 2 c) 3 a) 4 b) 5 c) 6 c) 7 b)
8 b) 9 a)10 a)11 c)12 a)13 b)14 b)
15 b)16 c)17 b)18 c)19 b)20 a)21 c)
22 b)23 a)24 a)25 a)26 b)27 b)28 b)
29 a)30 a)

Group I

1 a) 115° C (240° F)   b) 137° C (280° F)   c) 154° C (310° F)
2 a) 32° C (90° F)   b) 155° C (310° F)   c) 43° C (110° F)
3 a) Frangipane   b) Bavarois   c) Fresh whipped cream
                                        and black cherries.

4 Rice is common to all three.
5 Puff paste is used for producing all three.
6 a) Red   b) Green   c) Caramel (brown)
7 All three use choux paste.
8 They all require caramelized sugar.
9 Gâteau Religieuse; the other two are made with Genoese.
10 b) Omelette Soufflée

Group J

1 False   2 True   3 False   4 True   5 False
6 False   7 False   8 False   9 True   10 False

Group K

1 Petits fours   2 Potato   3 Whipped egg whites
4 Tempered   5 Ganache   6 Savarin   7 Swiss roll
8 Jam pancakes or Crêpes au confiture (French)
9 Gluten   10 Buffet

FURTHER READING AND REFERENCE GUIDE

The following publications are recommended for further reading. The student will benefit from the depth of study, recipes and methods found in other works which will allow them to develop their interest further.

Publications are listed and numbered. At the end of the list can be found a reference guide to information contained with each publication.

1 *Bakery questions answered.*
2 *Chef's compendium of professional recipes,* Fuller and Renold.
3 *Chocolate* (manufactures information) Cadbury's Ltd. and Lesme Ltd.
4 *Calculations for the hotel and catering industry.* G. Gee.
5 *Clean catering,* HMSO.
6 *Eggs,* Egg Marketing Board.
7 *Fats and oils* (manufacturers information) Craigmillar and British Creamery Ltd.
8 *Flours,* Flour Advisory Board.
9 *Food hygiene regulations,* HMSO.
10 *French for catering students,* J. Grisbrooke.
11 *Davis Consolidated Industries Ltd.*
12 *Law's grocers manual.*
13 *Metrication,* Metrication Board.
14 *Patissier,* Hanneman.
15 *Practical cookery,* V. Ceserani and R. Kinton.
16 *Professional Kitchen management,* Fuller.
17 *Raising agents, formula balance* (manufacturers information), Proctor and Gamble.
18 *Repertoire de la cuisine,* Saulnier and Brunet.
19 *Sugar,* British sugar bureau.
20 *Theory of catering,* Kinton and Ceserani.
21 *The modern patissier,* W. Barker.
22 *Understanding cookery,* Ceserani, Lundberg and Kotschevar.
23 *Yeast* (manufacturers information, United Yeast Company Ltd.
24 Information and codes of practice booklets on, health and hygiene, safe foods and safety at work are available from local Environmental Health Departments.

The following books although still in circulation are not easily available, but will make interesting and instructive reading.

25 *The complete patissier*, Kollist.

26 *The reasons why*, R. Daniel.

27 *The modern baker, confectioner and caterer*, (4 volumes) Kirkland.

■ REFERENCE GUIDE

Personal, kitchen and food hygiene 5, 9, 16, 20, 24, 27.

Food preparation and recipes 1, 2, 14, 15, 18, 21, 25, 27.

Commodities 1, 3, 6, 7, 8, 11, 12, 16, 17, 19, 20, 22, 23, 26, 27.

General theory 10, 16, 20, 22, 26, 27.

Equipment 14, 16, 20, 21, 26, 27.

Plus manufacturer's and suppliers' booklets.

INDEX